The
Sharpie Book

Florida sharpie yacht, about 1890. Courtesy of the
Library of Congress.

The
Sharpie Book

Reuel B. Parker

International Marine
Camden, Maine

Published by International Marine®

10   9   8   7   6   5   4   3   2

Copyright © 1994 International Marine, a division of McGraw-Hill, Inc.

Library of Congress Cataloging-in-Publication Data
Parker, Reuel B.
    The sharpie book / Reuel B. Parker.
    p.   cm.
    Includes bibliographical references (p.173 and Index)
    ISBN 0-87742-304-0
    1. Sharpies (Sailboats)—Design and construction—Amateurs' manuals. I. Title.
VM311.S53P37   1993
63.8'29—dc20   93-26032
                                                          CIP

Questions regarding the content of this book should be addressed to:
International Marine
P.O. Box 220
Camden, ME 04843

Questions regarding the ordering of this book should be addressed to:
McGraw-Hill, Inc.
Customer Service Department
P.O. Box 547
Blacklick, OH 43004
1-800-822-8158

The Sharpie Book is printed on acid-free paper.

Printed by Arcata Graphics, Fairfield, PA
Design by Faith Hague
Production and page layout by Janet Robbins
Edited by J.R. Babb, Jane Crosen, Tom McCarthy
Illustrations by the author unless otherwise noted

DEDICATION

To the memories of Howard I. Chapelle, Thomas Clapham, Larry Huntington, Lester Rowe, and Ralph M. Munroe, the sharpie masters.

CONTENTS

Acknowledgments ix

Introduction xi

One History and Evolution 1

Two Traditional Construction 30

Three Tools, Materials, Adhesives, Fasteners, and Safety 43

Four Modern Construction 50

Five Details and Accoutrements 70

Six Designs, Lofting, and Scantlings 97

Seven Sailing, Handling, and Maintenance 152

Appendices

   I Tables of Offsets for Adapted Sharpie Designs 163

   II Three Modern Sharpie Designs 166

   III Materials Suppliers 172

Bibliography 173

Index 174

ACKNOWLEDGMENTS

I would like to thank the following organizations, institutions, and individuals for their invaluable help and cooperation in compiling the drawings, photographs, and historical research material that made this book possible: the National Museum of Natural History, Smithsonian Institution; the Library of Congress; Mystic Seaport Museum; the North Carolina Maritime Museum; the Florida Parks Commission (Munroe "Barnacle"); the Historical Society of Southern Florida; the New Haven Colony Historical Society; the Chesapeake Bay Small Craft Museum; Gordon E. Hurley, Jr. (Clapham material); Bill Smith (*Lahoma* photos); Yves-Marie Tanton (*Le Sharpie* material); International Marine; W.W. Norton & Company; and *WoodenBoat* and *Yachting* magazines.

My sincere apologies to anyone I have carelessly omitted.

I would also like to thank the intrepid staff of International Marine for making this book a reality, in particular, Tom McCarthy and Jim Babb.

And finally, my heartfelt thanks to Jon Eaton at International Marine, who suggested writing a book about sharpies in the first place.

INTRODUCTION

The sharpie weaves an essential motif in the fabric of American history. It is exemplary of Yankee ingenuity, of the creative adaptability of the working man. Though the sharpie was born out of the needs of the Connecticut oyster industry in the mid-19th century, its form was remarkably diverse and grew with young America's needs until it occupied—in one mutation or another—much of America's inshore fishing industries. In the space of fifty years the sharpie spread farther and faster than any single boat type in history. Along with its many commercial applications, the sharpie was adapted as a cruising and racing yacht both in America and abroad, and eventually took to the open ocean.

This immense propagation was rooted in the dogged pragmatism of the American spirit of an earlier age, for sharpies are truly an American invention. They evolved to fill needs, and they filled them with grace, beauty, speed, and economy.

The late Howard I. Chapelle wrote that the sharpie's "rapid spread in use can be accounted for by its low cost, light draft, speed, handiness under sail, graceful appearance, and rather astonishing seaworthiness."

Sharpies are remarkably easy to build—easier, and in fact less expensive—than any other boat type. They are fast, simple, and fun to sail, surprisingly seaworthy, handy and versatile, can carry an impressive amount of weight, and are perfectly beachable and trailerable—an important and overlooked sharpie feature. Because sharpies are narrow for their length, fairly large boats are within the eight-foot highway width limitation imposed by most states. Hence a 28-foot pocket cruiser for a family of four, weighing less than 2,500 pounds equipped for cruising, can be trailered anywhere in America.

Like anything, the sharpie has a few limitations. All flat-bottomed boats will pound or slap against the water under certain circumstances, especially when being sailed to windward. This propensity is largely solved by sailing the boats heeled over, presenting the V formed by the bottom and leeward side of the hull to the waves. In general this pounding is a small price to pay for the other advantages of the sharpie, and seems to present a performance problem only when driving the boats into a short, steep chop—especially when the waves are disproportionately greater than the wind.

Another limitation is the sharpie's reputation as a "protected water" boat; it is not intended for general use in the open ocean. Let me qualify this by saying that very few yachtsmen willingly venture offshore in disagreeable weather, and that many sharpies are very capable coastal cruisers in most conditions. They are also capable of handling sudden squalls and getting to safety rapidly in deteriorating conditions. And in dire conditions when the shore must be met—either a breaking inlet or a stretch of beach that could spell death to all vessels with keels—no other large boat has the sharpie's abilities in the surf. Even very large sharpies can be surfed ashore through breakers and beached. With centerboard up, because of its light, buoyant hull and flat bottom, a sharpie behaves like a giant surfboard.

The third limitation, related to seaworthiness, is that most sharpies are not self-righting: If capsized, they don't come back to their feet. Even this limitation can be overcome, or at least prepared for, and many of the later sharpie designs were modified to be self-righting.

The sharpie has had many dedicated fans among American yachtsmen and marine historians. Following are some of their opinions:

> There is a good deal of "bunk" about the necessity of seaworthiness, and though numerous yachts suitable for riding out a winter gale on the Grand Banks are designed and built, yet their actual cruising is limited to protected water and to short 'longshore jumps in good weather. If, for business reasons or by inclination, one cruises under such conditions, it would seem poor judgement to demand a real sea-going yacht and to pay the required price. To those who admit that their cruising is thus limited, the sharpie offers a cheap and rather satisfactory type.

> —*Howard I. Chapelle*

> Sharpies are admirably adapted for floating over the bars and shallows of the rivers and coasts of Long Island Sound, and are stiff and seaworthy boats. They have been sent out for long cruises, and one drawing 12 inches has sailed in safety to the West Indies....The sharpie has had many uses, having been gainfully employed as oyster

boat, sponger, mail boat, cargo boat, Spanish mackerel fisherman, Cuban gun-runner, and, more lately, even as a "bootie." The chief recommendations of the sharpie are its cheapness, speed and ease of handling.

> —Report on the Ship-building Industry of the United States, *Tenth U.S. Census, 1880–85, Washington, D.C.*

In this corporate age of controlled environment, spiritual sterility, and plastic appliances, it is long past time to give back to the average person a piece of his or her American heritage—a useful, exciting thing to do by hand, with the help of family and friends, at home, with common household tools and cheap materials from the local lumberyard and hardware store. The result will be something to be proud of, to enjoy, to share and to learn from. It will reconnect people to the liquid environment from which their ancestors came. This is what the sharpie was always all about—a boat that belongs to the people—designed by, built by, and used by the common man.

See you on the water!

—*Reuel B. Parker*

Fort Pierce, Florida
Rockport, Maine
September 1993

CHAPTER 1
HISTORY AND EVOLUTION

Origins in Colonial Times

The exact origins of the sharpie are unknown. Flat-bottomed craft of many types and sizes are known to have existed before recorded history; archaeological digs along the banks of the Nile have unearthed portions of hulls resembling flat-bottomed cargo carriers and fishermen that are seen from China to Brazil even today. In times of antiquity, the limiting factor governing the creation of flat-bottomed craft was that they were generally formed from planks, or at least squared-off logs, requiring a higher level of tool use and fastening techniques than the more primitive rafts and log canoes that preceded them.

In America, flat-bottomed craft came across the Atlantic from Europe and the British Isles on the decks of ships, and were reproduced in the colonies in the forms of skiffs and scows of many types and sizes. These early craft were small, generally under 20 feet, and were limited by the availability of planking stock. As sawmills appeared, the number of skiffs and scows increased. In colonial times, planks were made either by driving a frow through a log with a mallet, literally slicing off planks, or by using a saw pit and large two-man ripsaws where one man worked the saw from above while the other worked from below in the pit.

In New England, particularly on the Connecticut coast, European settlers learned from the Indians how to make log canoes. The aboriginal canoes were sculpted and burned from coastal giant white pine trees. Colonial settlers in the New Haven area used log canoes to lighter goods from ships at anchor in the roadstead outside the shallow harbor into the town. Where the aboriginal canoe had a rounded bottom and was somewhat unstable, the colonists hewed the undersides of the logs flat, thereby decreasing draft and weight, and increasing stability.

The New Haven canoes ranged from 28 to 35 feet long, 3 feet to 3 feet 6 inches beam, 15 to 20 inches deep, and 3 to 4 inches in draft. The bottoms were about 3 inches thick and the sides 2½ inches thick. The canoes were rigged with one or two unstayed pole masts stepped through thwarts. The sails were leg-o'-mutton (jib-headed) type. A single leeboard was used to reduce leeway. A lanyard fastened from the bottom centerline of the canoe to the leeboard took strain off the sides of the canoe and eliminated the need for the usual leeboard fittings. In coming about, the leeboard was lifted from one side as the water pressure came off it, then lowered on the other side.

Figure 1-1. Sketch of an archaeological find from the Nile.

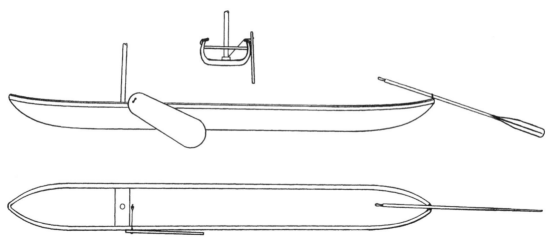

Figure 1-2. Connecticut log canoe.

The Oyster Fisheries

Although the log canoes were originally used for transportation and lightering cargo from ship to shore and vice versa, they found a new occupation by the second quarter of the 19th century. The following quote is from *The Fore-and-Aft Rig in America*, by E.P. Morris:

> Oysters were indigenous along the [Long Island] Sound, but the modern method of cultivation did not begin until 1823, when they were first brought up from the Chesapeake to be planted in the half-fresh waters of the Connecticut shore. New Haven harbor, wide and shallow, was then the center of the trade, which became an important industry....

The giant white pine trees of the New England coast were in high demand not only for log canoes but as masts for "the King's ships" and the construction of buildings, and before 1825 most of the easily accessible trees were gone. Around the same time, sawmills were being built along the coast and roads cut deeper into the forest to access the timber. As mills and lumberyards made planking readily available, the flatiron skiff came into favor. Although inexpensive and easy to build, the flatiron skiffs had limitations. In his article "The Sharpie," in the January 1927 issue of *Yachting*, W. P. Stephens stated,

"They were hard to row, bad performers in rough water, and a poor substitute for the log canoe."

The New Haven flatiron skiffs were from 15 to 18 feet long and had a beam of approximately one-third the length. Due to the flaring topsides, beam on the bottom was about one-fourth the length. The skiffs had broad, square sterns, and this is what made them hard to row.

Having a little personal experience with the type, I must say that with some modifications

Figure 1-3. Flatiron skiff. The model shown was built by Ed Glaser, captain of the Maine schooner *Isaac H. Evans*, to Chapelle's lines in *American Small Sailing Craft*.

they can be satisfactory; well-formed and lightly built flatiron skiffs of reasonably narrow beam (especially in the stern) row and sail well in most conditions. However, they do not do well driving to windward in short, steep chop. The really poor performers among the type are those with too much beam, unnecessarily high freeboard, and excessive weight.

The oyster industry created the need for very large skiffs. Through necessity, the flatiron skiff rapidly evolved into a longer, proportionately narrower and better-performing vessel. These craft were in evidence around New Haven in the late 1840s and came to be called sharpies because of their long, fine, or sharp bows.

Several of the vagaries of the shorter, beamier skiffs diminished as they were stretched out into sharpies. In his article mentioned above, W. P. Stephens went on to say, "When heeled deck-to, and sailing on the V formed by all of the lee side and half of the bottom, the actual breadth was lessened, the bad qualities of the ordinary flat-bottomed boat disappeared, and the actual immersed form was conducive to speed."

It is not known for certain who built the first sharpie, but there are two claims. In 1879, the January 23 issue of *Forest and Stream* attributed the first sharpie, *Trotter*, to a boat carpenter named Taylor. In the subsequent issue, the claim was disputed by one M. Goodsell, who claimed he and his brother built the first sharpie, *Telegraph*, in 1848. The second claim was not disputed.

Though no positive descriptions of the early sharpies exist, it may be assumed they were fairly long (20 to 30 feet), narrow, open, flat-bottomed skiffs with a square, raked transom and a centerboard. Like the log canoes, they carried one or

Figure 1-4. New Haven sharpie with log canoes on the Quinnipiac River, New Haven, Connecticut, around the turn of the century. Courtesy of the Library of Congress.

two freestanding pole masts stepped through thwarts, and used leg-o'-mutton sails.

Throughout their long history, sharpies have been built by amateurs and fishermen as well as professional boatwrights. The late Howard I. Chapelle, America's preeminent authority on small-craft design and history, believes the first leading New Haven builder was a man named Graves. The most prominent New Haven builder in the last quarter of the 19th century was Lester Rowe. It is Rowe who developed the New Haven sharpies to their highest evolution.

The earliest existing plans of New Haven sharpies depict boats about 27 or 28 feet long, with three maststeps providing the option of sailing the vessel as a cat-ketch or a sloop, depending on seasonal weather conditions.

The New Haven sharpie rapidly evolved into two sizes, sometimes referred to as a "one-man boat" and a "two-man boat." Their sizes were defined by the number of bushels of oysters they could carry: The smaller boats carried 75 to 100 bushels, were 26 to 28 feet in length, and typically (though not exclusively) carried one mast and sail. The larger boats carried 150 to 175 bushels, were 35 or 36 feet long, and were fitted

Figure 1-5. An early New Haven sharpie, circa 1870. Courtesy of the New Haven Colony Historical Society.

with three maststeps like the earlier and smaller versions. In summer, or in times of predictably gentle wind, two masts were carried. During windy seasons, generally in fall, winter, and spring, one mast was carried.

All the later New Haven sharpies were half-decked, with "washboards" or side decks and coamings to keep seas from shipping aboard when well heeled over in a fresh breeze. Oystering was done standing on the decks.

On the Connecticut coast, oysters were gathered with tongs—hinged rakes with opposing long tines and long wooden handles—from the side and stern areas of the boats. The tonger spread the handles open, plunged the tines into the soft, oyster-rich mud in shallow water (from 2 to about 10 feet depth), and worked the handles closed in pulling, rhythmic motions that separated the oysters from the mud. When closed and free from mud, the tongs were lifted on board, clear over the decks to the open hold where the handles were opened to deposit the oysters. Because the slow motion of the boat downwind often made it necessary to haul the loaded tongs in around the stern, most oystering sharpies had round sterns so the heavy tongs

Figure 1-6. The West Haven sharpie *Isabel* on a pleasure outing; note the square stern. Courtesy of the New Haven Colony Historical Society.

could be swung forward around the stern, along the sides, and up over the side decks. This way, the heavy load didn't have to be lifted as high (freeboard is lowest at the point where the tongs were swung aboard) and the oysters could be dropped closer to the middle of the hull.

The sharpies had high, tucked sterns, and the deepest part of the hull bottom was abaft amidships where the oysters were loaded. The combination of these two design elements allowed the sharpies to be heavily loaded in their after half without immersing either stern or stem, and maintaining the lowest center of gravity possible. It should be noted that sharpies designed for other purposes, such as racing and cruising, typically had lower sterns and differently rockered bottoms, with the lowest part of the hull body somewhat shifted forward, producing a flatter run and lower ultimate displacement potential.

Typically, oyster tonging was undertaken in smooth waters and light winds or calms. In *American Small Sailing Craft*, Howard I. Chapelle wrote:

> The sharpie was usually brought to windward of the tonging bed, and then, with her foresail set and her helm lashed, she was sailed slowly to leeward, and tonging began. The speed of the boat was readily controlled in light to moderate breezes by slacking off the sheet, and it was not uncommon for the sheet to be slacked all the way so that the foresail flapped over the bows, with its sprit projecting directly ahead. In calms the boat either drifted with the tide or was anchored and then shifted with sweeps; the sharpies rowed very easily. Underway, tonging was done from the side decks, of course.

Morris's description in *The Fore-and-Aft Rig in America* differs slightly:

> On the oystering grounds they are anchored by the stern,... the sheet is allowed to run out, and the sail swings forward over the bow. To one who does not know the rig it is an extraordinary and scarcely intelligible spectacle.

In my boyhood on Great South Bay, Long Island, I watched as clams were gathered by similar methods in beamy, motor-driven sharpies that still work the Bay today. Tongers would often start working their tongs forward, walking slowly down the side decks as the boat drifted, finally bringing their catch aboard near the stern. I assume the practice was similar on the New Haven sharpies, except when anchored: Being anchored at the stern, they would slack the anchor rode as an area around the boat was worked, allowing the boat to drift forward over a fresh area.

1850—New Haven

On the Connecticut coast the sharpie rapidly evolved, through trial and error, into a highly defined and practical craft. It was discovered, over the years, what worked best—and what didn't work. The fishermen had great pride in their vessels and, because they were fast and highly maneuverable, took to racing them. Chapelle described the New Haven sharpies as having standardized proportions. Their beam on the bottom was roughly one-sixth the hull length; topsides flare was 3½ to 4 inches per foot of depth amidships (or about 7¼ inches at a midlength height of 22 to 24 inches); bottom rocker (measured up to the bottoms of stem and stern from a base line parallel to the water line established at the deepest hull location) was about 12 inches forward and 18 or 19 inches aft (round stern) or 16 to 18 inches (square stern) for the 35 and 36-foot models.

Another description, appearing in Chapelle's government publication *Paper 25: The Migrations of an American Boat Type*, varies slightly:

> Kunhardt, writing in the mid-1880's, described the New Haven sharpie as being 33 to 35 feet long, about 5 feet 9 inches to 6 feet wide on the bottom, and with a depth of about 36 inches at stem, 24 inches amidships, and 12 inches at stern. The flare increased rapidly from

the bow toward amidships, where it became 3½ inches for every 12 inches of depth. The increase of flare was more gradual toward the stern, where the flare was equal to about 4 inches to the foot. According to Kunhardt, a 35-foot sharpie hull weighed 2,000 to 2,500 pounds and carried about 5 short tons [10,000 pounds!] in cargo.

The sharpie usually had its round stern carried out quite thin. If the stern was square, the transom was set at a rake of not less than 45 degrees. Although it cost about $15 more than the transom stern, the round stern was favored because tonging from it was easier; also, when the boat was tacked, the round stern did not foul the main sheet [today called mizzen sheet] and was also less likely to ship a sea than was the square stern. Kunhardt remarks that sharpies lay quiet when anchored by the stern, making the ground tackle easier to handle.

As his source, Chapelle cites *Small Yachts: Their Design and Construction, Exemplified by the Ruling Types of Modern Practice*, by C. P. Kunhardt. It's interesting to note that Kunhardt disliked sharpies, being instead a proponent of heavily ballasted, deep-keeled vessels.

A good deal of information on sharpies was documented by Henry Hall, Special Agent, 10th U.S. Census, in his *Report on the Ship-building Industry of the United States*:

> ...the sharpie...is so good a fishing boat and so fast a yacht that it has been adopted in a great many other localities throughout the United States where the waters are tolerably smooth and a safe, comfortable, and capacious boat is required. The sharpie is at present the oyster boat of Connecticut, and is also a favorite for all general pleasure rowing on the rivers and lakes of that state. The regular boatbuilders at Groton, New London, Norwich, Essex, and other places on the Connecticut River, and at Fair Haven, New Haven, Bridgeport, and South Norwalk, make as many as from 10 to 50 of this class of boats a year. A large number are also made by fishermen, one at

a time, for their own use, and many are also made each year by young men for pleasure rowing and sailing, some getting out the stuff themselves from the lumber yard of the town, others sending to New York for it [early "kit" boats?].

> The small sharpie for rowing is from 12 to 15 feet long, about 3 feet wide, and 18 inches deep, and has three thwarts. It will carry 3 or 4 men, and costs $20 or $25 to build complete. Boats from 20 feet in length upward are usually made for sailing. The size used by oystermen would average about 30 feet in length; they vary, however, from 20 to 40 feet. The breadth of the boats is from 0.17 L. to 0.25 L., and the depth amidships about 0.11 L. in small boats and 0.06 or 0.08 L. in large ones, the proportions varying slightly with the fancy of the owners, some wanting large and capacious craft, others fast craft. In the latter case the beam is made narrower. Large sharpies cost from $200 to $400. A schooner-rigged boat of this class, built for racing on the Shrewsbury River, in New Jersey, fitted with cabin and berths, cost $500, the high price being due to the furniture in the cabin. For sharpies used in oystering the cost seldom exceeds $200. The principal place where the sharpie can be seen is at Fair Haven, Connecticut, where at nightfall in the oyster season nearly 200 of them can sometimes be seen alongside of the wharves.

In *Paper 25*, Chapelle explains the migration and popularity of the sharpie type:

> The sharpie was so distinctive in form, proportion and appearance that her movements from area to area can be traced with confidence. This boat type was particularly well suited to oyster fishing, and during the last four decades of the 19th century its use spread along the Atlantic coast of North America as new oyster fisheries and markets opened....

> The sharpie's rapid spread in use can be accounted for by its low cost, light draft, speed, handiness under sail, graceful appearance, and rather astonishing seaworthiness. Since oyster

tonging was never carried on in heavy weather, it was by chance rather than intent that the seaworthiness of this New Haven tonging boat was discovered. There is a case on record in which a tonging sharpie rescued the crew of a coasting schooner at Branford, Connecticut, during a severe gale, after other boats had proved unable to approach the wreck.

In *The Fore-and-Aft Rig in America*, E. P. Morris describes the eventual demise of oystering from sharpies in New Haven:

> ...as late as 1870 the flats of the harbor bristled with flexible stakes that marked the oyster beds, and there was a large fleet of sharpies, certainly not less than a hundred, afloat in the river. As the town grew into a city, the water of the harbor became polluted, the oysters were moved out into the Sound and the dredging was done from steamers. I need scarcely say that the flavor of the oyster is not what it was "when I was a boy"; and the sharpie has almost disappeared.

1855—Long Island and New York City

The sharpie almost immediately crossed the Long Island Sound, and 100-bushel boats were built and employed on the north shore of Long Island, New York, starting in 1855. Chapelle reports that by 1857, 150-bushel two-masted sharpies were in use in lower New York harbor. Both west and east of New Haven, smaller and slightly beamier sharpies came into extensive use in local oyster fisheries; these craft were sloop-rigged, and came to be known as "flatties." The flatties were "popular on the north shore of Long Island, on the Chesapeake Bay, and in Florida at Key West and Tampa." The flattie type later developed a deadrise stern (V-bottom aft), and finally evolved into the skipjack and batteau on the Chesapeake, and the V-bottom boat elsewhere.

The first known large sharpie yacht was *Lucky*, whose half-model used to be (and may

still be) in the Model Room of the New York Yacht Club. *Lucky* was built in 1855 from a model by Robert Fish, 51 feet long by 13 feet beam by 2 feet 10 inches draft. "According to firsthand reports," said Chapelle, again in *Paper 25*, "she was a satisfactory cruiser, except that she was not very weatherly because her centerboard was too small."

Chapelle describes schooner-rigged sharpies as being similar to but larger than the New Haven boats. These craft developed on Long Island Sound starting around 1870, and appeared later on the Chesapeake, in the Florida Keys, the Carolinas, and even the West Indies. A natural size limitation of around 50 feet soon became evident, due to structural problems. By using tie-rods, some with turnbuckles to set up tension, and edge-fasteners in the sides, it eventually became feasible to build larger hulls. The sharpie schooner became more popular on Great South Bay than on Long Island Sound. Many of these schooners had watertight bulkheads at each end of the hold; the hull between was drilled with holes to create a wet-well. These vessels, called "smacks," could carry live fish in their wet-holds, and became known on the Chesapeake as "Terrapin smacks." Most of the early sharpie schooners were small, ranging between 30 and 38

Figure 1-7. Drawing of Terrapin smack by Kunhardt, from *Forest and Stream*, 1885.

feet. Later, as construction methods permitted, larger sharpie schooners developed. Some of these reached the 60- and 70-foot range, and at least one carried three masts.

1860s—New Jersey

One of the few places near Connecticut where the sharpie didn't become popular was Barnegat Bay. The garvey, a local type, was in favor there. The garvey is a small sailing scow, punt-shaped, with flaring sides and a sled-like profile; it is half-decked, and the bow is narrower than the stern. Garveys varied in length from 24 to 26 feet, in beam from 6 feet 4 inches to 6 feet 6 inches (5 feet to 5 feet 3 inches on the bottom), could carry more oysters for their length than the sharpies, and performed well. The rig consisted of two spritsails, the forward being larger. While the popularity of garveys prevented the sharpie from gaining prominence on the New Jersey coast, they didn't compete with the sharpies' wide use elsewhere in the eastern United States. I have found no lines of sharpies from New Jersey; Chapelle states that garveys were so economical, popular, and handy that the sharpie was not greatly needed.

However, several paragraphs of Henry Hall's report are devoted to the prominence of small oyster skiffs on the Jersey coast during the latter half of the 19th century:

> On the Jersey coast there is nothing built except fishing and oyster boats, with occasionally a coal barge, from Staten Island to the region of Barnegat and Absecon. At Amboy a great many oyster skiffs are employed by the fishermen of that busy locality, and probably 125 of them can be seen every day at nightfall gathering about the landing places on both sides of the Kill at that point. Two or three boat shops are steadily employed in their production. Unlike the Connecticut skiffs, these boats are regularly framed, and have a strip of flat bottom, taper-ing to a point at each end, with clinker-built [lapstrake] sides nailed to frame timbers inside, placed about 20 inches apart, the sides being full and round and the stern perpendicular but V-shaped, as in a yawl. There are three sizes of these oyster skiffs, 18, 19, and 20 feet respectively. This is the length of the bottom. The boats over all are 4 and 4½ feet longer. The beam is about 6 feet, and the depth from 20 to 22 inches. The planking is pine or cedar, strongly fastened with copper rivets through each lap; the frames are roots of the white oak tree, selected as having the proper curvature naturally, squared and fitted to their places; and the bottom is floored over and the thwarts made removable, so that a large pile of oysters in the shell can be heaped up in the boat amidships. Most of the skiffs have a pole with a small fore-and-aft sail, the mast being planted a little forward of amidships, but not in the bow. When there is a sail, there is generally a center-board also. About 250 feet of cedar are cut up for the planking and flooring. The boats cost $90 and $100 each, and one man with an assistant can make 20 of them in a year. The building of new boats and the repair of old ones is a pleasant and profitable industry.

From Hall's description, these New Jersey oyster skiffs sound like sloop-rigged surf dories, or wherries, with their rounded sides. According to Hall, the skiffs were of lapstrake construction, with copper-riveted sides and, I assume, single-plank bottoms and V-shaped transoms. Although Hall calls these craft "skiffs," mean-ing, by definition, small (under 20 feet) flat-bottomed craft, I suspect they may have really been dories or wherries, which were popular on the Jersey coast at that time. Marine terminology through history is frequently vague, confusing, and often very misleading. Regional definitions varied greatly.

Early 1870s—France

According to Chapelle (*American Sailing Craft*), the sharpie was introduced into France between

1870 and 1880 by a French yachtsman and writer by the name of L. More. It seems ironic to me that the sharpie became popular as a yacht in Europe before it did so at home, but such is the case. More made two trips to Long Island Sound, and each time he brought a sharpie back to France, the second one being of the "Nonpareil" type. (The term "Nonpareil" refers to sharpies built by Thomas Clapham at Roslyn, Long Island, which had shallow V bottoms.) These craft caused quite a commotion, resulting in the spread of the sharpie through western Europe.

Other than this, I have not been able to find more information about early sharpies in France. But the type is still, to this day, popular there, and I found a book in the office of my friend, naval architect Yves-Marie Tanton, called *Le Sharpie, Son Histoire et Son Evolution*, by Maurice Amiet. This remarkable book consists of plans for sharpies and modified sharpies from several countries spanning a full century.

Early 1870s—The Chesapeake

On the Chesapeake Bay, as on the Connecticut shore, the log canoe, adopted from the Indians, was a very popular small craft for most purposes. The log canoe evolved much further on the Chesapeake, however, into rather large vessels made from several logs joined together. It is unclear exactly how and when the sharpie first appeared on the Chesapeake, and whether the type migrated from Connecticut or was independently "invented" there, as it was in New

Figure 1-8. Chesapeake Bay 28-foot sharpie. Courtesy of the Library of Congress and Wirth Munroe.

Haven. The latter is quite possible, as there were small flat-bottomed skiffs employed in oyster tonging prior to 1870. But sharpies were on the Bay in the early 1870s, and Chapelle (in *Paper 25*) relates the following story:

> There is a tradition that sometime in the early 1870's a New Haven sharpie named Frolic was found adrift on the Bay near Tangier Island. Some copies of the *Frolic* were made locally, and modifications were added later. This tradition is supported by certain circumstantial evidence.

The Tangier Island skiffs resembled New Haven sharpies above the water, including round sterns and cat-ketch rigs, but had shallow V-bottoms.

A distinct form of Chesapeake Bay sharpie, a large sailing skiff, became popular on many parts of the Bay in the last quarter of the 19th century. These very handsome sharpies had square sterns, curved stems, strong flare, flat bottoms, sharply raking transoms, daggerboards, and were rigged with two leg-o'-mutton sails. The masts were raked more than those of the Connecticut sharpies, and the sprit booms were set higher on the masts. Sometimes the rig included a short bowsprit and "balance" jib, which I will explain later. The rudder was hung outboard on a large skeg. (A skeg is a plank-keel aft, usually longer than deep.) The type varied from 18 feet to 28 feet; the bigger boats were half-decked, and the smaller boats were open.

Schooner-rigged sharpies similar to those seen in New York were popular on the Chesapeake Bay in the 1880s. Many of these were "smacks," having wet-wells, and Chapelle drafted an example of the type, shown in Figure 1-9. This is the famous Maryland Terrapin smack, whose lines I have copied from *Paper 25*. Chapelle states that

Figure 1-9. Maryland Terrapin smack, from Chapelle, based on sketches and dimensions given by C. P. Kunhardt in *Small Yachts: Their Design and Construction, Exemplified by the Rules of Modern Practice*. Courtesy of the Library of Congress *(Paper 25)*.

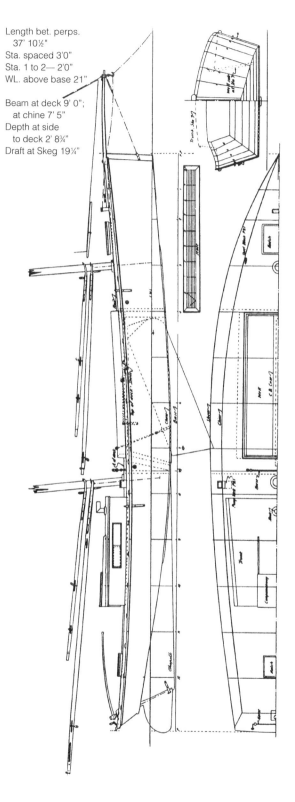

Length bet. perps.
37' 10½"
Sta. spaced 3'0"
Sta. 1 to 2— 2'0"
WL. above base 21"

Beam at deck 9' 0";
at chine 7' 5"
Depth at side
to deck 2' 8¾"
Draft at Skeg 19¼"

he relied on old photographs for source material in addition to that from Kunhardt.

Perhaps because of the rough waters on the Bay, or to obtain more capacity, V-bottomed craft, such as bateaux and skipjacks, eventually replaced most of the large sharpies on the Bay by 1890. However, various types of skiffs (sharpies under 20 feet) have survived to the present day. Among these were several double-ended types described by Chapelle (*Paper 25*):

> The use of the principles of flatiron skiff design in sharp-stern, or "double-ended" boats has been common. On the Chesapeake Bay a number of small, double-ended sailing skiffs, usually fitted with a centerboard and a single leg-of-mutton sail, were in use in the 1880's. It is doubtful, however, that these skiffs had any real relationship to the New Haven sharpie. They may have developed from the "three-plank" canoe used on the Bay in colonial times. [One plank formed the bottom; the other two the sides.]
>
> The "cabin skiff," a double-ended, half-decked, trunk-cabin boat with a long head and a cuddy forward, was also in use on the Bay in the 1880's. This boat, which was rigged like a bugeye, had a bottom of planks that were over 3 inches thick, laid fore-and-aft, and edge-bolted. In spite of its slightly cambered bottom, this boat, though truly a flatiron skiff in midsection form, had no real relation to the New Haven sharpie; it probably owed its origin to the Chesapeake log canoe, for which it was an inexpensive substitute.

Figure 1-10. The author's Maryland crabbing skiff *Mallard*.

One of the double-ended skiff types in the first category was the Maryland crabbing skiff. These exquisitely graceful small craft varied from 17 to about 24 feet in length, and were popular in various locations on the Bay, including Hooper Island and Smith Island, on the Eastern Shore. The crabbing skiffs had single, raking masts and sprits, often with a short, vertical club at the clew, and many carried a short bowsprit with a "balance jib."

In *Paper 25*, Chapelle gives interesting evidence of the use of mass media in disseminating information on sharpies:

> Since the 1880's the magazine *Forest and Stream* and, later, magazines such as *Outing, Rudder,* and *Yachting* have been the media by which ideas concerning all kinds of watercraft from pleasure boats to work boats have been transmitted. By studying such periodicals, Chesapeake Bay boatbuilders managed to keep abreast of the progress in boat design being made in new yachts.

1874—North Carolina

After the Civil War, the region of the North Carolina Sounds was economically depressed, with very little boatbuilding activity. Chapelle tells us that in 1874, George C. Ives had Graves, in New Haven, build a 34-foot sharpie, which he introduced at Beaufort in 1875. This sharpie outsailed the local "Albemarle Sound boats," used in the shad fisheries, and proved herself able to work in "the fierce gales that sweep the Carolina Sounds in the fall and spring." The sharpie was also better suited for oyster harvesting than the Albemarle Sound boat, which had higher freeboard (height above the water), greater draft (permitting less access in the Sounds), and less working area on deck. Hence, with the introduction of the sharpie, extensive harvesting of the heavily-populated oyster beds became a major industry.

Local builders took up sharpie building using the Ives boat as a point of departure. As happened elsewhere, the sharpie rapidly evolved to meet the local conditions and demands.

Late 1870s—Vermont and Lake Champlain

A prominent writer for *Forest and Stream* in the last quarter of the 19th century was the Reverend W. H. H. Murray, who wrote under the sobriquet of 'Adirondack Murray.' Murray introduced sharpie yachts on Lake Champlain in the late '70s, though they soon found commercial application as well. Chapelle tells us that "The boats were chiefly remarkable for their variety of experimental rigs. . . . Racing sharpies were popular, and Burlington, Vermont, was the center of sharpie building on the lake." I regret I haven't found any surviving plans of these craft; I would dearly love to see some of these experimental rigs.

Late 1870s—The Great Lakes (Ohio)

Henry Hall's *Report on the Ship-building Industry of the United States* gives the following description of the Ohio sharpies:

Fishing on the (Great) Lakes is an along-shore occupation. It is not necessary, as a rule, for the men to be out overnight in their boats, as they put out from the mouth of the river, or from the bay where they belong, in the early morning, and

Figure 1-11. The North Carolina sharpie *Three Friends*. Courtesy of the North Carolina Maritime Museum.

Figure 1-12. The author's 19-foot Ohio pound-net sharpie *Gato Negro*.

calculate to be back again perhaps in time for supper. Carried on in this way, the business does not require boats with decks and houses, and the fishing craft of the lakes, therefore, do not as a general rule have either, nearly all of them being open boats.

A great many boats are the work of men half fisherman, half carpenter, who make only one boat, or at the most two or three boats in a year. The patterns of boats used on the Lakes all come from the sea-coasts...

This last statement is open to question. When studying the type, one quickly notes that the Lakes sharpies are markedly different in both hull and rig from sharpies anywhere else. The hulls were proportionately beamier and heavier and had square, raking transoms. The rigs were very lofty and looked for all the world like gaff-riggers with tops'ls set. This illusion was created by the use of full-length battens below the heads of the sails set at a peak angle as a gaff would be, extending the leech of the sail back as if it were the peak of a gaff.
Hall continues:

Along the Ohio coast the sharpie is the favorite of the fishermen. The mouths of the Huron, Black, and other rivers are full of this class of boats, which are often pulled up into the bulrushes on the flats when not in use.... The average size of a sharpie is 36 feet long, 10½ feet wide, and 3 feet deep, thus being a fuller, heavier, and more capacious boat than a Connecticut sharpie of the same length. It takes two men 17 days to build one, and its value, when finished, is about $225.... the boats vary in size, some being not over 24 feet in length and others as high as 42 feet....

...A 32-foot sharpie is fitted with 36- and 34-foot masts; a 36-foot boat with masts 48 and 46 feet long. The masts rake considerably, and carry the same style of sail as the Erie boats [with gaff/batten and single halyard].

The capacity of the Ohio sharpie is quite unusual. It carries from 7½ to 12 tons of pound-

nets, fish, and apparatus, besides the crew; and, in addition to its ability in this direction, it is also a very fast and manageable boat.

With sails and rigging, a 36-footer weighed approximately 3,500 pounds. It is fascinating to note that a vessel of that weight could carry a payload of up to 24,000 pounds and still sail at all.

Evidently Ohio was settled largely by people from Connecticut and Massachusetts, and it would seem probable that there is a link between the Lakes sharpies and the New England boats. Chapelle speculates that the Erie sharpie originated in Ohio, and Henry Hall tells us that the most noted builder at Sandusky in 1881 was George Littleton, originally from Virginia. The boats were built without plans or models by fishermen as well as boatbuilders, at Huron, Green Bay, and Dover Bay in addition to Sandusky. It is fascinating to track these tidbits of information and speculate upon their influence on the development of the sharpie.

Sharpies used on the Great Lakes varied considerably in size, shape, proportion and rig, as well as in commercial application. They varied in length from 20 to at least 42 feet, and were consistently heavier and fuller bodied than the New Haven boats. Because of their size, shape and capacity, they appear to me to be distant relatives of the New England flatiron skiff.

Further descriptions of these powerful sharpies come from Chapelle's *American Sailing Craft*:

Hall and other observers agree that the boats were very stiff and able, and, with their very large rigs, were very fast sailers in spite of their beam. It is probable that the adverse effects of the great beam in these sharpies were counteracted by the very heavy loads they habitually carried in their business. They appear to have employed some stone ballast as did most of the sharpies, which usually had a small tier of stone paving block or sandbags as ballast to give momentum in tacking. The weight carried by the lake sharpies was

Figure 1-13. Ohio pound-net boat under sail, 1890. Courtesy of the National Museum of American History, Smithsonian Institution.

respectively, length, beam, and depth of body amidships. From these examples, it is clear how much larger the Lakes sharpies were, proportionately, than most other sharpies.

In *The Fore-and-Aft Rig in America*, Morris mentions a North Carolina sharpie with a boomless foresail using double sheets, but otherwise very similar in rig to the Ohio pound-net boat. He presents evidence (a possible migrating boatbuilder?) that perhaps the hull form of the Ohio pound-net boat came from the Carolinas, or New England, and the rig from the Sandusky, Ohio, boats. The Mackinac rig, as it was known, disappeared from the coast, but survived on the Lakes. Perhaps the rig evolved from the spritsail rig, as used with the four-sided sail, which was still in occasional use on the Lakes when the sharpie first became popular there. I find this unlikely, and suspect that the rig evolved from the gaff topsail rig, which was in use everywhere in America. In any case, it may be seen that various hull and rig types spread rapidly back and forth across America.

probably great enough to overcome the drag of the balanced rudder, set at so sharp a rake.

The rig of the lake sharpies is an interesting one, combining the advantages of the gaff with those of the true leg-of-mutton....a simple single halyard serves and the gaff becomes no more than a light batten, requiring no bands, jaws, or other hardware....the gaff is a double-batten, screw-bolted through the sail. Few boats had a set of jaws on this double batten; the heel was usually seized to a mast hoop.

Some boats, among the smaller of the type, were sloop-rigged.

In his research (*American Small Sailing Craft*), Chapelle documented the sizes of some Lakes sharpies as follows: 36 feet x 10 feet x 3 feet; 32 feet x 9 feet x 3 feet; 28 feet x 9 feet 6 inches x 3 feet; 20 feet x 7 feet 9 inches x 28 inches; 26 feet x 9 feet 6 inches x 3 feet. The dimensions are for,

1881—The Carolina Sounds

After the sharpie was introduced at Beaufort, North Carolina, as mentioned earlier, the type spread both up and down the coast. Take a quick look at some maps and charts of the Carolina coast, and you'll have an idea of the vast aquatic resources of these water-rich states; the Carolinas contain dozens of bays and sounds protected from the Atlantic by long strips of barrier islands. Much of this water is tidal estuary, rich with shellfish in very shallow water, often little more than three feet deep.

The sharpie was the perfect craft to work the oyster beds of these estuaries, and by 1881 the Carolina Sounds sharpies had developed their own characteristics. As the oyster grounds were far from market ports, larger boats than the regular New Haven sharpies were needed.

By 1890, many of the Carolina sharpies were 40 to 45 feet in length, had low cabins, and carried gaff rigs. As dredging gradually replaced tonging as the oyster-harvesting method of choice, the sharpie schooners became even larger. The obvious choice of rig for the dredging sharpies was the bald-headed gaff-rigged schooner, and these boats became commonplace after 1890. The gaff-schooner rig was required for dredging because of its power. Chapelle states that during the '90s the Sounds dredging schooners "were usually between 42 and 50 feet long and 10 to 12 feet beam." Though these big sharpie schooners were not as fast as the New Haven boats, they were safer and more powerful. Many of the schooners had cabins: Some had a

cramped fo'c's'le under the foredeck, others had a cuddy or trunk aft, and a few of the larger vessels had trunks forward and aft. U-shaped cargo hatches and cockpits were common to the Carolina sharpies.

The New Haven rig retained its popularity with Carolina tongers, but the schooner rig was preferred for dredging. In addition to greater power, the gaff rig's strengths included more adjustment of sail area and better handling under all weather conditions. It should be noted that oyster dredging could be carried on in rough weather, while tonging could not. Chapelle wrote (*Paper 25*):

Figure 1-14a. Deck of a North Carolina sharpie, showing the U-shaped main hatch typical of sharpies used in the Carolina Sounds. Courtesy of the Library of Congress.

These schooners remained in use well into the 20th century and, in fact, did not go out of use entirely until about 1938. In the 1920's and 30's many such boats were converted to yachts. They were fast under sail and very stiff, and with auxiliary engines they were equally as fast and required a relatively small amount of power. Large Carolina sharpie schooners often made long coasting voyages, such as between New York and the West Indies.

In their final development in the Carolinas, the sharpies reached 60 feet in length, "and many of these looked like small coasting schooners above water, having strong sheer and fiddleheads." It is interesting to note that a few of these big sharpies retained the marconi rig, including a jib and bowsprit, but were narrower of beam than the gaffers.

1881—Florida

The widely held notion that Commodore Ralph M. Munroe introduced the sharpie *Egret* to Florida in the late 1870s is erroneous. The truth is that Munroe brought the first sharpie to Florida in the fall of 1881. Following is Munroe's

Figure 1-14b. The large schooner-rigged North Carolina sharpie *Iowa*. Courtesy of the North Carolina Maritime Museum.

account, from *The Commodore's Story*, by Munroe and Gilpin:

> With us on the steamer's deck went a 30-foot sharpie sailboat, which was a complete novelty in Key West waters, and excited much comment. The general opinion was that owing to her excessively light draft (8 inches) she would be useless except in running before the wind, and their astonishment was great when they found none among the native craft able to beat her to windward. They dubbed her Skipperee, and the name stuck.

During the summer of 1883 Munroe designed a 33-foot sharpie, which was built by Brown of Staten Island, and which Munroe subsequently brought to St. Augustine, Florida, in December of that year on board the schooner *W. H. Van Brunt*. The sharpie, named *Kingfish*, was rigged as a gaff ketch with sprit booms. Munroe and a companion sailed her south to Coconut Grove through a wide variety of weather conditions. I have included a story of this voyage in Chapter Seven.

In the summer of 1886 Munroe designed the double-ended 28-foot sharpie *Egret*, specifically for running the shallow Florida inlets and handling the rough Gulf Stream offshore waters in almost any weather. *Egret* had a deep, narrow

Figure 1-15. *Kingfish* running wing-and-wing, from *The Commodore's Story*. Courtesy of the Historical Society of Southern Florida; Ralph Munroe Collection.

Figure 1-16. Commodore Ralph Munroe's "sharpie lifeboat" *Egret*. Courtesy of the Historical Society of Southern Florida; Ralph Munroe Collection.

erel, snapper and grouper on the reefs, sponging, turtling, and trapping alligators and crocodiles. Sharpies carried mail, cargo, passengers, survey and mapping crews, and various government officials. A wide variety of rigs were used on the different-sized boats, including full-size schooners with bowsprits and head rigs of the clipper bow. In *Paper 25*, Chapelle wrote, "On the Gulf Coast at Tampa, two-masted sharpies and sharpie schooners were used to carry fish to market, but they had only very faint resemblance to the original New Haven boat." And in

bottom and very flaring topsides, and might be considered to combine some of the best qualities of the dory with those of the sharpie. She was built at Brown's on Staten Island, and brought by Mallory Boat to Key West, where she distinguished herself in many ways, including transporting the mail from Palm Beach to Miami in all seasons. There is more about *Egret* in Chapter Seven.

Munroe referred to *Egret* as a "sharpie-lifeboat . . . very strongly but lightly constructed. She drew eight inches, and had only fifty to seventy-five bricks, laid under her floor, for ballast. She was fitted with all the appurtenances needed to keep the sea in almost any weather, and if necessary to be put on the beach without harm."

Egret stands as a unique sharpie, and it is too bad that no accurate lines of her hull have survived. Her remains are somewhere under Miami City Park, patiently waiting to be discovered by some future archaeologist. In Munroe's words: "The big suction dredges gently buried her, and there, beneath the pleasure seekers in the breezy park, she lies at peace, after her long life of adventure. Requiescat!"

Sharpies of all sizes and types became popular in Florida after Munroe's dramatic introductions of the type. These included fishermen for all fisheries: coastal kingfish and Spanish mack-

Figure 1-17. *Egret* from astern. Courtesy of the Historical Society of Southern Florida; Ralph Munroe Collection.

American Small Sailing Craft he states: "The Coast and Geodetic Survey long employed two large sailing sharpies, the *Spy* and *Transit*, on the Florida coast."

Many sharpie yachts were built, by Munroe and others, and these traveled all over the Keys, both Florida coasts, the Texas Gulf, the Bahamas, and even down into the West Indies.

It seems to me that Florida saw the greatest popularity and proliferation of the sharpie type. In present times the Florida Keys are one of the few places where there are still quite a number of sharpie yachts around, including one or two fleets of charter bareboats.

An example of a later Florida sharpie is the 1894 Cedar Keys sharpie, whose lines were taken off by Larry Huntington at Howard Chapelle's request, and which are printed in *American Small Sailing Craft*. At 32 feet in length, this Cedar Keys sharpie was larger than usual. Chapelle states that Cedar Keys sharpies typically ranged from 18 to 22 feet and were rigged as gaff cat-

Figure 1-18. The sharpie yacht *Pelican*, built in 1885 for Florida waters. Courtesy of the Library of Congress and Wirth Munroe.

boats, a very rare choice of rig for sharpies. It is fascinating to note that this rig was also used on Lake Champlain. An example of this craft is shown in figure 6-7.

Late 1880s—Washington State and the San Juan Islands

In *American Small Sailing Craft*, Chapelle describes an unusual type of double-ended sharpie which was used "in the halibut fishery in Juan de Fuca Strait and neighboring waters." These sharpies were beamier and heavier (carrying substantial ballast) than the East Coast sharpies; they were not intended for great speed, but were intended to be seaworthy. Of the example shown, it is interesting to note that the stem base is below the waterline, a marked departure from the design of most sharpies, which religiously keep their stem base just out of the water, even when laden.

There seems to be no known history of these craft, or of how they came to be used in Washington State. We can only guess that a perceptive fisherman read an article about the type in one of the periodicals of the day, probably in *Forest and Stream*. The type carried a bald-headed schooner rig, complete with a long bowsprit and cuddy cabin forward.

This model, a 36-footer, is an excellent example of a seaworthy sharpie design; to my knowledge, these lines are the only surviving plan of a large 19th-century double-ended sharpie in existence.

At the end of the 19th century, the sharpie had spread throughout the United States, and was in use in Canada and Europe. Any place where a shoal-draft, inexpensive workboat might be employed—sounds, rivers, lakes and bays—had sharpies. Even within the seemingly narrow design parameters of the type, variations to hull and rig of every imaginable extreme had developed. No other single boat type in the history of humankind has seen such diversity, popularity and widespread application.

Henry Hall made the following comments in his 1880–85 report:

> Many experiments have been made with the model, and light-draft schooners, intended to run in the shallow rivers of the southern states, have

Length bet. perps
36' 1¼"
Beam on deck
9' 1"
Beam on bottom
7' 6"

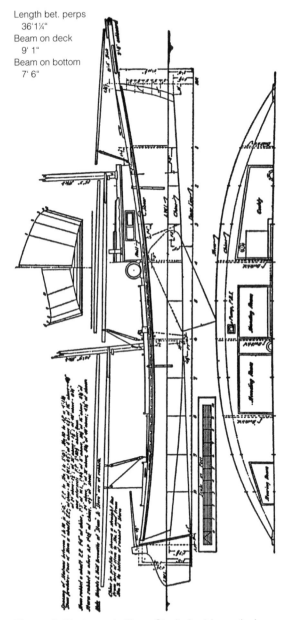

Figure 1-19. Juan de Fuca Strait double-ended sharpie. Courtesy of W. W. Norton Publishing Co.

been built of 200 tons register for the lumber and other trades; but for large vessels the model has failed to do what was expected. It is now generally understood that a sharpie should not be built more than 50 feet long, but the best results are obtained from 35 foot boats.

As I mentioned earlier in describing the development of sharpie schooners on Long Island Sound and elsewhere, the use of edge-fasteners and steel reinforcement, including tie rods with turnbuckles, eventually allowed the construction of larger sharpies. But the difficulties inherent in gaining a strong backbone or longitudinal structure in a narrow, flat-bottomed craft with no substantial keel remain a design challenge. I believe the answer lies in cold-molded plywood construction, though aluminum and steel would work nearly as well.

1890s—Yacht Development, and the Modified Sharpie

Because of the sharpie's many qualities, yachtsmen took to the type wholeheartedly. Sharpies of all sizes and types came into use all over America and France, but it soon became evident that the working sharpies had evolved form and rig to an extremely high degree of development, and alterations of time-proven proportions often resulted in disastrous failures. Chapelle commented in *Paper 25*:

> …efforts to improve on the sharpie resulted in the construction of boats that had neither the beauty nor the other advantages of the original type. This was particularly true of sharpies built as yachts with large cabins and heavy rigs. Because the stability of the sharpie's shoal hull was limited, the added weight of high, long cabin trunks and attendant furniture reduced the boat's safety potential. Windage of the topsides structure necessary on sharpie yachts also affected speed, particularly in sailing to windward. Hence, there was an immediate trend toward deadrise [V-bottom] in the bottom of the yachts, a feature that suffi-

ciently increased displacement and draft so that the superstructure and rig could be better carried. Because of its large cabin, the sharpie yacht when under sail was generally less workable than the fishing sharpie. Although it was harmful to the sailing of the boat, many of the sharpie yachts had markedly increased beam.

Because sharpies were so fast, they soon became popular for racing, especially on the Connecticut coast. At first the working oyster boats were raced; then, in a competitive spirit, craft were designed and built strictly for speed. Chapelle described these in *American Small Sailing Craft*:

> The racing sharpies were built on working-boat lines and construction and were, by common consent, of the same approximate dimensions. There were minor departures: the run was usually flatter, giving a deeper stern than in the working sharpies, and the beam was often greater amidships, particularly in the last of the type. The hulls were usually better finished and black walnut bulkheads and seats were common. The coamings were usually varnished, and some attempt was made to approach yachting standards in paint work. The racing rig was much greater than in any working sharpie, as the racers used "springboards" to outrig the weight of their crew to increase sail-carrying power.

The typical New Haven oyster boats did change shape somewhat as the type evolved for racing. The carrying capacity of the oyster boats was manifested by a high stern, and the deepest part of the hull was well aft. This allowed loading of oysters in the stern of the craft, where it was easier to deposit them during tonging. As weight increased, the stern would sink, and the high stern would remain above water, as would the base of the stem—important for good sailing. In other words, as the hulls were loaded, the waterline rose aft but remained nearly fixed forward. Because racing craft did not have this requirement, the sterns were gradually made lower and the runs flatter, the rocker of the bottoms flattened somewhat, and the deepest part of the bottom shifted slightly forward. In some cases the beam was increased very slightly also, to allow more sail to be carried. Springboards, or long planks, were fitted from the centerboards across the rail outboard to windward, upon which sat the heaviest of the crew members—human movable ballast. The rigs of these "hot-rods" became truly outrageous, including long plank bowsprits, boomkins, oversize sails, lofty masts, and even yards with huge square sails for running. On some of these rigs the paired fore sprits actually extended beyond the mainmasts, requiring that they be eased forward by slacking the snotters when coming about. Thus, accidental jibing was fatal—it could take out the whole rig.

The sharpies were already well known for their speed and weatherliness, but the racing models set records that few monohulls can achieve even today. The following from *American Small Sailing Craft* gives some examples, though it is not clear whether the speeds given were for racing sharpies or working craft:

> The speed of the sharpies has ample testimony, and some of the large boats were found to have sailed at remarkable rates: one sharpie covered eleven nautical miles in thirty-four minutes [over 19 knots!], and another averaged 16 knots for three consecutive hours. These high speeds were obviously with started sheets and with the hull in a planing attitude.

Although the true sharpie was lost as the hull evolved into other types, the early modifications were modest and often increased speed, seaworthiness, and the ability to carry sail. Because of the flat bottom, the waterlines of all but the double-ended sharpies ended in a rectangular (or trapezoidal) shape. As this shape caused some drag due to large wetted surface, the first modifications of the sharpie hull consisted of incorporating a V-bottom shape in the stern. The V started after the flat midship section and increased aft. This resulted in a somewhat pointed waterline plane aft, with less wetted surface. Thomas Clapham of Roslyn, Long Island, New York, is generally credited with this innovation (although it also appeared in the Hampton flatties, popular in Virginian waters since before the Civil War), and he named the resulting type the "Nonpareil sharpie." The addition of V-bottom, or deadrise, to the sharpie hull soon included the entire length of the boat. Clapham experimented extensively with this, varying the amount and location of deadrise in his models, and often increasing the beam slightly also. These craft continued to be called Nonpareil sharpies. Chapelle described Thomas Clapham as "a well-educated man and prolific writer." The Nonpareil sharpies also became known as "Roslyn sharpies" and "Roslyn yawls" after Clapham's hometown.

Another logical modification was curving the bottom athwartships into an arc. The effect of this is similar to the V-bottom: it adds deadrise. This allows increased beam, making the hull stiffer and able to carry more sail, and creates a somewhat pointed waterline plane aft with less drag than that of flat-bottomed models. I have incorporated the arc-bottom in many of my own sharpie designs because it adds great strength and lends itself to both plywood and cold-molded wood construction.

In *American Sailing Craft*, Chapelle wrote:

> During the nineties Larry Huntington began experimenting with sharpies, building them on Long Island, and he, too, developed a modified type. Where Clapham had employed straight deadrise, which soon evolved into the skipjack or V-bottom, Huntington used a rounded bottom athwartships, retaining the flat sides and chines of the orthodox sharpie. The Huntington type remained a true sharpie, except for the slight camber in the bottom athwartships. Usually this was an arc of a circle amidships, the amount of camber being quite small there and decreasing towards bow and stern. This feature increased the

speed in light airs. After the half-rater *Question* "cleaned up" on the Sound the Huntington type was widely copied.

During the late 19th century, a great controversy raged between the "plank-on-edge" fans and the "skimming-dish" fans. Basically, yachtsmen were divided in preference between deep-keeled, heavily ballasted hulls and shoal-bodied, centerboard hulls. The latter were always faster, but isolated accidents often resulted in their condemnation as unsafe. Even though such acci-

dents were almost always the result of errors in judgment, the fact remained that shoal-bodied hulls were almost never self-righting, whereas deep-keeled hulls almost always were. (This has changed somewhat in the late 20th century due to modern designs, construction methods, and materials.)

It is interesting to note C. P. Kunhardt's role in popularizing sharpie yachts (*Small Yachts: Their Design and Construction*) even though he was a fanatical supporter of the deep keel and heavily ballasted hull used in the English cutter

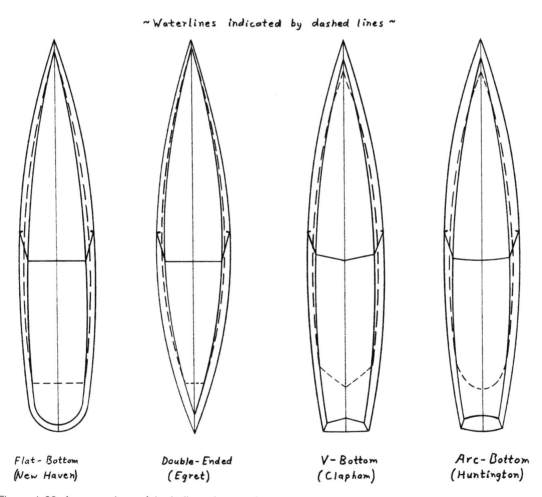

~ Waterlines indicated by dashed lines ~

Flat-Bottom (New Haven) Double-Ended (Egret) V-Bottom (Clapham) Arc-Bottom (Huntington)

Figure 1-20. A comparison of the hull sections and waterline planes of different sharpie hulls.

yachts in this period. Kunhardt published several designs and drawings of sharpies and did much to promote them by writing about them, even though he was opposed to the type.

In addition to his Nonpareil sharpies, Thomas Clapham is credited with many other innovations in yacht design. He developed a highly successful rig, which he called the Roslyn yawl, and he incorporated the use of outside ballast. His shallow, V-bottomed Nonpareil sharpie hulls, with their outside ballast shoes and flaring topsides, were evidently uncapsizable.

At the time of the American "cutter craze" (the above-mentioned affinity for the English "plank-on-edge" type), Clapham had the following letter published in *Forest and Stream*, February 14, 1879:

> I am at present building a sharpie, on experimental lines, and if the captain of any cutter or deep keel yacht is anxious to prove a shaky theory I will be most happy to give him a turn to windward and home in any kind of weather and the rougher it is, the more sanguine I am of demonstrating that 15" is better than 15' in the way of draught.

It didn't take long until sharpies were banned from racing any craft but other sharpies. They simply were always the fastest boats.

As for the seaworthiness issue, Clapham published this statement in 1879:

> Reported that a sharpie went out from Branford [Connecticut] to the reef off that harbor and rescued the crew of a schooner wrecked there when neither smack nor tug could be found in New Haven to venture out.

In 1881, Clapham's comments were more pointed:

> There is not the slightest difficulty in producing an uncapsizable light draft yacht that will equal or surpass the cutter in seaworthiness and speed, yet be absolutely unsinkable. Why, then,

should we turn to England and borrow a loggy, slow and unhandy model when at our own water's edge we have something better at far less cost?

And in the September 22, 1881, issue of *Forest and Stream*, he wrote:

> A "Nonpareil" sharpie, 61 feet overall by 14 feet beam, about completed for a member of the New York Yacht Club, intended for sea work and cruising, has a large cabin with 6 feet headroom, will take a party of ten in comfort and draws but 18" of water and will work to windward with dry decks when a cutter of like dimensions would wallow under water half the time. The cutter would cost $10,000 or more; the "Nonpareil" sharpie, with outfit complete, may cost anywhere from $1800 to $2500.

Clapham's boats improved as he evolved the type. Numerous of his craft made offshore passages, even in winter gales, safely and rapidly, without shipping seas. He also experimented with the arc-bottomed hull, and Chapelle points out in *American Small Sailing Craft* that Clapham "should perhaps receive credit for the innovation." Many of Clapham's racing designs were arc-bottomed with hard chines and flat, flaring topsides. It is interesting that many racing and cruising yachts of today incorporate those same features, including quite a few of my own designs.

Clapham's boats were extremely fast and won many races, some having to be withdrawn because they couldn't be beat. It has also been noted that his boats balanced so well that they often steered themselves, even in rough weather, with the tiller free, or could be steered by the sheets alone.

Another interesting design footnote is that Thomas Clapham always argued in favor of the angular bilge in preference to the rounded bilge, claiming a number of advantages for that model, especially in a light-draft boat.

G. Griffith Clapham says the following in the December 1938 issue of *Yachting* in an article he wrote about his father:

The yawl rig seems best adapted to the light draft single-hander. It is easy for one man to make sail and, when the wind gets strong, it is easy to lower the mainsail and proceed under jib and jigger. I have done this many times when out on the Sound in a northeast gale and a heavy sea, with no other craft in sight. She often sailed under mainsail alone. *Minocqua* worked perfectly under full sail or any portion of it, was steady, stiff and fast and also dry, no matter what the weather.

Clapham's Nonpareil sharpies had 1,100-pound outside ballast shoes, and were considered uncapsizable. The hulls, Roslyn-yawl-rigged, were remarkably stable. Wrote William J. Starr in "An Appreciation," written the year of

Figure 1-21. *Minocqua*, a 38-foot Clapham "Roslyn yawl" Nonpareil sharpie. Courtesy of Gordon E. Hurley, Jr.

Clapham's death (*Yachting*, November 1915):

> ...flaring sides and lifting type of overhanging ends gave them much reserve buoyancy and stability in spite of their relatively narrow breadth.... In form of section these Clapham sharpies were the V-bottom boats of today— nothing more, nothing less—starting with a sharp V entrance forward (originally used to prevent pounding), with a good amount of straight deadrise amidships, and flattening somewhat aft into a very clean run. The secret of their speed with small driving power and their clean sailing was the perfectly fair segmental rockering of their bottoms from forward to aft, and perhaps fully as important, the perfect diagonal formed by the sweep of their sharp bilge when heeled under sail.

Without going too far into the principles of naval architecture, this mention of "perfectly fair segmental rockering" and "perfect diagonal" can be appreciated by imagining one of Clapham's hulls heeled over in a moderate breeze such that the submerged chine acts like a second keel, and the windward side of the boat bottom and submerged leeward topside are nearly symmetrical to each other. If you hold a straightedge across the body plan (design stations) of *Minocqua* (Figure 6-16 in Chapter Six), intersecting the deck edge on the right and the chine on the left, you will see the value of this symmetry. Water flowing under this hull has the minimum possible impediment.

Thomas Clapham also built models and tested them in the trout pond behind his shop. William Starr explains:

> Having experimented so much with working models, it was natural that Thomas Clapham should prefer the half-breadth model to the drawing in building; but all these models were faired by straight-grained pine battens, so there might be no concealed humps or hollows to stop the clean run of the water.... Mr. Clapham used to say, "If a man can't make a boat balance without hours of 'calculations,' he'd better quit." There

was another precept of his, doubtless the secret of his fair hulls: "Work all your fore-and-aft sailing lines to the sweep of a white pine batten, and let the so-called 'water-lines' take care of themselves." ... [and] "For a given sail area, the sharp-bilged boat will be faster than the one with rounded bilge, if both are equally well modeled."

Starr's last point is a fact still demonstrated in New England lobsterboat races.

I think Clapham, right along with Nathanael Greene Herreshoff, must share the title of "the father of the modern American yacht." Included among Clapham's innovations are the reverse sheer, the fin keel, the racing scow rectangular deck plan, circle-segment chines, arc-bottoms, and the Roslyn yawl rig—to say nothing of making extensive use of sailing models.

The Sharpie in the Twentieth Century

Relatively few new developments have been made with the sharpie in the last hundred years, for a number of reasons. With the decline of the onshore oyster industry in Long Island Sound, oysters were cultivated farther offshore and harvested using steam-powered vessels. In the Chesapeake, the V-bottom model eventually found more favor. The advent of gasoline power saw the end of the age of sail. Then, two world wars hastened the development of new boat types. And finally, fiberglass replaced wood in construction almost completely, encouraging different hull shapes. The flat sections of the sharpie do not lend themselves to fiberglass construction; the inherent weakness of fiberglass requires extensive use of compound curves to develop strength.

The flat bottom has survived, however, mostly in workboats and small plywood skiffs. Because these types are generally engine powered, they are beamier, heavier, and rarely exhibit the beauty and efficiency of the sharpies. In essence, the type has "devolved" to a condition considerably worse than that from which it began: the flatiron skiff and Colonial log canoe.

The sharpie has been kept alive, though, by a few who read history, and by rare examples of surviving boats. There is always a demand for fast, beautiful, economical, and simple sailing craft, and occasionally the type is "rediscovered." Designers such as Chapelle in the first half of this century and Phil Bolger in the second half have done much to promote sharpies. I believe all the qualities of the sharpie have as much value today, in our age of shrinking resources and limited time, as they have ever had. Perhaps of equal importance is the personal value of creating something with your own hands instead of buying it off a shelf or out of a catalogue. Sharpies are still popular in France, and I think the type is just about ready to sail back across the Atlantic and once again take up residence where it started. America—are you ready?

CHAPTER 2
TRADITIONAL CONSTRUCTION

The Basic Sharpie

Of the numerous factors that influenced the design of sharpies as they evolved, simplicity of construction was by no means the least. The boats remain to this day the simplest of all to build. In its most basic form, sharpie construction can be described in the eight steps of Figure 2-1 on page 31.

Hull Construction

Sharpie construction, in the words of W. P. Stephens (*Yachting*, January 1927), "was very simple, the bottom planks running athwartship, and for a man familiar with the ordinary tools of the house carpenter but little knowledge of boatbuilding was required."

Of course, the larger boats were more sophisticated, but the basic principles of construction remained the same. Instead of using one plank for the sides, two or more planks were tied together with strips of hardwood—frames—across them. If the hull was so long that full-length planks couldn't be found, butt blocks were used to tie the ends of planks together.

In the New Haven sharpie, the keelson, or inner keel, was made up of three vertical planks through the middle portion of the hull. The centerboard trunk was fastened above the center portion of these planks (a segment of the middle plank being omitted for the centerboard to

pass through). The bottom edges of the three planks were cut to the curve, or rocker, of the boat bottom. The ends of these vertical keelson planks were notched to fit over flat keelson planks that extended to the extreme ends of the hull. Vertical centerboard trunk posts were placed between the vertical planks at each end of the opening for the centerboard. The vertical planks were through-bolted (or riveted) and spiked together. For the sake of clarity, I am going to call the "inner keel" the "keelson" throughout this book. Thus the "keel" would be outside, though few sharpies had more than a "skeg," or "skeg-type keel."

Except for only a few small sharpies, the boats had chine logs—longitudinal battens that reinforced the joint between hull bottom and sides. The hull sides were fastened to a stem and sprung around one or more trapezoidal molds and/or bulkheads and fastened to the stern. There was a bulkhead at the forward end of the centerboard trunk, made of edge-fastened planks. Scuppers were cut in the bottom to let water out, a thwart-like step was placed about halfway up, and the upper half of the bulkhead was set above the forward edge of the step (viewed in section athwartships, this bulkhead/step/bulkhead zigzagged). In the early New Haven boats, the upper part of the bulkhead curved athwartships and was made of tongue-and-groove material; later boats used edge-

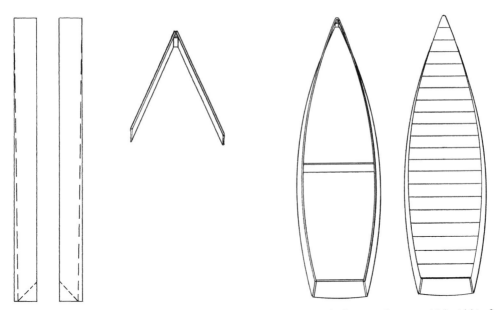

1) Take two long, identical, tapering planks, and cut the narrow ends to an angle.
2) Fasten the wide ends to a triangular stem.

3) Spring the planks around a trapezoidal midship form and fasten them to a trapezoidal transom.
4) Fasten planks across the bottom (cut to fit).

5) Add battens around the outside of the sheer.

6) Add boards across the inside at the height and location desired for seats.

7) Set pegs (tholepins) for oars, drill a hole through the stem for a painter (bow line), and add a skeg to the bottom.

8) Paint or oil the wood.

Figure 2-1. Sharpie building sequence.

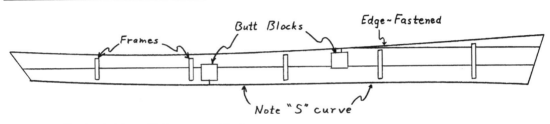

Figure 2-2. Planked sides with frames and butt blocks.

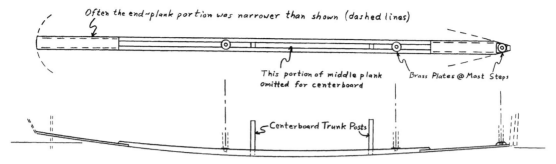

Figure 2-3. The keelson or backbone of a large sharpie.

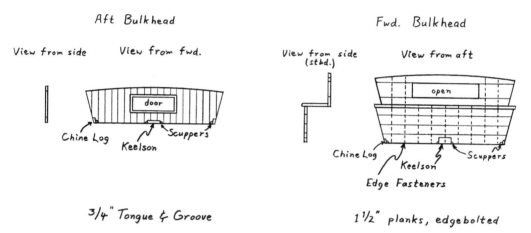

Figure 2-4. Bulkhead details.

fastened planks running athwartships, similar to the lower half of the bulkhead. Vent holes were often cut in the upper bulkhead. Of course, some sharpies just had continuous bulkheads in front of the centerboard trunk, and some had none at all, relying on a thwart and perhaps knees to brace the forward trunk post. Very large sharpies had another bulkhead at the after end of the centerboard trunk also. In the smacks, holes were drilled in the hull bottom planking between these two bulkheads, flooding the holds on both sides of the trunk to create "wet-wells" in which fish would stay alive while being transported to market. Some large sharpies had a

bulkhead aft, just abaft the cockpit coaming, to enclose a lazarette in the stern. This was planked with vertical tongue-and-groove material and included a door or opening for access aft. In the early boats this bulkhead was curved athwartships in mirror image of the curved upper portion of the forward bulkhead.

In double-enders, the stern was simply another stem; in transom vessels, the stern was a plank or planks with cleats to reinforce the joint to the sides; and in round-sterned vessels, the sides tied into sets of top and bottom horizontal frames scarfed together in semicircles, around which vertical "staves" were fastened.

Since almost all sharpies were decked, there were generally (though not always) sheer clamps or beam shelves. These were fastened above or to the side frames (see Figure 2-6), and the deck beams abutted or rested on them. The beams were notched for carlins (fore-and-aft deck timbers located under hatches, cabin trunks, and occasionally coamings). The narrow side decks, or "washboards," were typically supported by knees instead of beams. The larger boats had mast partners—fore-and-aft planks mortised into adjacent deck beams—where a mast penetrated the deck. If the mast penetrated in the extreme bow, a large breasthook acted in place of partners. If a mast was placed where there was no deck, it passed instead through a thwart, or seat. There were some decked sharpies in which the sheer clamps or beam shelves appeared only in the ends of the boat, under the fully decked parts, and others in which there appear to be no clamps or shelves at all. Simplicity was paramount.

Decking consisted of planks laid fore-and-aft. Fancy deck planking was absent on working sharpies; the planks were generally of white pine, fairly thick and wide for the boat sizes. "King" or center planks and "margin" planks at the deck edges were rarely, if ever, used in sharpies. Deck planking overlapped the hull sides and was trimmed to the angle of the topside planking,

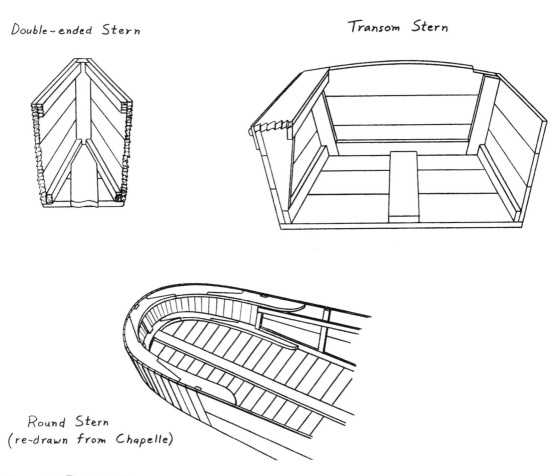

Double-ended Stern

Transom Stern

Round Stern
(re-drawn from Chapelle)

Figure 2-5. Three sterns.

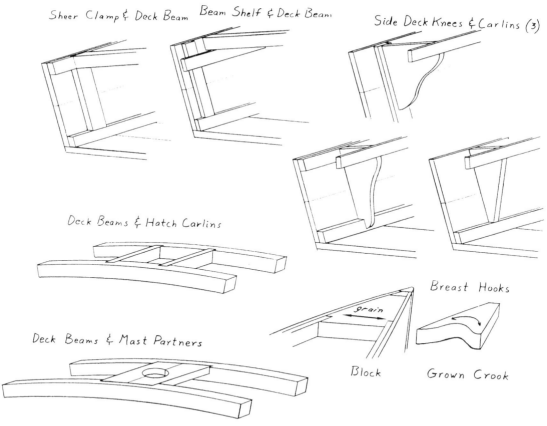

Figure 2-6. Sheer clamps, beam shelves, deck beams, carlins, knees, mast partners, and breasthooks.

and the edge was covered over by a wale—a wide, thin plank that ran the length of the hull covering the deck-to-hull joint. A half-round hardwood rubrail was placed at the top of the wale, and a toerail with scuppers cut in its bottom edge at the low point of the deck was set above the deck edge. While on some boats details differed, the rubrail and toerail were rarely absent. On small sharpies, the wale was often omitted and the rubrail covered the deck edge. On round-sterned hulls, the wale was typically made of segments aft. The inboard deck edge was generally covered by a coaming that extended several inches both above and below the deck planking, or was simply fastened above the deck edge. Sometimes a cove strip was fitted outside to cover the joint

between coaming and deck; this seems to be the only "fancy" trim used, and even it performs the function of keeping water out of the joint. On some boats the coaming was bent or steamed to a curve; on others it was squared off and had mitered or rabbeted corners. Most of the boats had a hatch on the foredeck, consisting of a "box-top" type fitted over a square coaming.

Interior Components

Interior structure consisted of the centerboard trunk, maststeps, and thwarts, besides the bulkheads and deck components already mentioned. The centerboard trunk's vertical end-posts were set between the vertical keelson planks, and the

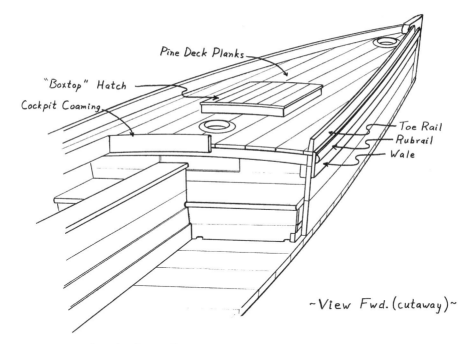

Pine Deck Planks

"Boxtop" Hatch

Cockpit Coaming

Toe Rail
Rubrail
Wale

~View Fwd. (cutaway)~

Figure 2-7. Decking, wale, rubrail, toerail, coaming, and hatch.

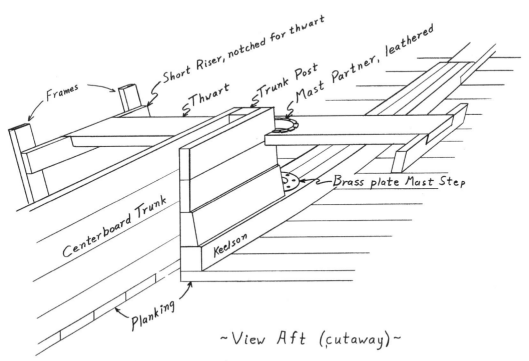

Frames

Short Riser, notched for thwart

Thwart

Trunk Post

Mast Partner, leathered

Centerboard Trunk

Brass plate Mast Step

Keelson

Planking

~View Aft (cutaway)~

Figure 2-8. Centerboard trunk, maststeps, and thwarts.

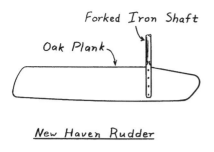

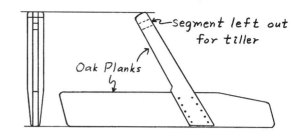

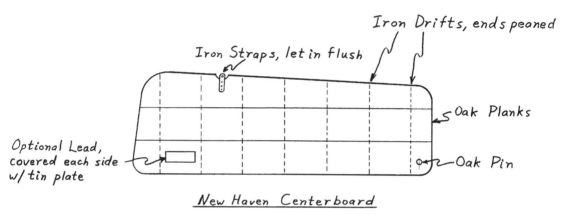

Figure 2-9. Rudders and centerboards.

trunk side planks were fastened to the posts. The first trunk plank was the same thickness as the keelson plank, with its top edge beveled to the smaller thickness of the planks above it. Often the trunk planks were edge-fastened with long bolts that also went through the keelson planks. A cap was fastened to the top, with appropriate openings in it for means to raise and lower the centerboard. In many sharpies, part of the raised board protruded above the cap, which was slotted to accommodate this.

Often the maststeps consisted only of holes drilled in the center of the three vertical keelson planks. The forwardmost step was either a hole in the keelson, or a block fastened on the flat keelson plank with its sides beveled to fit snugly against the side planking.

Thwarts were used as seats, steps, mast supports, and compression/tension structural ties between the hull sides. Cleats, or thwart risers, were fastened to the frames immediately forward and aft of the thwarts; it seems the frames were spaced deliberately to lie equidistant from each edge of each thwart for this purpose. Whereas in traditional small-boat construction thwart risers ran nearly the length of the hull, this seems rarely to be the case in sharpies. Most boats had only one thwart, through which passed the after mast. A "doughnut-shaped" wooden ring was fastened above every mast hole, and the mast holes were lined with greased rawhide. In some sharpies, particularly those without decks, there were more thwarts. The zigzag forward bulkheads common to the New

Haven boats incorporated a thwart as a step, as described above.

Rudders and Centerboards

The rudder consisted of a plank (typically oak) attached to an iron shaft in the round-sterned hulls, or was built up of edge-fastened planks (dinghy-style) in the double-ended hulls. The transom-sterned hulls used both rudder types. Centerboards were made from edge-fastened oak planks. The pivot pin was an oak dowel. Some boards had lead weight inset near their lowest corners; most relied on the weight of their fasteners and waterlogging to overcome buoyancy. The boards were raised either with a lanyard or a handle. If a handle was used, it locked under a thumb cleat to hold the board down, and folded on a hinge to hold the board up.

Hardware

Metalwork and hardware were simple on the sharpies. If a rudder shaft was used, it was made of iron, with a clevis or paired flanges to fit over each side of the rudder blade. The tiller, usually of oak, was fixed to the rudder shaft by means of an iron fitting. This fitting was forged with a squared-off hole to fit onto the squared-off head of the rudder shaft, and was riveted to the tiller. An iron pipe with a flange above the deck passed through the hull vertically and supported the rudder. Several holes were drilled in the shaft to allow the rudder depth to be adjusted for different conditions by moving a pin. A clevis or pair of straps with an eye was used to lift the centerboard, though some of the smaller boats had a tall vertical plank with a hole at the top, and the large Chesapeake Bay sharpies used daggerboards with handles on top. A third method used a metal plate set into a fore-and-aft slot in

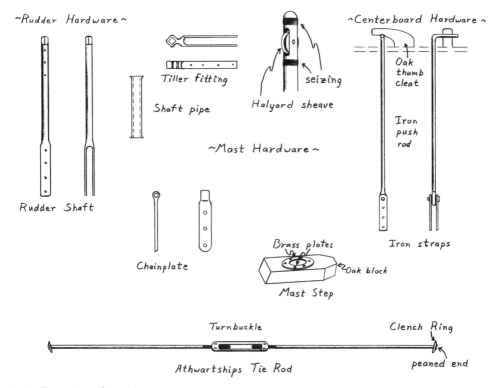

Figure 2-10. Examples of hardware.

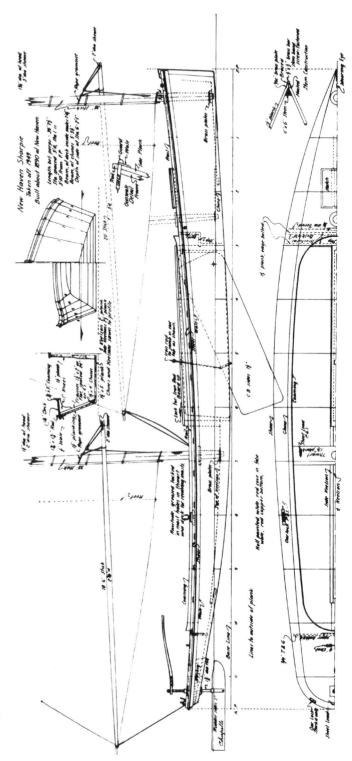

Figure 2-11. Plan of a typical New Haven sharpie, showing design and construction characteristics. From Chapelle's *Paper 25: The Migrations of an American Boat Type.* Courtesy of the Library of Congress.

the top of the centerboard; the plate was riveted in place, and the board was notched to expose a lifting hole drilled in the plate.

The New Haven boats had heavy tierods just abaft the tall forward masts. These were iron, with a turnbuckle in the middle to adjust tension, and the ends were peened over or "up-set" over large clench rings outside the planking just below deck level. These clench rings were placed on the faces of the oak false wales or rubrails. The larger boats employed more tierods as needed, usually at the mast locations. Very large sharpies suffered from structural problems and fatigue; for this reason they were rarely built over 50 feet long.

Brass rings were used on the maststeps and mast bases as bearings to allow the masts to rotate freely. Rowlock sockets were fitted port and starboard, sometimes two pair, and a single socket was placed on the stern a little to port for sculling. Often sheaves were fitted in slots in the mastheads for halyards and in the forward sprit ends for snotters. Fairleads, blocks, cleats, and chocks varied in different localities and included wood, iron, and brass or bronze. Anchors and grapples were iron; anchors were of the fisherman type. Most of this hardware was forged by the local blacksmith.

Spars

Masts were lofty, freestanding, and tapered. Sprits or booms, gaffs, and yards (used in racing sharpies) were tapered at each end. Spar material included Southern yellow pine, spruce, white pine and fir; information on this is sparse. The following, from *American Small Sailing Craft*, is Chapelle's description of spar dimensions for the New Haven boats:

The foremast of a 35-foot boat was between 28 and 36 feet in length; the main was between 26 and 34 feet; the fore sprit was 19 to 20 feet; the main sprit averaged a foot shorter. The masts in the 1880's were about 4½ inches in diameter at

the partners, but later this became 5½ inches, and the head was between 1½ and 2 inches in diameter. . . . The sprits were about 3 inches at the middle and 2½ inches at the fore end; the after end was about 2 inches at the shoulder. [The spliced rope grommet clew of the sail fit over the reduced end of the sprit and lay on this shoulder.]

The one-man sharpies usually had single masts somewhere between 24 and 28 feet long, 4 to 4½ inches in diameter at partners and 1½ inches in diameter at head. The sprit was usually between 15 and 17 feet long and about 2½ inches in its greatest diameter.

Scantlings and Historic Notes

In his *Report on the Ship-building Industry of the United States*, Henry Hall described sharpie construction as follows:

[For small sharpies] The bottom is made of 1-inch white pine, the sides of ⅞-inch pine or cedar, the thwarts of 1-inch pine. The stem, 3 by 4 inches; bilge streak, 1 by 2 inches; frames, 1 by ¾ inches; and skag, ⅞ inch thick, are made of white oak; the knees are of oak or cedar. These boats weigh from 150 to 200 pounds, and about 200 board feet of stuff is cut up in making them. The only tools required by the builder are a hammer, brad-awl, hand-saw, tenon-saw, jack-plane, smoothing plane, rule, square, bevel, and perhaps a screw-driver, and the addition of a putty knife and a paint brush would make the kit complete.

The larger sharpies require no greater outfit of tools on the part of the carpenter, but they do call for more judgement in regard to the keenness of the bow, the rounding up of the stern, and the location of the various parts. . . . A sailing sharpie carries a pole mast, and if more than 20 or 25 feet long two pole masts, without shrouds, except in a very large one, when one small wire shroud is rigged on either side of each mast. A centerboard is generally fitted into a large boat, as also a narrow strip of decking, or wash-board, along by the gunwales, with a low hatch-coaming on the inner edge. The sails are narrow or pointed at the top, and are spread at the foot by sprits in the smaller boats, but by booms in the larger ones. The sides flare 10 or 12 inches. In small boats the sides are each made of one plank; in deeper ones, of two planks, the sheer being given by the addition of a third and narrow streak forward and aft. They are made throughout of white pine, except the framing pieces, which are of oak or chestnut. The floor is invariably planked across the boat. The capacity and small draft of the sharpie are astonishing, a large one, with the addition of a cabin, and with everything on board, seldom drawing over 3 inches forward and a foot aft. Sharpies are admirably adapted for floating over the bars and shallows of the rivers and coasts of Long Island sound, and are stiff and seaworthy boats. They have been sent out for long cruises, and one drawing 12 inches has sailed in safety to the West Indies. Their speed under sail is one of their good qualities, and when matched against the deep-draught sail boats and yachts which continually cruise through Long Island sound in the summer time they rarely fail to beat a rival of the same length. The sharpie is pre-eminently an oyster boat, but its speed has led to its introduction into yacht races and to its being now generally debarred from admission into such contests. Many experiments have been made with the model, and light-draught schooners, intended to run in the shallow rivers of the southern states, have been built of 200 tons register for the lumber and other trades; but for large vessels the model has failed to do what was expected. It is now generally understood that a sharpie should not be built more than 50 feet long, but the best results are obtained from 35-foot boats.

It should be noted again that the problems involved in building sharpies over 50 feet were structural. Because the hulls were long and narrow, they would twist and flex alarmingly when driven hard in a seaway. To a degree, these problems were overcome in construction of some of the later large sharpies—in some cases by using more truss rods. Modern cold-molded plywood, steel, and aluminum construction all transcend the structural problems faced a century ago. These days, there is no real limit to the size sharpies can be designed and built—other than practical considerations of just how *useful* a truly gigantic flat-bottomed boat might be. I personally think 75 feet or so might be a practical size limit for cruising, charter, commercial fishing, or coastal cargo-carrying sharpies.

Gathered from various works of Howard I. Chapelle, as previously cited, are his notes on scantlings for traditional sharpie construction. I include them here as much for their historical value as practical, and hope you will be able to follow them after reading the preceding descriptions.

The structure of N. H. [New Haven] sharpies was strong and rather heavy, consisting of white pine plank and oak framing. The sides were commonly wide plank. Each side had two or three strakes that were pieced up at the ends to form the sheer. The sides of large sharpies were commonly 1½ inches thick before finishing, while those of the smaller sharpies were 1¼ inches thick. The sharpie's bottom was planked athwartships with planking of the same thickness as the sides and of 6 to 8 inches in width. That part of the bottom that cleared the water, at the bow and under the stern, was often made of tongue-and-groove planking, or else the seams athwartship would be splined....The chines of the sharpie were of oak planks that were of about the same thickness as the side planks and 4 to 7 inches deep when finished. The chine logs were sawn to the profile of the bottom and sprung to the sweep of the sides in plan view. The side frames were mere cleats, 1½ by 3 inches. In the 1880's these cleats were shaped so that the inboard face was 2 inches wide and the outboard face 3 inches wide, but later this shaping was generally omitted. At the fore end of the sharpie's centerboard case there was an edge-bolted bulkhead of solid white pine, 1¼ or 1½ inches thick....The decking of the sharpie was made of white pine 1¼ inches thick and 7 to 10 inches wide. The stem was a triangular-sectioned piece of oak measuring 6 by 9 inches before it was finished. The side plank ran past the forward edge of the stem and was mitered to form a sharp cutwater. The miter was covered by a brass bar stemband to which was brazed two side plates ³⁄₃₂ or ¼ inch thick. This stemband, which was tacked to the side plank, usually measured ½ or ⅝ inch by ¾ inch and it turned under the stem, running under the bottom for a foot or two. The band also passed over a stemhead and ran to the deck, having been shaped over the head of the stem by heating and molding over a pattern.

The sharpies required a great deal of longitudinal strength, and this was obtained by the use of a built-up keelson structure which was made of three planks on edge. The middle one was a filler that stopped short at each end of the centerboard slot. The keelson did not run to the ends of the hull; a couple of feet abaft the foremast it was scarfed to a flat keelson plank and on this was placed the mast-step block. The flat plank usually extended under the large V-shaped stem liner. Aft, a similar flat-plank keelson was scarfed in, the scarf usually being about at the after end of the load water line, and through this plank passed the iron pipe rudder-tube, the plank forming a reinforcement to the bottom at this point.

The sharpie's stern was composed of two horizontal oak frames, one at chine and one at sheer; each was about 1½ inches thick. The outer faces of these frames were beveled. The planking around the stern on these frames was vertical staving that had been tapered, hollowed, and shaped to fit the flare of the stern. This vertical staving was usually 1¾ inches thick before it was finished. The raw edges of the deck plank were covered by a false wale ½ to ¾ inch thick and 3 or 4 inches deep, and by an oak guard strip that was half-oval in section and tapered toward the ends. Vertical staving was used to carry the wale around the stern. [I don't know that this was always the case.] The guard around the stern was usually of steamed oak.

The cockpit ran from the bulkhead at the centerboard case to within 4 or 5 feet of the stern, where there was a light joiner bulkhead. A low coaming was fitted around the cockpit and a finger rail ran along the sides of the deck. The boat had a small square hatch in the foredeck and two mast holes, one at the stem and one at the forward bulkhead. A tie rod, ⅜ inch in diameter, passed through the hull athwartships, just forward of the forward bulkhead; the ends of the tie rod were "up-set" or headed over the clench rings on the outside of the wale. The hull was usually painted white or gray, and the interior color was usually buff or gray.

The two working masts of a 35- to 36-foot sharpie were made of spruce or white pine and had a diameter of 4½ to 5 inches at deck and 1½ inches at head. Their sail hoists were 28 to 30 feet, and the sail spread was about 65 yards. Instead of booms, sprits were used; these were set up at the heels with tackles to the masts. In most sharpies the sails were hoisted to a single-sheave block at the mast heads and were fitted with wood or metal mast hoops. Because of the use of the sprit and heel tackle, the conventional method of reefing was not possible. The reef bands of the sails were parallel to the masts, and reefing was accomplished by lowering a sail and tying the reef points while rehoisting. The mast revolved in tacking in order to prevent binding of the sprit under tension of the heel tackle. The tenon at the foot of the mast was round, and to the shoulder of the tenon a brass ring was nailed or screwed. Another brass ring was fastened around the mast step. These rings acted as bearings on which the mast could revolve.

As the heart of sharpie production was centered around New Haven, it is instructive to know the construction methods used there. As mentioned in Chapter One, the leading New Haven builder at the end of the century was Lester Rowe. His son told Chapelle that "it was not uncommon for his father and two helpers to build a sharpie, hull and spars, in six working days, and that one year his father and two helpers built 31 sharpies." By this time some power tools were in use, at least in the mills, and "the heavy cutting and finishing" was done from patterns at the mill. The following description from *Paper 25* tells of the construction methods used:

Sharpie builders in New Haven very early developed a "production" method. In the initial stages of building, the hull was built upside down. First, the sides were assembled and the planking and frames secured; then the inner stem was built, and the sides were nailed to it, after which the bulkhead and a few rough temporary molds were made and put in place and the boat's sides bent to the desired curve in plan view. For bending the sides a "Spanish windlass" of rope or chain was used. The chine pieces were inserted in notches in the molds inside the side planking and fastened, then the keelson was made and placed in notches in the molds and bulkhead along centerline. Next, the upper and lower stern frames were made and secured, and the stern staved vertically. Plank extensions of the keelson were fitted, the bottom laid, and the boat turned over. Sometimes the case was made and fitted with the keelson structure, but sometimes this was not done until the deck and inboard works were finished.

Hall, in his *Report on the Ship-building Industry*, explains that the sharpies were so easily built that many fishermen and yachtsmen built their own, and the type thus migrated easily, being "adopted" for smooth-water application. This widespread amateur and semiprofessional sharpie building, so geographically diverse, was considered a great natural resource in the 19th century:

If the immediate construction of a large number of sharpies were demanded by a sudden emergency Connecticut would be found to contain hundreds of young men (mechanics, clerks in stores, students, and others) who could at once build large and excellent boats; in fact, all through the United States the amateur boatbuilders are by no means an unimportant element in the population....It is the saying in New Jersey that the first thing a boy learns is how to use a gun and go hunting; the next, how to sail a boat; the next, how to build one.

The construction methods explained in this chapter are primarily specific to New Haven sharpies. Because the sharpie originated there and enjoyed long and popular use, more is known about its particular construction than that of other regional boats. However, many of the other sharpies were similar in construction; those that were not similar were built using construction fairly common to workboats anywhere in America. In Chapter Six, cross sections of numerous sharpies, though adapted for plywood, will show the slight deviations in construction. I would like to mention that there are many excellent ways to build boats, and the time-honored, traditional methods outlined here are by no means a poor ancestor to the more modern methods described in the next chapters. Great personal satisfaction, as well as longevity, strength, utility, and beauty can be achieved by building a traditional sharpie, even going so far as to reproduce the original wrought-iron hardware and canvas sails. Or any in-between blending of technologies, materials, and methods might be used. Certainly, many modern sharpie components are likely to be traditional in any case—masts, sprits, thwarts, rudder, tiller, rubrails, toerails, and coamings, for example.

CHAPTER 3
TOOLS, MATERIALS, ADHESIVES, FASTENERS, AND SAFETY

Tools

The tools described by Henry Hall may not be totally adequate for sharpie building, but they are undoubtedly close. In modern times of electric everything, the average home workshop probably very nearly contains all the tools required to build a cold-molded plywood sharpie with considerably more speed and ease than a century ago.

First, I will list the essential power tools:

- **Circular saw** with (fine) 24-tooth carbide blade and ripping guide attachment.
- Hand-held **saber saw** or scroll saw, with adjustable bed for bevel cuts.
- ⅜-inch variable-speed reversing **electric drill motor** with a drill index, hardened #2 Phillips screwdriver bits, and assorted paddle bits as needed.

The following are desirable but nonessential power tools:

- **Orbital sander.**
- Low-speed **body grinder** with 8-inch soft pad.
- **Table saw.**
- **Router.**
- **Bandsaw.**
- **Power plane.**
- A shop-type industrial **vacuum cleaner**— wet/dry is best.
- One or two box-type **exhaust fans.**
- **Staple gun**—either electric, hand-powered, or pneumatic.

Some kind of power sander will save elbow grease, but you can certainly get by without one. The orbital sander is really just a finishing tool; the body grinder has many more uses, but requires skill and care.

Ripping guides are available for most circular saws. They consist of a metal fence held in place by a bracket and thumbscrew, and work very well after a couple of practice cuts. The ripping guide will do most jobs involved in building a sharpie that would otherwise require a table saw.

The router is a luxury. The same work can be done with a block plane and sandpaper, or, in the case of mortising, with a mallet and chisels.

The work of a bandsaw can be done with a good hand-held reciprocating saber saw. *It is essential that your saber saw have an adjustable bed*; many of the cuts you make will be bevel cuts—that is, not vertical. The bandsaw is truly a luxury.

Staple guns are very handy for fastening plywood planking. If you build a round-sterned sharpie, an electric one could fasten the layers of doorskin (⅛-inch plywood) in place. Hand-powered staple guns (such as the Arrow T-50) will also penetrate doorskins, but you will need to hammer the staples flush. The hand-powered staple gun is also useful for stretching out Xynole-polyester cloth, if you use it to cover your plywood. A professional pneumatic staple gun is a luxury limited to the production wood-shop; if you happen to have access to one, it will substantially reduce construction time. This tool requires an air compressor to run it, which gets us into the realm of air-powered tools and paint-spraying equipment. While these are wonderful tools, you certainly don't need them to build one sharpie in your garage.

The power plane is a dangerous tool—both to human flesh and to wood. The inexperienced worker can do amazing damage in a heartbeat with this tool. It does what a hand plane can do, but very much faster and with almost no effort. Its principal application in small-boat construction is to make scarf joints. If you elect to scarf your plywood planking together instead of using butt blocks, the power plane is very handy. However, plywood scarfs can also be made with the body grinder and an 8-inch soft pad with 36-grit sandpaper, and the body grinder will perform more functions than the power plane. Note that an 8-inch soft pad with 36-grit paper can do a lot of damage also—to both wood and human flesh—and will require some practice to use safely.

The hand tools you'll need are more numerous. These are the essential ones:

- **Tape measure**—1 inch by 25 feet, if you are building a big sharpie.
- **Rafter squares**—16 by 24 inches, and 9 by 12 inches.
- **Hammer**—20-oz. straight-claw is my favorite.
- **Screwdrivers**—Small, medium, and large slot-heads, and #2 Phillips-head.
- **Pliers** and **Vise-Grips**

- Four-in-hand **rasp/file**—This has four different cutting surfaces.
- **Hand saws**—A 10- or 12-point crosscut saw, kept sharp, can do everything you need. A back saw, for cutting trim, would be nice if you are building a cruising sharpie with an interior.
- **Planes**—A small palm-size block plane and a 10-inch jack plane are both essential. Keep these razor sharp, and they will serve you well.
- **Mallet** and **chisels**—A wooden mallet is essential for driving good-quality wood-handled chisels. If you already have cheap plastic- or metal-handled chisels and are happy with them, they can be driven with your claw hammer. Assorted chisels in ¼-, ½-, ¾-, and 1-inch sizes will come in very handy. You can easily get by with ¼-inch and ¾-inch chisels if you can't afford the others. Keep these razor sharp, and handle with extreme care.
- **Sharpening stone**—A two-sided synthetic stone, available in hardware stores, is adequate. I use WD-40 for cutting oil. A rolling sharpening guide, made by General Tool Corp., is very handy for maintaining accurate edges on planes and chisels.
- **Sanding block**—Hand-held rubber type.
- **Putty knives**—Flexible type; 1½-inch, 3-inch, and 8-inch (for fairing).
- **Large shears**—If you are going to cover the hull and decks with fabric.
- 9-inch **roller frames** and heavy-duty **plastic trays** (for glue and paint).
- 6-inch **bubble rollers**—If you fabric-cover; for rolling out air bubbles.
- **C-clamps**—A good assortment, from 4-inch (at least four) to 8-inch (two) opening.
- **Drawing battens**—Make two from long, straight-grained spruce, white pine, or Douglas-fir. One should be about ⅜ inch by 1½ inch by as long as possible (18 or

20 feet); make the other ¼ inch by 1 inch by 8 feet. There is no fixed rule for these battens—you may want more or different-sized ones. A 4-foot straightedge will come in handy also; I often use my 4-foot level. Use an old fiberglass fishing rod to draw tight curves and curves of changing radius (for knees, round sterns, etc.).

- **Levels**—It is ideal to have a 4-foot level, a 2-foot one, and an accurate line level. You can get by with just a 2-foot level; when leveling things far apart, tape the level to a perfectly straight 2 x 4 and use it for whatever size level you need.
- **Bevel square**—This is a hardware store item. The currently common ones have a plastic handle and wingnut adjustment.
- **Compass**—Carpenter's type; can be used as a scribe or compass.
- **Chalkline**—For striking long, straight edges.
- **Sawhorses**—You will have to make these: The ones for your strongback should be 24 inches high, narrow enough not to interfere with planking (depends on boat size), and very sturdy. Make at least two more, 27 or 28 inches high by 42 to 46 inches wide. Avoid those metal brackets—they are wobbly and will damage your saw blade.

Optional hand tools include the following:

- **Saw protractor**—Just a large protractor with an adjustable straight arm; acts as a fence for mitered saw cuts using a circular saw or for marking angles, reading angles, and transferring angles in degrees.
- Rolling **sharpening guide**—Mentioned above as a companion to your sharpening stone; made by General Tool Corp.
- A sturdy bench-mounted **vise** is very handy.

- A carpenter's **wood vise** is also handy, though nonessential.

Materials

For "utility" wood—used in making sawhorses, strongbacks, molds, etc.—use common lumberyard stock local to your area. This might include spruce, hem-fir (a variety of softwoods), white pine, Southern yellow pine, and Douglas-fir.

For construction wood—primarily "longitudinals" such as chine logs, sheer clamps, and keelson plank—try to use "better" woods such as Southern yellow pine and Douglas-fir. White pine and spruce may be used, but they are more prone to rot and don't hold fasteners well. If you use them, seal them well with epoxy or use wood preservative, and paint them. For long lengths of good-quality wood for longitudinals, you may have to buy unusual stock and re-cut it—for example, tongue-and-groove (yellow pine or Douglas-fir), stair tread stock (same), and ¾-inch stock (finished to 1-inch). Use these better-quality woods for cleats, stems, maststeps and partners, toerails, centerboards and rudders (if not plywood sheathed), trunk logs, and thwarts. Pine or spruce are fine for deck beams, but must be well sealed.

I used to condemn the use of pressure-treated, or "Wolmanized" Southern yellow pine in boat construction, but have since found that it can be used if the stock has good grain and is air-dried. For example, you might buy long, straight, pressure-treated 2 x 12 planks that have been stored under cover in a lumberyard for a month or more, and are fairly dry. These planks can be ripped on a table saw or with a circular saw and ripping guide to the dimensions you require, and allowed to dry further prior to use. Keep them away from the sun, stack the cut pieces with spacers, and allow air to circulate around them. The dry material can be glued with epoxy and 3M 5200, but use fasteners also. *Be aware that pressure-treated wood is highly toxic*: Wear a dust mask when cutting and sanding, clean the sawdust up often and dispose of it correctly, and paint over finished woodwork.

Make your rubrails from white oak or Southern yellow pine. Many sharpies used "half-round" material. You can make this from standard stock, using a router or plane and sandpaper, or you may be able to purchase it.

Note that the difference between red and white oak is profound: The former is much more prone to rot.

The rubrails and toerails may be made from pressure-treated material to great advantage, as these two components take a lot of abuse and are prone to rot. If you make scarfs, cut them long (minimum 8 to 1), glue them with epoxy, and retain fasteners in both ends of the scarfs.

Masts and sprits or booms should be made of high-quality Douglas-fir. Sitka spruce may also be used, but it is hard to get and very expensive; it is also not as strong as the fir. Douglas-fir can be bought from large lumberyards all over the U.S. in 4 x 4 and 6 x 6 timbers up to 30 feet long, though you frequently have to custom-order it. Masts can be laminated also, either hollow or solid, from the same materials in smaller dimensions. Note that scarfs in masts must be very long (12 to 1), so order long-enough stock to allow for scarfs. Spar-quality lumber might be technically described as #1 grade, select structural, architectural grade, or clear/heart/vertical-grain. The idea is to avoid large, badly placed (near the edge) knots. Often a good piece of #2 material will be perfectly adequate, but you will need to carefully inspect it. Grain should be long, straight, and parallel to the timber, without deep checks and other deformities. Small, fixed (firm) knots present no problem.

Aluminum is today's common choice for masts, but, frankly, I dislike it. Aluminum is not very strong, fatigues and breaks easily, and corrodes rapidly. It is, however, very light. Because sharpies have freestanding (unstayed) masts, aluminum sharpie masts must be round, tapered, and very strong. Good-quality small, tapered flagpoles are often used for masts of this type,

but they are expensive, less durable, less trustworthy, and not as flexible as wooden masts. This last is a serious concern: Sharpie masts are designed to "spill the wind" near the top in strong puffs, thereby making for safer sailing. Aluminum masts will not do this; wooden ones will. The wooden masts are also tapered to a very small diameter aloft (1½ inches, even on large sharpies), while very few flagpoles taper that much; if they did, they would break.

Planking may be solid stock or plywood. In these modern times, there is little reason for solid planking unless you want to build an authentic reproduction, or "just love it." The big problem is availability and cost of boat construction–quality lumber. Most wood today is "kiln-dried" (to decrease production time), which makes it more rot-prone and less flexible than air-dried lumber.

Plywood will make a stronger, lighter, potentially more durable boat. If the plywood is carefully joined and sealed with good waterproof adhesives and covered with fabric and epoxy, it will last as long as it is maintained.

Marine plywood is the best to use, but I have built many boats from ACX and BCX construction-grade plywood, as well as BBOES plywood, made for concrete forming. For building a sharpie on a budget, go to your local lumberyard and hand-pick the best plywood you can afford.

If your hull and decks are to be fabric/epoxy covered, place the good plywood face inside. The C face is then filled with epoxy, sanded, and covered, while the good face is only sealed and painted.

Adhesives

Epoxy, in various forms, makes the best all-around adhesive, sealant, fairing compound, and primer. WEST System and System Three seem to dominate the market these days, but there are many other sources. I use industrial epoxies, such as those made by Shell Oil Corporation.

One of the little-known truths about epoxy is that there are only about four major manufacturers in the world. Many of the various competing marketers simply buy it in truckloads, put their label on it, and dramatically raise the price, particularly if the epoxy is for "marine use." Shop around locally and see what is available. Because you are most likely building one boat, one time (careful—it's addictive), you may be best off using one of the expensive big-name distributors, just for reliability, convenience, and availability of the various things you will need with epoxy, such as thixogens. Avoid one-to-one mix-ratio epoxies—they are not as strong as the others.

Thixogens are compounds used to thicken the epoxy. The commonly needed ones are Cab-O-Sil or Aerosil (expanded silica), and microballoons or Q-cells. Cab-O-Sil is used for making glue, filler, fillets, and structural mixes. It is not "hydroscopic" (does not absorb water) and can be used underwater. Microballoons are tiny, hollow plastic spheres used for glazing, fairing compound, filling, and fillets above the water. They are hydroscopic to a minor degree on the surface or when damaged, and their use is avoided underwater. Microballoons are not as strong as Cab-O-Sil, and are rarely used to make glue. Microballoons are lightweight and easy to sand; Cab-O-Sil is denser, heavier, and very hard to sand.

Pure cured epoxy is also very hard to sand, so be sure to work neatly with it, scraping off excess from work surfaces.

Another thixogen is "fibers," available in various kinds from various suppliers. These are used in making glue, for adding tensile strength to the joint. I use them only for scarf joints, in conjunction with Cab-O-Sil, taking care not to mix the glue too thick, which makes it weak (wood will soak up a lot of epoxy, leaving the glue joint too dry).

Send away for the booklets that are offered by most epoxy distributors, and study the methods and products they recommend.

Note that *all epoxy is toxic and hyperallergenic, as are the reducers and many of the thixogens used with it.* Use these materials with great care, and keep them away from children and pets. Wear a dust mask or respirator, latex gloves, and protective clothing, and place exhaust fans in shop windows.

Plastic resin glues, such as Weldwood and resorcinol, are excellent for wood. However, your joints must be of good quality, and components must be firmly clamped until the glue is cured.

There are some excellent **polyurethane-type adhesives** available, such as 3M 5200, Bostik 920, and Sikaflex. The 5200 and Bostik can be cleaned up with mineral spirits—a big plus—but these adhesives are toxic and must be handled with gloves and with good ventilation.

"Semi-disposable" boats may use **aliphatic-resin carpenter's glue**, such as Titebond or Titebond II (virtually waterproof). With good paint jobs and close attention to maintenance, such boats may last a lifetime. But for hard, continuous service and long exposure to water, they will eventually fail.

For maximum durability, cover all exterior plywood with **Xynole-polyester fabric** saturated with epoxy. Fiberglass is not as strong or durable over wood, is more difficult to work with, is toxic and hideously irritating (you don't want it anywhere near your home), and costs about the same. More about this later, in Chapter Five.

Fiberglass tape is useful for covering butt joints in plywood. Grind or sand a hollow depression a little wider than the cloth (2-inch cloth tape is recommended); lay the tape in, and soak it with epoxy. **Polyester tape** (superior but a little more expensive) is available from John R. Sweet Co. (see Appendix III).

Avoid completely the use of polyester resins and fillers in your boat.

Fasteners

The new "quick-and-dirty" fastener in boat-building is the **deck screw**, or cold-galvanized drywall screw. It comes in a great variety of sizes, is self-tapping (no holes needed), and will last indefinitely if sealed in epoxy. This means your best use for them is holding glue joints while they cure, after which you either remove them or countersink the heads (if they aren't already below the surface) and fill over them with thickened epoxy, then cover the lamination involved with fabric and epoxy. If not protected, they will eventually rust out and fail. For the backyard and garage sharpie, I don't think they can be beat. Drive them in using your variable-speed electric drill motor with hardened #2 Phillips-head bits. Stainless steel square-drive deck screws are available from Chesapeake Marine Fasteners (see Appendix III), but they are expensive.

Ring-shank (annular) nails, available in bronze, stainless steel, and galvanized steel, are also excellent fasteners for boat construction. They should be countersunk with hammer and punch and filled with epoxy. The shock and vibration involved in hammering are hard on the strongback and frame, and these should be made very strong if nails are used. A useful tool for nailing is a "plumber's lead," a hand-sized octagonal weight of lead that is held behind the area to be nailed. It holds the structure in place and absorbs most of the shock, driving the nail in faster.

Staples are good for fastening plywood planking in place, but they don't have the holding or drawing power that screws and ring-shank nails have. However, they are excellent if the plywood is thin (particularly doorskins), and if used in conjunction with clamps and other fasteners. If the plywood planking is flat, and if weight can be applied to it, such as with bottom planking and decking, staples are very effective alone. As mentioned in "Tools," pneumatic staple guns are best, but they are expensive and require an air compressor. Electric staplers and some hand-powered staple guns will help with doorskins (you will have to sink the staples with a hammer) and for temporarily stretching out Xynole-polyester cloth, as mentioned above. Cement-

coated, zinc-electroplated staples are common and are fine to use as long as they are countersunk, filled with epoxy, and covered with fabric and epoxy; if not, they should be removed. Or, use Monel staples.

Through-bolts are rarely needed in modern sharpie construction. **Eyebolts** and **lag-eyebolts**, if used, should have a shoulder and be hot-dipped galvanized steel, bronze, or stainless steel, as should through-bolts. Avoid cadmium- or zinc-plated steel.

Bronze fasteners of all kinds are excellent, but very expensive. If you build a traditional sharpie, they are the best to use.

Safety

Perhaps your biggest concern for a home project should be safety. Because of the rigors of the marine environment, many of the materials, coatings, and chemicals used in boat construction are toxic, hyperallergenic, and carcinogenic. This is the sad truth. Working with these substances in a controlled professional environment is one thing; bringing them into your home is quite another. Even plywood is toxic because of formaldehyde in the glue. These are some general guidelines to make your project as safe as possible; I urge you to follow them, look for more, and be conscious at all times of your safety and that of your loved ones and home:

- Keep at least two all-rated **fire extinguishers** in your shop—one near each exit.
- Get a good first-aid kit and keep it stocked. The "stretchy" fabric-reinforced **bandages** work much better than plastic ones; keep plenty of these on hand in different sizes. Use **hydrogen peroxide** to wash cuts and scratches. Even though it may be inconvenient, as soon as you get cut or scratched, clean the wound and bandage it. Keep an **eye cup** with your kit, along with a bottle of saline **eyewash**.

- Know where your **nearest hospital** is and two quick, safe routes to it.
- Wear appropriate **protective clothing**. This should include **particle masks**, **safety glasses**, **latex rubber gloves**, a **respirator**, and **coveralls** (I use paper suits from an automotive paint supplier). **Ear protection** is a must if you use power tools. I myself am quite hard of hearing in my middle age, because I didn't protect my ears.
- Provide **good lighting**. Evenly diffused sunlight is best, but 48-inch double-tube shop lights are inexpensive and very useful, as are clamp-on utility lights.
- If you work inside, use one or two box-type **exhaust fans** to provide ventilation.
- *Never use chemical solvents to clean epoxy from your skin.* **White vinegar** works perfectly—keep a bottle in your shop cleanup area, and another in your shower (there often seems to be that spot you missed).
- **Remove dirty clothing** before going into the house and sitting down. Your spouse will be less likely to divorce you halfway through your boatbuilding project. **Coveralls** are great because you can remove them when leaving the work area. I like to shower and change my clothes before getting in my truck or going into the house; if you have a shower in your garage or basement, using it will promote domestic harmony.
- **Latex gloves** can be bought by the box from your local drugstore. Use **baby powder** to lubricate your hands and absorb sweat. For long projects, like planking, put on two pairs of gloves. This way, when the outer pair tears or gets too fouled with epoxy, you can strip them off without having to stop to change gloves.
- Keep your shop clean and well organized. Remember: *You can't screw up when you clean up.* Dispose of scrap, sawdust, and dirty rags regularly and carefully. Before starting your project, take a long, thoughtful look at your work area and **organize** it. Keep in mind that you will need a space for the boat, a staging or work area beside it, a workbench of some kind, room to work around the boat on all sides, and storage areas for plywood, lumber, glues, and paint products. Fasteners can be kept in labeled plastic buckets or cans, and tools can be kept on a shelf under your workbench.
- Get a good supply of **quart plastic mixing buckets** for glue, and keep plenty of **clean rags** on hand for cleaning up.
- Use good **extension cords**, preferably the grounded type, if your tools are grounded (three-prong), and keep them in good condition (avoid knots, kinks, heavy weights, and epoxy fouling). It is a good practice to **disconnect** cords and tools when finishing work, or shut off electricity to the area.

The most important thing to remember is, *have a good attitude.* Be positive and systematic and thorough in your work. Cultivate good work habits. Try not to get frustrated or discouraged—take your time, and enjoy the work. After all, you are doing this for yourself, for the personal growth and experience as well as for the finished project. Remember to enjoy the process as much as its goal—isn't that the real reward of a good life well lived?

CHAPTER 4
MODERN CONSTRUCTION

Modern Construction Methods

There is one crucial structural difference between traditional construction and modern construction, and that involves hull planking and plank seams. In traditional planked construction, individual boards are tied together, the seams between them being sealed somehow to prevent water from passing through. There is very little inherent diagonal strength across the seams; no matter how well secured individual planks may be, at some point the edges will try to work and slide against each other, a process that, once started, can only deteriorate.

Over the ages, many attempts have been made to prevent this process. Tying planks together with frames or lashings is perhaps the oldest method. Caulking—driving cotton or oakum tightly into the seams between planks with a mallet and iron—is ancient. Lapstrake planking, where the plank edges overlap each other and are riveted together, works very well. Double-planking, where a second planking layer is fastened over the first, with seams staggered, in many ways represents the beginning of modern cold-molded construction. Splining and tongue-and-groove milling are somewhat effective, particularly when combined with use of a water-resistant adhesive. Using full-length internal seam battens fastened in place is a variation of double-planking. Finally, the use of diagonal structural members, like straps and truss rods, came into use late in the last century, followed by diagonal planking in this century.

By modern construction I mean cold-molded wood, steel, aluminum, and fiberglass construction. Cold-molded construction involves the use of plywood, which is itself cold-molded wood. The term *cold-molded* is a little awkward, as it derives from a gluing method already obscure and rarely used. Early water-resistant glues had to be heated before use. With the invention of urea-formaldehyde glues, which did not have to be heated, using them in gluing became known as "cold-molding." When epoxy resins were invented, allowing great latitude in lamination techniques, the term *cold-molding* was applied to their use. Obscure or not, the term has stayed with us.

The advantage of cold-molded lamination, so aptly demonstrated by plywood, is fairly uniform strength in all directions, including diagonal. A sheet of plywood, once fastened around its perimeters, has omnidirectional tensile and compressive strengths. It has no seams that can work against each other or flex in or out, it is waterproof, and the layers of wood grain alternately placed at right angles to each other create a membrane vastly stronger than a material with primarily unidirectional strength—like a plank. In fact, well-executed plywood planking has structural characteristics, for its weight, that compare very favorably to those of steel and aluminum.

Perhaps the real beauty of plywood construction is that the necessary materials, tools, equipment, fasteners, and adhesives are common to nearly every civilized location on Earth; and the skills required to use them are almost universal, to at least some degree. In other words, if you want to, *you* can build your own plywood boat. With the advent of fabric-covering systems for wood and highly evolved paint systems, cold-molded wood construction can also have longevity and durability that rival and even go beyond what is possible in steel, aluminum, and fiberglass construction.

How does all this apply to sharpie construction? The only big difference between old and new is the planking. The basic structural components of a 19th-century sharpie remain basically the same, with a few exceptions, in a contemporary cold-molded plywood sharpie. The big advantages of plywood planking are strength, durability, light weight, absence of leaking, simplicity of construction, and low cost. Other than planking material, much of plywood sharpie construction remains very similar to traditional sharpie construction.

Because plywood construction has so much inherent quality, and because steel, aluminum, and fiberglass are much more complex and specialized methods, this book will concentrate on cold-molded plywood construction. However, I should briefly mention some facts about steel, aluminum, and fiberglass. Because of the weights involved, steel construction is too heavy for most small-boat construction. Particularly where sharpies are concerned, I would not consider steel construction for a vessel much under 40 feet. Aluminum is much lighter, and is an excellent material for small and large boats alike. But aluminum requires exotic welding equipment, highly developed welding skills, and is generally an expensive medium. If you can afford it or have the equipment and skills, aluminum is an excellent material for sharpie construction. Be aware, though, that aluminum is very vulnerable to corrosion, and requires meticulous maintenance. Fiberglass works best in mass production, as it requires a mold in which to be laid up. Fiberglass is at its structural best when used to form compound curves—shapes that have curvature in all directions. Because sharpie hulls have long, flat hull sections, fiberglass is a poor choice of material, requiring a relatively heavy layup with internal reinforcement structures. And so, cold-molded plywood, properly protected from the elements, is really the best all-around choice for sharpie construction.

The Strongback

All but the smallest of boats need a strongback upon which to be built. Because sharpies are so simple, they require the simplest of strongbacks. The small sharpie described in the beginning of Chapter Two can be built on two sawhorses. Even rather large sharpies can be built on stout sawhorses anchored securely to the shop floor, or staked to the ground. (See the beginning of Chapter Three, under "Tools," for suggested dimensions for sawhorses.)

A pair of long planks fastened to the sides of identical sawhorses will form a strongback upon which any size sharpie can be built. For boats under 18 feet, use two 2 x 6s, about 2 feet shorter than the hull, screwed to the sides of two sawhorses. For boats 18 to 25 feet, use 2 x 6 planks screwed to the sides of three sawhorses (you will probably have two planks on each side with a butt on the middle sawhorse). For each additional 5 feet in length, add another sawhorse and increase the width of your strongback planks. Align the horses carefully, anchor them securely, and use straight planks for the sides.

Figure 4-1. The strongback.

Level the tops of the planks, and *make sure both sides are parallel.*

An important consideration when building the strongback is that it be 4 inches narrower than the bottom of the narrowest mold-frame, bulkhead, or transom that it will support during construction. For small sharpies, this will require building narrower-than-usual sawhorses.

Hull Sides

Instead of being assembled from planks, the hull sides are made from sheet plywood. The only problem here is that plywood is very hard to get in lengths over 8 feet, so we have to join panels together. This can be done either by scarfing or with butt blocks. Scarfing can be intimidating to the amateur, so let's discuss butt blocks first.

Make your butt blocks from plywood the same thickness or the next size thicker than the plywood you want to join. Your hull side panels will have to be laid out and cut out (I'll explain lofting and panel layout in Chapter Six). Join the panels together on a flat surface—the floor is fine—and measure the height at each butt joint. Subtract the width of the chine log from the bottom and the width of the sheer clamp from the top. Cut out your pair of butt blocks (port and starboard) to that height. Make their length 6 inches for small boats, up to 12 inches for big boats. Glue the butt blocks in place, centered on the joint, placed to accommodate the chine log and sheer clamp. Use some fasteners on larger boats; these can be staples, bronze ring-shank nails, or small screws. If you fasten from the butt block into the planking and don't break through the other side, so much the better. If your glue is a plastic resin type, such as Weldwood, weight the block securely with something heavy to act as a clamp, like a big toolbox or some lead pigs. If your glue is epoxy or a polyurethane like 3M 5200, Bostick, or Sikaflex, weight is not so critical. *Before doing this, reread the section "Adhesives" in Chapter Three.* You don't really need fasteners here at all (except in large

sharpies) if your glue joint is good. Remember to coat the butting edges of the plywood before gluing the butt block in place.

After the glue cures, turn the planks over and sand off any excess, making a slight hollow trough the height of the joint and about 2½ inches wide. This can be easily done using a hand rubber-block sander with 36- or 40-grit sandpaper. Lay 2-inch fiberglass or polyester tape (see Appendix III for materials suppliers) in this trough and soak it thoroughly with epoxy. Even if you don't fabric-cover your hull and deck, doing this will greatly increase the life of your boat. *Be aware that epoxy is toxic—wear gloves whenever you handle it.*

I have explained side planking prematurely here to match the sequence described in Chapter Two. In practice, you don't yet need your side planks, and may prefer to wait until your molds

Figure 4-2. Glass-taping outside butt blocks.

and stem and stern components are set up on your strongback. Furthermore, if you don't have patterns or panel layout instructions for side planks, you will have to at least temporarily spring your chine logs and sheer clamps into place and trace your planking directly from the hull frame. I will explain how to do this a little later in this chapter.

The Stem

Make your triangular stem (or apron) from a block of solid wood. For boats under 20 feet, this could be a nominal (lumberyard size) 3 x 3, which measures 2½ inches square. The size and orientation of the stem or apron is described in the "construction notes" for each individual boat in this book. On some sharpies—those with flaring (bowed-out) topsides—the bottom of the stem will be a smaller triangle than the top. If so, cut out the whole stem to the top triangle and whittle it down gradually to the bottom triangle using a block plane. This twisting angular cut is called a "rolling bevel."

The easiest way to cut the stem sides is on a table saw. If you don't have one, use a circular saw as follows: Lay the stem block on your workbench with the inner (after) face up, having drawn your largest (top) triangle on both ends, and having drawn two lines connecting the tri-

angle's corners to cut along. Clamp two blocks to your workbench: one at the far end of your stem, to push against while cutting; the other on the left or right side (this depends on what kind of saw you have), to set the stem against, so you can keep your fingers away from that saw blade. If your saw can't get all the way through the stem, after cutting both inner-face cuts (turn the block around once), turn the stem over so that the outer (forward) face is up. Draw the centerline that connects the points of your triangles, and cut twice more to finish getting all the way through. This is the first hard thing you will have to do; if you get through this, you can build the boat! On boats with inner stems—called "aprons" or "liners"—and outer stems, the apron may not come to a point, being trapezoidal instead. The layout and cutting process is the same, however, except that there will be two lines on the outer face of the apron. You will notice that for many aprons, the stock you use will be rectangular in section, and its orientation in the hull is "on the flat," meaning it is wider than deep.

Molds and Bulkheads

Depending on the size of your hull, you will have from one to several temporary frames or *molds*. If your boat has bulkheads, you can make

Figure 4-3. Laying out the stem-apron and inner-sternpost bevels: (left) from the top; (right) view of a finished stem apron showing a rolling bevel, from the bottom.

them now and use them for molds. The dimensions for molds and bulkheads will need to come from a table of offsets, from a lofting, or both (these are discussed in Chapter Six). Temporary molds can be of sheet plywood or made up from lumber—usually 1 x 4 stock, except on large (over 30 feet) hulls, which require 1 x 6 or 2 x 6 stock. When you lay out your molds or bulkheads from your lofting, *remember to subtract the thickness of the hull planking.* The corners of molds made of planks can be overlapped or butted and reinforced with plywood gussets. Nail and glue them together (yellow carpenter's glue is fine). Cut notches in the bottom corners to allow for the chine logs, in the top corners for sheer clamps, and in the middle of the bottoms for the keelson. If the keelson is deeper than your frame material (it will be for traditional New Haven sharpies), make plywood gussets to receive the keelson and hold the frame halves together.

For small boats especially, I often cut out my plywood bulkheads smaller than the lofting indicates by *twice* the hull thickness, and make false butt blocks to go between the bulkhead edges and the planking. This will prevent "hard" spots (bumps) on the planking from the compression of the sharp plywood bulkhead edge. These hard spots show up primarily on very "curvy" hull sections, hence doing this is not always necessary, particularly on hull bottoms (which are nearly flat) or on larger boats with thicker planking. But the false butt blocks help distribute load (especially on the bottom), and make a stronger, more fair hull. If your sharpie is going to be a workboat, or a serious "pocket cruiser," I recommend using them. Take care not to notch too deeply for your chine logs and sheer clamps, which still must interface with the planking. *Use a batten to draw the bulkhead bottom edges, and add a slight curve to the boat bottom—this will add strength to the plywood bottom planking.* Cut out scuppers, if desired, in the bottom corners and middle-bottom (on each side of the keelson notch) of your bulkheads. Make a deck beam template, and use it to mark and cut the tops of your bulkheads (instructions for making this template are included later in this chapter in the part about decking).

Mark your waterlines (from the lofting) carefully on both sides of all molds and bulkheads, and likewise mark your centerlines. You will use these marks to align the molds to each other. Finally, mark where the strongback stanchions

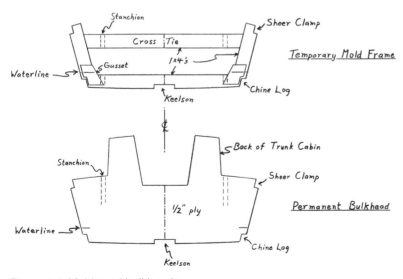

Figure 4-4. Molds and bulkheads.

(mold supports) will lie on the frames (half the distance across the strongback), measured out from the mold centerlines.

Setting up the Molds

Use a scale to measure the distances between the design stations on your plans that were used to make molds and bulkheads. Lay out the locations of your molds and bulkheads on the strongback. Some common sense is required here in figuring out how the boat will fit over the strongback. In general, the strongback is a couple of feet shorter than the hull; this means the stem should end up a little forward of one end of the strongback, while the stern overhangs the other end. If your sharpie has a transom, this would be temporarily fastened to stanchions—upright 1 x 4 or 2 x 4 planks—whose tops are cut at a sharp angle. The stanchions must be high enough to support the molds but not stick out above them, and you must decide how high to place your molds on the stanchions. To do this, measure on the plans the distance from the top of the stem to the waterline; draw waterline marks on your stanchions at that distance above your strongback, and make the stanchions longer than that distance by an amount to reach the bottom of each mold-frame or bulkhead (hence, each pair of stanchions is different).

Screw the stanchions to the outer faces of your strongback planks. Attach the mold-frames and bulkheads top and bottom to the stanchions. Use a level to make sure the stanchions are plumb, and use a level to make sure all the waterline marks are level to each other. You can see why it is important that the strongback be straight and true. When placing the stanchions, set the forward ones forward of your station marks on the strongback, and set the after ones aft of the station marks. Conversely, when you "hang" your molds and bulkheads on the stanchions, set the forward molds aft of the stanchions and set the after molds forward of the stanchions. Doing this eliminates any need to

Figure 4-5. Hanging the molds on the stanchions.

bevel the molds: as the planking is sprung around the molds, the contact points will be equivalent to the design stations, assuring that the hull will be accurate to the design. The slight gap that remains is filled with glue. Carefully align the waterlines marked on the molds to those on the stanchions; likewise, align the stanchion marks (half the strongback width from the centerlines) to the stanchions. Sight down your molds from each end of the strongback and visually confirm that the waterlines and centerlines are in line with each other. Unless you have severe astigmatism, your eyes are your most accurate tools—learn to use them and trust them. Apply cellophane packing tape to temporary molds where excess glue might make their removal a problem. Note that the term *molds* includes mold-frames and bulkheads.

The Stern

If your sharpie is double-ended, make an inner stern post much the way you made the bow stem or apron, and have it ready to join to the after end of the side planks.

If your boat is transom sterned, make the transom from the "expanded transom" drawing on your plans or lofting (see Chapter Six). Remember to subtract for the planking thickness when laying out your transom. Do your layout on the after (out) side of your material, and mark the bevel angles on the sides, bottom, and top (critical if there is to be a deck). Take these angles off the plans with a bevel square—if they aren't perfect, you can adjust them in place later with a plane. Build a little curve into the bottom of the transom—it will make the hull stronger and look nice. Your transom can be made from plywood (twice the side-planking thickness) or solid wood, if you want to varnish it later. If you use solid wood, be sure it is well seasoned so it doesn't check, and seal the grain with wood sealer as soon as you can. Make cleats to reinforce all four sides of the transom, of wood the same thickness as the transom. Run the side cleats all the way from top to bottom, and butt the top and bottom cleats to these. Bevel the outer edges the same as the outer edges of the transom. If you don't have side-plank layouts, and will be installing chine logs and sheer clamps prior to planking, or if the boat is large, notch your transom cleats to provide mortises for the logs and clamps. If your sharpie is over 25 feet or so, and has a keelson, notch the bottom cleat for the keelson also. This is particularly helpful on hulls that have deadrise (V) in their sterns. Make two stanchions cut to the "angle of rake" of the transom, and screw these to the sides of the end of your strongback stringers. Mount the transom on these, taking care to set it at the right height, angle, and centerline. To find the "angle of rake," measure the angle between transom and any vertical line on your plans with your bevel square.

Transom height is found by measuring with a scale from the bottom of the transom to the waterline on your plans. Transferring this dimension to the boat is a little tricky: Tie strings across two molds between the waterline marks on each side; hold a tape measure up from the bottom of the transom (actually the top, because the boat's upside down) extending upward, and sight across the tape to the two strings. When the strings are in line, where your eye looks across the tape will be the waterline below the transom. Slide the transom up or down until the dimension is correct. *Remember to add in the planking thickness.* Screw the transom securely to the stanchion tops—if it is solid wood, "toe"-screw it from inside so as not to damage the outer face.

If you are building a round stern (it's not that hard, really), make up your top and bottom flat stern frames. These will each consist of five pieces scarfed together, unless you make them from plywood (much easier). Lay out the appropriate radius circles (one for top, one for bottom) on plywood, and take the flare angle (bottom to sides) off the plans with your bevel square. For simplicity, most sharpies used the same bevel angle all the way around the stern. If the angle varies a little, the glue should fill the slight gap. Whether you make the frames from plywood or

A) Double~ended Stern

B) Transom Stern

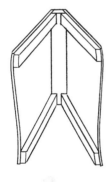
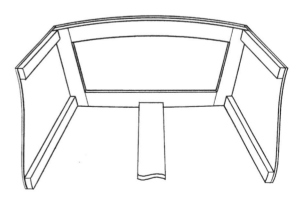

Figure 4-6. Sterns: (left) double-ended; (right) transom.

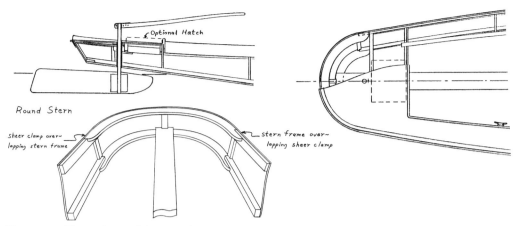

Figure 4-7. Three views of the round stern.

scarfed-together planks, the dimensions will be about the same. For a 28-foot sharpie, the frames should be 1½ inches thick by 5 or 6 inches wide. If you use plywood, laminate two layers of ⅝- or ¾-inch plywood together; if solid wood, cut the pieces out from 2 x 8 stock and 2 x 12 stock for the back section. For a 35-foot sharpie, make the frames the same thickness and an inch or two wider. Laminate the curved frames together and sand the sides smooth. The frames should be made to overlap (extend along) the insides of the side planks 6 to 12 inches, depending on the size of the boat; the chine logs and sheer clamps will be notched by this same amount where they overlap the frames. An alternate method is to notch the ends of the curved frames to overlap the chine logs and sheer clamps (see figure 4-7).

Planking the Sides

To plank the sides, you will need some floor space and a helper. Stand the side planks on edge (upside down), one on each side of the stem (or apron), stretching out from the stem in a big V. Glue and fasten the sides to the stem, aligning the bow plank edges to the point of the stem block. If your fasteners are strong (you might use clamps also), you can now lift the assembly onto the strongback and spring the sides around your molds. This is actually desirable if your stem has different-shaped triangle sections top and bottom due to flare in the topsides; springing the sides into place will help the planking lie flat on the stem sides. Otherwise, you can let the glue cure and start planking the next day.

The easiest way to spring stiff sides around is with a "Spanish windlass"—a loop of rope twisted tight with a stick like a tourniquet—but for most craft, the plywood planks will be limber enough for two people to bend by hand. Position the planks by taking a measurement off the plans from the bottom of the stem to the first design station used (often the forward bulkhead). Slide the planks around until this measurement is reached, and clamp the sides to one or more molds. Go to the stem and sight back along your marked centerlines, adjusting the planks until the stem is centered. Double-check your distance from the stem to the first frame or bulkhead, and clamp the sides to the frames such that the bottom edges (on top, because you are building upside down) of the sides protrude very slightly beyond the molds and bulkheads to allow for trimming and beveling. If you are building a transom-stern sharpie, the after ends of your side planking, when in position on the transom, should automatically locate the stem properly. Double-check the distance and make sure the stem is on center.

To glue the sides to the bulkheads, wedge the

sides away a little and coat all mating surfaces with glue. You should have your false butt blocks ready to go—make sure they won't interfere with the chine log or sheer clamp—and slide them up into place from the chine (at the top now). Fasten the sides through the false butt blocks into the bulkheads with ring-shank nails, staples, or screws (big boats only). Fasten near the top and bottom only—let the middle bulge out slightly if it wants to.

If your sharpie is a double-ender, pull the sides together in the stern and glue and fasten them to the sternpost, taking care to align the edges. Double-check distances and centers.

For transom sterns, simply pull the side planks in to the transom, align their after ends to the transom's after face, and glue and fasten them in place. If the sides are a little long (better than a little short), you can trim them after the glue dries.

For round sterns, fasten the top and bottom plank edges to the sides of the flat stern frames at the marked points (6 to 12 inches aft from the forward ends of the frames, depending on boat size). Check fairness by eye to make sure the frames follow the lines of the sheer and chine; the frames will converge aft.

Installing the Chine Logs

On the traditional New Haven boats, the chine logs were much wider than thick, and they were typically equal in thickness to the planking. Because of the much greater strength of plywood, we will not follow that rule of making the logs as thin as the planking, but rather the logs will be similar in size to those traditionally used. Consult your plans for the appropriate log sizes for your hull.

In most cases it will not be necessary to cut the bottom edges to the side planks—they can be "tortured" or "edge-set" into place. You will, however, have to bevel the bottom edges of the logs to the flare angle between bottom planking and side planking. If you have a table saw, rip the top edges to the same angle as the bottom edges so they won't hold water (in section, then, the chine logs will be shaped like parallelograms). This can be done with a circular saw by using a clamp-on guide made by the saw manufacturer. I still use my guide for cuts where the table saw is inconvenient. For small sharpies, you can use a jack plane or block plane to bevel the log bottoms after they are installed. For boats over 20 feet, it will be necessary to scarf two or more planks together to achieve the required length. This should be a simple diagonal scarf, four times the width of the chine log (the diagonal saw cuts would be 12 inches long for a log 3 inches wide, for example). Cut these scarfs accurately, and glue them carefully on a flat surface; sight down the scarf to make sure the wood continues straight on both sides of the scarf. Using fasteners at each end of the scarf won't hurt, especially on large boats, but shouldn't be necessary if you make a good glue joint with epoxy or plastic resin glue. After curing, sand off excess glue and smooth the joint.

Cut the bow ends of the logs to fit against the back of the stem. This is a "compound bevel" cut: using a bevel square, take the angle on the bottom (hull side to the back of the stem—the bevel square is oriented flat) and mark it on the bottoms of the logs; use the bevel square again to take the vertical angle between the plank bottom and the back of the stem, and mark that on the sides of the logs. Use a handsaw to make the cuts. It's easier than it sounds. After you do this once, you will say, "Oh, sure, that's just a compound bevel cut." If it's off a little, just take extra care sealing the end-grain when you install the logs—no one will ever know—and the next time you do it, it will come out better.

Now, spring the chine logs into place. This will be a "dry fit." Slide them forward so your cut ends butt the back of the stem, and let the aft ends "run wild." If your sharpie is double-ended, with one log running wild above the stern post, use a small square to transfer the bottom outer edge of the post up to the bottom outer edge of the log, and mark it. Then use your bevel square to take off and transfer the angles to make your new compound bevel cut. You will need some help pulling the middle of your chine log up and away from the side to force the end down inside the hull where it will butt against the sternpost. Repeat the operation for the other log. If you are building a transom-sterned boat, do everything the same, except your compound bevel will mate to a side transom cleat, and it will be easy to spring the log-end inboard to pop it into place (you won't need help lifting the middle away from the boat). For round sterns, cut a long notch in the bottom of the end of the log for the flat stern frame to fit into (unless you opted for cutting notches in the frames instead). Cut the logs off about where the side planks end; the notches should be from 6 to 12 inches long, depending on the size of the boat. The forward end of the notch will be directly above the end of the bottom flat stern frame, already in place. When you fit the chine logs, you may have to slide the after ends in under the stern frame first, then slide them forward to butt against the stem. When everything fits right, glue and fasten the logs in place.

If you are building a sharpie for which you have no layout information for side planking,

Figure 4-9. Longitudinals installed prior to planking.

you will need to install your chine logs and sheer clamps first (at least temporarily), instead of sliding them into place after the side planks are on. This involves positioning your stem apron in the right location relative to the molds and frame, and fixing it there so you can attach the ends of the logs and clamps to it. Then spring the logs and clamps into place and fit the aft ends to whichever stern you have, and fasten them temporarily in place. Now bend your plywood around the longitudinals and trace the stem, stern, sheer, and chine onto it. You can do this with full plywood sheets, with help; you can "rough cut" the side planking oversize to make things more manageable; or you can make templates with doorskins, cardboard, or heavy paper. After cutting out the side planking, check your fits (particularly at butt blocks). You can now either remove the longitudinals and proceed as the text describes (best for smaller boats), or permanently attach the longitudinals and plank over them (best for big boats).

Figure 4-8. Side planks and chine logs.

The Keelson Plank

In most cases, the keelson will simply be a flat plank laid in notches in the molds and bulkheads. Trim the ends to fit closely at the bow and stern. This may involve several careful cuts where keel plank meets the stem apron, as the sides will have to be trimmed to interface with the chine logs. Allow the keelson plank to "stand proud" a little where it passes through the notches in the molds: this will force a little curvature into the bottom planking, making the hull stronger. Since you have already cut the bottoms of your bulkheads and transom to a slight curve, do not let the keelson stand proud at those stations. In big New Haven sharpies, you need only build the traditional three-plank-on-edge keelson if the boat is going to be completely open. If it will have bulkheads, flotation boxes under the thwarts, or be otherwise reinforced, a simple flat-plank keelson will suffice.

In small sharpies, under 20 feet, the keelson may be absent in some boats, unless the after section of the hull develops a V-bottom. In this case you will need a keelson plank with bottom edges beveled (use a plane) out from the centerline to the angle of the planking. This bevel will "roll" or increase going aft, and the keelson will have to stand increasingly proud going aft to allow for this increase. It's not as hard as it sounds: the bottom of the keelson plank at the centerline will end right at the point of the bottom of the transom. Plane off the corners of the plank to meet the bottom edges of the transom. The bevel will roll from its deepest at the transom to nothing (flat) at the midship mold-frame or bulkhead. If you build a Clapham Nonpareil sharpie with V-bottom throughout, the keelson plank can be ripped on a table saw to the least bevel (usually constant except in the bow); areas of increased bevel can be hand-planed after the keelson is in place.

If you do build a large, open New Haven sharpie along traditional lines, refer to Chapter Two for construction of the elaborate keelsons used. Instead of through-bolting and spiking it together, use glue and nails or screws. You may have to scarf planks together to achieve the widths and lengths required. This built-up keelson seems to be peculiar to the New Haven craft; large sharpies in other localities relied on the flat-plank keelson. Because of the greater strength and lighter weight inherent in cold-molded plywood construction, I would recommend just using flat-plank keelsons in conjunction with compression posts under the thwarts, or, better still, bulkheads under both edges of the thwarts to form enclosed flotation boxes.

Planking a Round Stern with Doorskins

At this point the round sterns should be planked. The simplest way to do this is to use layers of exterior-grade ⅛-inch plywood mahogany doorskin.

To form a strong joint between the stern planking and side planking, make a "step" scarf by rabbeting the ends of the side planking. Depending on the size of the hull and plank thickness, you will need from one to three of these rabbets. Each rabbet should be ¼ inch deep by at least 2 inches long, to receive two layers of doorskin. To further reinforce this joint, make a cleat and install it vertically behind the seam between stern and side planking inside the hull. Install another cleat between the top and bottom stern frames at the centerline aft to stiffen the structure. This cleat may also act as a butt block for plank layers.

To trace the shape of the stern planking onto a doorskin, bend a full sheet right around the stern (or one side of it) with the grain of the plywood oriented vertically (basically at right angles to the flat stern frames). Trace the top and bottom stern frames and the end of the side planking onto the doorskin, and cut it out.

Glue and fasten the cleats in place, and glue and fasten the doorskin in place. Continue in this manner, wrapping doorskins around the stern and cutting, fitting, and gluing them in place. Stagger your butt seams at least 6 inches apart, and terminate each successive layer in the appropriate side plank rabbet. For example, if you are building a 35-foot New Haven sharpie, the side planking might be ¾-inch marine plywood. Your side plank ends would have two-step rabbets, and your stern planking would be made up of six layers of ⅛-inch doorskin. The first two layers would butt the side plank ends over the cleat; the second two layers would lie in the first and deepest rabbet; the third two layers would lie in the second and shallowest rabbet. The vertical joints of each doorskin layer, about one-third of the way around the stern, would be staggered about 6 inches apart. For convenience, every fourth layer may be allowed to have a joint in approximately the same place.

During lamination, apply glue liberally to both interfacing doorskin surfaces, and work the doorskins into place from the rabbets aft, forcing out all air while fastening the perimeters to the stern frames with staples or nails. When finished and cured, sand the stern smooth, paying careful attention to the fairness of the joints. If the stern planking stands a little proud from the side planking, use a block plane to shave it down and fair it out. Plane and sand the stern plank edges fair to the bottom stern frame.

Bottom Planking

The hull is nearly ready for bottom planking. Use a hand plane and sanding block to "true up" the edges of hull, chine logs, bulkhead bottoms, and keelson. This will ensure a fair bottom and good glue joints.

Because of the limitations imposed by manufactured plywood sizes, the bottom planking will need to be scarfed or butted together in sections. If the bottom of your sharpie is 4 feet wide or less, the bottom planking may run fore-and-aft—otherwise, it will run across the hull. If you elect to scarf the panels together, use the following process: A scarf in plywood should be at least 10 to 1; that is, the length of the scarf must be 10 times the thickness of the material. For example,

suppose your bottom plywood is ½ inch thick, and the length of the hull on the bottom is 15 feet with a maximum width of 4 feet. Two sheets of plywood will cover it with one scarf, and the scarf will need to be 5 inches long. To cut the scarfs, stack your plywood on a table or sawhorses such that the top sheet's edge is set back 5 inches from the edge below, and draw a line across the top sheet 5 inches from the edge of the top sheet. Note that one of these sheets will be upside down. If you have a particular plywood face you want to be on the outside, orient the sheets appropriately (if using ACX plywood in conjunction with a fabric/epoxy covering, face the "C" side out). Use a power plane or body grinder to cut a long, even inclined plane from the bottom edge of the bottom sheet to the pencil line on the top sheet. Glue the scarf carefully on a flat surface, such as the floor, with a piece of waxed paper under it to keep it from sticking. Set a nail through each side of the scarf to keep the joint from slipping, and set weights on the scarf to clamp it while the glue cures. After curing, sand off excess glue and fair the joint smooth.

If you elect to use butt blocks, lay out on the hull bottom—chines and keelson—where the butts will be located, and measure their width. There will generally be two for each joint, as the keelson will divide them. Cut the butt blocks from plywood the same thickness as the planking, 2 inches shorter than the dimension between the chine log and keelson. When gluing the butt blocks to the planking, place them so that there will be a 1-inch gap between the butt block and the chine log on one end, and between the butt block and keelson on the other end; this is to allow bilgewater to flow along the hull bottom. After the glue has cured, turn the planking over and sand a shallow trough along the joint, as explained above when we prepared the side planks, and lay up fiberglass or polyester tape and epoxy in the trough.

Set the bottom planking on the hull, align it, and trace the outside perimeter with a pencil. Remove it, turn it back over on sawhorses, and cut out the bottom. Set your circular saw to the bevel of the side flare, and cut a fraction outside your pencil lines. An alternate method of planking the bottom is to lay up each section in place, cutting and fitting one at a time, and fastening the sections together in place on the hull. The butt blocks will then need to be installed from inside. This may be a little awkward with the hull upside down, but it will be necessary with large hulls. Don't forget your false butt blocks between bottom and bulkheads, if you elected to use them.

If your hull has a V-bottom, the planking will be made in two halves. If only the stern is V-shaped, as in the Chesapeake Flattie, you can make a curved, V-shaped cut in the after part of the planking so that each half can be laid up on the keelson. First cut a slot along the centerline aft; then, with the planking on the hull, spring each half into place separately, trace it to the hull (use a batten over the keelson centerline), remove it, and cut it out.

Check for a good fit, and glue and fasten the bottom planking to the hull. After curing, trim the edges of the bottom to the sides and "ease" them—round them off to a radius approximately equal to the thickness of the bottom planking. You can do this with a block plane, coarse sandpaper, or a router.

On large sharpies, it may be desirable to "double-plank" the bottom to achieve higher strength. If so, simply butt the plywood sheet edges and stagger the butts of the second planking layer at least 18 inches away from the first butts. Grind and epoxy/glass-tape the joints both inside and outside the hull. If the sheets are long enough to plank each layer in opposite diagonals, this will make for a stronger hull, even if the diagonal angle is only a few degrees.

The Centerboard Slot, Gripe, Skeg, Sternpost, and Outer Stem

Using a long, straight batten, carefully lay out a centerline on the hull bottom. Locate the centerboard slot, lay it out, and cut it out with a cir-cular saw. The ends can be cut with a saber saw or by drilling large holes with a paddle bit. (When using a paddle bit, stop drilling just as the point breaks through and finish drilling the hole from the other side.) Clean up the slot with coarse sandpaper. If a slot already exists in the keelson (as with the New Haven triple-plank-on-edge keelson), use a long ⅛-inch twist drill to locate the corners of the slot by drilling through the bottom from inside the hull.

If your boat is to have a skeg, cut it from solid lumber to the approximate size, locate it on the hull, and "scribe" a line along the top edge of the skeg from the hull with a compass or carpenter's flat pencil held on edge. Cut this line, and fit the skeg to the hull; glue and fasten it. Near the after end, it may be more convenient to run long screws through the keelson and hull into the skeg from inside the boat.

Many sharpies with transoms, as well as double-enders, have an external sternpost. Make this

Figure 4-10. Outer stem and gripe.

Figure 4-11. A double-ender's sternpost and skeg.

to interlock with the skeg and install it now; fasten transom-mounted sternposts from inside.

Most sharpies have outer stems. If so, plane the rough bow or stern edges flat, and fit the outer stem in place. Use long, large-diameter screws to fasten outer stems—and epoxy glue is best for this job. Some sharpies also have small plank keels or keel battens outside; make and install these now. A small keel batten placed forward of the centerboard slot and extending under the stem is called a *gripe*.

Fabric/Epoxy-Covering

After a thorough sanding, spot-filling and re-sanding of any flaws, the hull is ready for fabric-covering. I recommend using Xynole-polyester cloth, available from Defender Industries (see Appendix III), with epoxy resin. Polyester cloth is stronger, safer, and much easier to work with

Figure 4-12. Xynole-polyester cloth draped in place prior to wetting out with epoxy.

than fiberglass. Do not, however, use polyester *resin* anywhere on your boat—it is not compatible with wood and will eventually delaminate.

Stretch the polyester cloth tightly over your hull fore and aft, but not athwartship, and hold it in place with masking tape, push pins or temporary staples. Wet out the cloth with epoxy, using a ⅜-inch nap roller (cheap roller covers may come apart in epoxy), working from the middle out toward the ends. Roll on two or three coats, taking care to saturate the cloth thoroughly.

Fabric/epoxy-covering your hull is optional. The job is messy, and epoxy fumes are toxic. The catalyst is hyperallergenic and can cause severe reactions. Use epoxy in a well-ventilated area, and wear protective clothing, including latex gloves and a respirator (*not* a dust mask). Covering the hull will greatly increase its durability, as well as decreasing maintenance. The alternative is to coat all exterior surfaces with liberal amounts of wood preservative, which is also toxic and requires the same precautions and protective clothing as epoxy. Allow wood preservative to dry thoroughly, preferably for several weeks, before applying paint. There are several other ways to fabric-cover the hull: I have had success with cotton, linen, window screen, polypropylene, and nylon (such as fine-mesh curtain fabric) saturated with oil-based paint, epoxy, or arabol (liquid latex rubber lagging compound). If you decide to experiment, please do so on *samples*, rather than your hull, to see if the methods and materials work.

The last step before turning over the hull is to apply a good primer to the surface (unless you are waiting for preservatives to dry). If you covered the hull with fabric and epoxy, you may elect to "glaze" the hull now with a mixture of epoxy and thixogens; this process and mixture are explained in Chapter Five.

It is helpful at this point to locate the waterline on the outside of the hull by transferring measurements from your marks on the molds and bulkheads to the outside of the hull. Add a height of 1 to 3 inches, depending on the size of

Figure 4-13. Finished fabric covering, glazed and primed.

the hull, above the designed waterline to your scribed waterline (where the bottom paint ends). A good visual effect is to add a little more height to the scribed waterline at the bow and stern (check your plans, too). Spring a long, straight batten through the points you have marked on the hull, and very carefully scribe your waterline with a fine-tip magic marker.

The Sheer Clamp

You will need help turning over the hull. From underneath, disconnect your stanchions from molds and bulkheads. Lift the hull straight up off the strongback and turn it over onto another pair of horses. Unscrew the stanchions from the strongback sides and set the hull back on the strongback right-side up. You will need some bracing under the ends of the hull to support it; fasten bracing pieces in place after "truing" the hull to her waterline by measuring up from the strongback to the waterlines of the stem and stern.

You will need a sheer clamp around the inside perimeter of your hull sides. In many traditional craft, the sheer clamp was set down below the sheer, and the deck beams rested on it. In our cold-molded sharpies, the sheer clamp is placed right at the top, where it acts as a cleat between the plywood planking and plywood deck. Bevel the top edge of the sheer clamp to the angle at which the deck intersects the hull topsides. Take this off your bulkheads with a bevel square, noting that the angle may vary from bow to stern. If so, cut to the least angle using a table saw or circular saw with a ripping guide, and plane the sharper angles in place.

Cut the ends of the sheer clamp to fit bow and stern, in a similar manner to how you cut the chine logs—those compound bevel cuts again. If your stern is round, notch the after end of the clamp to fit under the flat upper stern frame (or vice versa). After a dry fit, glue and fasten the sheer clamps in place. When cured, plane and sand the surfaces true. The easiest time to sand and paint the inside of the hull is now, before the deck goes together.

Deck Beams

Make a deck beam template as follows: Using a piece of plywood equal to the boat's maximum beam, measure down from the top edge at each end the amount of deck crown. This figure should be included in construction notes for your design. If not, make the crown equal to ½ inch per foot of beam—therefore, a vessel with an 8-foot beam will have a 4-inch deck crown.

After marking the amount of crown at each end of the plywood template, set nails at the marks, and set another nail in the middle of the template the thickness of your flexible drawing batten from the top. Spring a batten through the nails, and add two more nails halfway out toward each end of the template from the middle, pushing the batten upward slightly by identical amounts each side. Study this curve to make sure it is fair and symmetrical, and trace it on the template. Repeat the process below the first line by the desired thickness of the deck beams, but make the new curve slightly flatter, so the deck beam tapers slightly at the ends. Trace the second line, and cut the template out. You will use it to mark the tops of your bulkheads, and to trace onto stock for your deck beams. Note that, for many of the boats, the deck beam ends should be approximately the same height as the sheer clamps they will rest against. Shorter beams toward the ends of the hull will stand proud of the sheer line (because of taper, they are higher nearer the center); plane a little off the *bottom* edges until they fit.

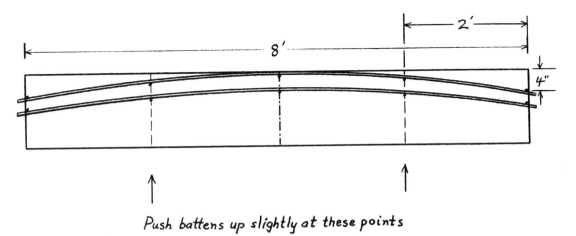

Push battens up slightly at these points

Figure 4-14. Making a deck beam template.

Deck beam scantlings will come from your plans. All but large sharpies will have very few deck beams. Figure the number and their location, and measure their lengths across the hull after marking on the sheer clamp where they will be placed.

The easiest way to lay them out is by measuring forward or aft from the bulkheads or molds. Cut out the beams from the right-sized stock by scribing from the template—scribe the longest beam at the top of your stock, and scribe progressively shorter beams under each other to maximize stock use. In some cases, you may get all your beams from one piece of wide plank the length of the boat's beam. After cutting them out, route, chamfer (bevel), or ease the under edges of the beams, and sand them smooth. Cut the beam ends to fit snugly to the sheer clamps—compound bevel cuts again. Make plywood gussets, called beam shelves, to join the beams to the undersides of the sheer clamps. These will look like triangles with lopped-off corners. You can skip these on small sharpies, but they are important on large ones.

Glue and fasten the deck beams in place. Use long screws in pairs at each end, from outside the hull, through the clamp into the beam ends. Fasten the gussets under the clamps and beams with screws and glue. You may have to plane a little off the underside of the ends of the shorter beams, as previously mentioned, to get a snug fit, and you may also have to plane a bevel on the outboard ends and tops of the gussets to get them to lie snug to the hull and the undersides of the clamps.

Deck Substructure

Make your breasthook from timber the same thickness as your deck beams. Run the grain across the hull. Where applicable, extend the breasthook far enough aft to include the foremast hole—the breasthook also functions here as a mast partner. On big sharpies, you may need several widths of timber to do this. You can also build up several layers of plywood to make a breasthook; this is indeed the best way to do it.

Cut your mast hole (at least ½ inch larger than the mast diameter, if you intend to leather the hole), before installing the breasthook. If you stack plywood, cut and trace the holes layer-to-layer. Take care that the hole penetrates at the correct angle; on many boats, it doesn't go straight through. Use a rasp, file, and sandpaper to true up the hole.

If there is a second mast hole, or if the only mast hole is farther aft, make a mast partner to fit between the adjacent deck beams twice the width of the mast hole. This can be a solid plank, plywood, or stacked plywood. On large boats, it is good practice to make the partner 1 inch longer than the distance between adjacent beams, and to notch the beams such that the partner drops into place and fits snugly. The top surfaces of the breasthook and mast partners must finish flush to the deck beam and sheer clamp top surfaces. Plane and sand the surface smooth and fair.

Make plywood knees to support the side decks. Because there are no side frames for these to lie against, as in some of the traditional boats, you can either make some side frames for them or cut them out big enough to reach the bottom of the hull, thereby acting as partial bulkheads (very strong). On the big sharpies, laminate knees from two layers of ¾-inch plywood. Notch the knees for sheer clamps and chine logs, and notch the inboard heads for carlins, if used.

In some sharpies the side decks vary in width, and each pair of knees will need to be a different width. In all cases the knees will be of different heights and must be carefully fitted to the hull. The top angles should, however, be approximately the same throughout.

Space the knees every 2 or 3 feet, or according to the plans, and glue them in place. Fasten the top edges through the hull and sheer clamp from outside with one large screw for each knee. If you mount the knees perpendicular to the hull, you won't have to bevel any edges.

Side deck carlins were traditionally used only on large sharpies, but will be needed for most cold-molded sharpies to support the relatively thin plywood deck edge. Notch your bulkheads at the correct angles for the carlin ends, and spring the carlins into place along the inboard heads of the knees, letting the ends of the carlins run wild several inches beyond the bulkheads. After a dry fit, glue and fasten the carlins in place.

On large sharpies with hatches, cut hatch carlins 1 inch longer than the distance between adjacent beams, and notch the beams for the carlin ends. Make the carlins from stock the same thickness and height as that of the deck beams, and glue and fasten the carlins with screws or nails through the beams into the carlin ends.

If your sharpie will have a vertical rudder shaft, make a plywood deck stiffener to run from the appropriate deck beam to the stern. Notch this into the beam(s) and stern frame on large boats. Small sharpies can make use of a deck stiffener forward—this can run from the bulkhead right to the stem, being in essence mast partner, breasthook, and backup block for cleats, bowsprit, or mooring bitt. Its use may eliminate the need for the forwardmost deck beam; the stiffener can be plywood or a solid plank. The most convenient time to finish (sand, paint or varnish) the deck substructure is now, before laying the deck.

The Deck

Plane and sand the top surfaces of the deck substructure, and you are ready for the deck. Lay out sheet plywood to cover the deck with as few seams as possible, and arrange the seams to lie on deck substructure whenever possible. On large sharpies, you may have fore-and-aft seams; these may be butted and reinforced from inside with seam battens placed between the deck beams. If they are short and isolated (as at the sides of the foredeck), and if the deck is to be covered with fabric and epoxy, they may simply be butted and glued with epoxy. After laying out plywood to cover the deck, scribe it from underneath with a sharp pencil, including openings for hatches, masts, etc., and cut it out. The best time to paint the deck underside is before laying it. Prime, sand and paint the areas you traced from below, overlapping your pencil lines by about ⅛ inch, leaving raw wood for the glue joints to the deck substructure. Make sure the cut pieces fit, and glue and fasten the deck in place. Take care to clean up squeezed-out glue inside under the deck.

Plane and sand all edges, and ease or bullnose the outboard deck edges to a radius equal to the thickness of the deck. Fill fastener holes and seams with thickened epoxy, sand smooth, and fabric-cover the deck. Although the traditional method used canvas and paint, Xynole-polyester and epoxy are better by far, providing a tough, waterproof, strong, and permanent surface. If you prefer to have a traditional planked deck, refer to Chapter Two.

Figure 4-15. Deck substructure.

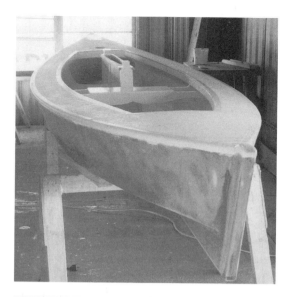

Figure 4-16. The deck: (top) plywood; (bottom) traditional.

The Centerboard Trunk, Thwarts, and Maststeps

These are the final major components of the open sharpie.

The centerboard trunk is made in halves. Lay out the trunk on plywood, leaving a little extra along the bottom to scribe and trim it to the keelson, and cut it out. Take care to get the angles for the posts at each end of the trunk right—usually the forward post is set plumb and the after post rakes forward or is also plumb. Duplicate the other half from the first, after scribing to the keelson and trimming the bottom edge. Make the trunk logs from solid stock the appropriate size and length indicated by the plans, and scribe and trim them to the keelson also. Fasten the plywood trunk halves to the logs with screws or nails and epoxy, and smooth epoxy putty over the screw holes. Fabric/epoxy-cover the inside surfaces of the trunk halves (or saturate with wood preservative). Make trunk posts, and mortise them halfway through the keelson at each end of the centerboard slot with a chisel and mallet (or router and flute bit). Glue the posts into the mortised holes, being very careful to make them plumb side-to-side, and plumb or raked at the correct angles fore-and-aft. Fabric/epoxy cover (or seal with wood preservative) the inner faces of the posts.

After curing, glue and fasten the trunk halves in place. Use short screws through the plywood trunk halves into the posts, and long screws down through the trunk logs into the keelson plank. Use plenty of glue, and don't allow voids. Crawl under the hull and carefully clean the inside joint between trunk and keelson, also filling any voids. For an alternative adhesive to epoxy, 3M 5200 or Bostik is excellent for this application, and it can be cleaned up with mineral spirits. Be sure to fabric/epoxy cover the joint inside the centerboard trunk between the trunk, keelson and hull planking. This joint is succeptible to worms, rot, and water saturation. It should be protected even if you don't fabric/epoxy cover your hull.

Make the appropriate cap for the trunk, according to your design, and glue and fasten it in place, unless you desire to have all or some portion of it removable (desirable for large sharpies with long trunks). Removable sections should be well-fastened and might employ sponge-rubber gaskets.

Lay out the position of the thwarts on the insides of the hull, and measure the distances across and angles of intersection between thwarts and hull. Subtract for plywood stiffeners or notch for side frames to be placed between the thwart-ends and hull, and cut out the thwarts. If a thwart is holed for a mast, lay out the center and cut the hole oversize. Cut and fit the plywood hull stiffeners (at least the width of the thwart) to fit snugly from sheer clamp to chine log. If your boat has a thwart riser (longitudinal batten), end your thwarts shy of the hull and skip the stiffeners.

If there is room to install it as a unit, fasten the ends of the thwart to the stiffeners with screws or nails through the stiffeners into the ends of the thwarts, using epoxy or 3M 5200 adhesive. If not, make cleats for the thwart to rest on (bevel the top edges), and glue and fasten these to the stiffeners. If you want to be able to remove the thwart, make the cleats large and plan to screw or through-bolt the thwart to the cleats. Glue the stiffeners to the hull, and fasten the thwarts in place.

If you use paired side frames at the end of each thwart, cut these to fit between chine logs and sheer clamps, and notch the thwart-ends to fit between the side frames. Fasten a cleat to the frames for the thwart to rest on. In open boats without side decks, knees are traditionally placed above the thwarts in pairs at each end. Make these from solid stock or plywood, and notch them to fit the sheer clamp or inwale. It won't hurt to make all the components above the

thwart risers removable for easier maintenance. If you do, use bedding compound in all joints to prevent rot.

Stern sheets are the U-shaped seats in the stern of an open boat. They consist of a series of planks, typically a little thinner than thwarts, placed fore-and-aft. They are supported by thwart risers or cleats on the sides, by a cleat fastened to the transom, and by a small beam placed athwartships between the risers. This beam is usually cut to a decorative pattern (virtually a "signature" of many old-time builders), and it supports the middle of the stern sheets. You can make stern sheets of planks in the traditional manner (they often form a "fan" pattern), particularly if you intend to finish all your seating "bright" (varnished or oiled). Or you can make them from one piece of ½-inch plywood.

Make maststeps from three or more layers of ¾-inch plywood or from solid blocks. Make the steps square or rectangular and equal to the dimension across the keelson plank. Cut holes to receive the mast tenons in all but the bottom layer of plywood (or don't go through the block bottom). Drill a ¼-inch hole through the center of the bottom layer, and cut a ¼-inch by ¼-inch slot across the bottom so that water will drain out of the step. Glue the layers together, and glue and fasten the step to the keelson. If there is a step in the extreme bow, fit the step tightly to the hull planking also. Use epoxy or 3M 5200 to glue the assembly in place. Use epoxy or plastic resin glue for the individual layers. Thoroughly seal and paint the step to prevent rot.

The basic structure of the boat is now complete, and ready for exterior primer and paint.

CHAPTER 5
DETAILS AND ACCOUTREMENTS

Realistically, a bare hull and deck is a long way from being a boat. Now we need to make all the myriad components, as well as finishing, painting, rigging, and fitting out.

Rudders, Centerboards, and Tillers

The most practical way I have found to make rudders and centerboards, for all size craft, is to build "cores" out of lumber stock, shape them, and cover them with plywood sheathing. I then apply a skin of polyester cloth and epoxy to seal and protect the wood, overlapping the cloth on the edges such that all end-grain has two layers of cloth and epoxy over it. For all but very small craft, I add at least one more layer of cloth on abrasion surfaces—the bottom edges of rudder and centerboard. For vessels over 30 feet, I build up five or six layers of cloth on the lowest corner of the centerboard; and during yearly haulouts I add an additional layer or more, depending on how much has been abraded away during the season's use.

For simplicity, the designs in this book have centerboards of two different thicknesses: 2¼ inches and 3⅛ inches, finished. These are the maximum thicknesses that will safely fit in the trunks; actual thicknesses may end up slightly thicker or thinner, depending on materials used and finishing techniques. These two thicknesses are determined by the inside trunk widths,

which are in turn determined by the trunk posts, which are either 2½ inches square (the nominal 3 x 3) or 3½ inches square (4 x 4).

Both centerboards and rudders are cored with nominal 2-inch stock (1½ inches thick). The stock width will vary in my plans, but it is not critical. Avoid 2 x 12 stock in all but large boats, because it is more prone to warping. Using 2 x 6s, 2 x 8s and 2 x 10s seems to work best. Lay out the stock according to the plan drawings (traditional or cold-molded layouts are similar), cut the edges to shape, and glue the components together on a flat surface; use plastic film (Visqueen) or waxed paper to prevent sticking. To clamp the components together, use pipe clamps or cleats and wedges around the perimeter. If you use plastic resin glue, make your joints very tight and double-coat all end-grain joints.

If your rudder has a shaft, the core is built up on each side of it for all but small craft. For the latter, drill a hole for the shaft through the rudder plank, and drill another hole of smaller diameter through the leading edge of the rudder plank, right through the rudder shaft and a couple of inches beyond. You won't be able to drill through the stainless steel shaft in place: Let the drill point scratch the shaft in place (be sure to drill on center), remove the shaft and drill it on a drill press at low speed. Use water liberally to lubricate and cool the drill.

Epoxy the shaft (1-inch diameter, let's say) in

Figure 5-1. (top) Rudder core, and (bottom) centerboard core layup.

balanced rudders should be "foiled" somewhat like an airplane wing, and post-hung rudders should taper aft. The trailing edges may come nearly to a point, as the plywood sheathing will build them back up. Don't go nuts with all this; tests have shown that at the low speeds of most sailboats, the performance differences between a fully NACA-foiled fin and a squared-off one are subtle. However, a little shaping is known to help. It should also be noted that razor-edge trailing edges, besides being vulnerable to damage, actually create more drag than a narrow, squared-off trailing edge. Sharpies are, however, capable of high-enough speeds that they deserve more care in shaping than, say, a displacement-type cruiser. If you are building a real go-fast machine, take more trouble than if you are building a daysailer for picnics on the lake.

Use a power plane, hand plane, adze (unlikely, I realize), or body grinder to shape your foils. Take care that both sides of your cores match. Curved surfaces are better than flat ones; use a batten to check your progress.

a

b

Figure 5-2. Foil development for rudders and centerboards: (a) Rough shaping, cheek and tiller slot for a crabbing skiff rudder. (b) This crabbing skiff centerboard is shaped more like a dagger-board because it swings down nearly vertical.

place, and drive the smaller-diameter pin (⅜-inch) in place with epoxy. For larger craft, weld ⅛- or ¼-inch thick tangs on each edge of the rudder shaft and cut slots in the core material such that the core components slide over the tangs and butt tight to the shaft. On very large craft, add fasteners through the core and tangs—I usually use ¼-inch flathead machine screws in pre-tapped holes in the tangs.

After curing, pencil in centerlines around the perimeter, and shape the core. Centerboards and

Figure 5-3. Rudder with head for tiller socket—sanded and ready for epoxy/fabric covering.

After shaping, trace the core onto plywood, orienting the grain fore-and-aft if convenient (it's not critical), and cut out the two plywood sheaths. Glue, fasten, and clamp the sheaths onto both sides of the core simultaneously to avoid warping.

For rudderheads, use thicker plywood than the sheathing material for the head plates at the tiller socket. On larger sharpies, use both thicknesses, cutting the first sheathing layer away at the socket to provide for greater tiller thickness. On very large sharpies, double up on the head plates for strength. Use long, large-diameter screws to fasten the head plates on the rudderhead; on large craft, use through-bolts.

On very small skiffs, you may simply fabric/epoxy-cover the rudder core, avoiding the plywood altogether. Or you might elect to make your rudder from plywood, though it's harder to shape.

Take care in fitting your centerboard to the trunk. Make sure it fits loosely before you cover it with fabric and epoxy, which may add nearly ⅛ inch in thickness. Locate the pin holes carefully, and use a square or pair of squares and a long (12-inch) ¼-inch twist drill to drill a pilot hole through both trunk and board simultaneously. To do this, place the board in the trunk in the up position and wedge it firmly in place while drilling the pilot hole. Remove the board

and drill the pin holes with a spade bit or hole saw. I use PVC pipe segments epoxied in place as pin bushings for smaller vessels, and stainless-steel pipe for large craft (over 30 feet). Put bushings in both the centerboard and trunk.

Make cover plates for the pin from plywood, stainless steel, or brass/bronze. The pin itself should be stainless steel, brass, or bronze; a piece of old shaft will work perfectly. Match any metals—never place dissimilar metals in contact with each other unless you have no choice (such as a bronze propeller on a stainless shaft). At least one cover plate, and preferably both on larger craft, should be removable. Use screws to hold them in place (not too long!), and bedding compound or sealant (nonadhesive type) to prevent leakage. Seal the plates with epoxy or preservative and paint them.

Make the tiller from high-quality (straight grain/no knots), strong wood—I prefer oak or ash. Give it some curve, with the grain if possible, and taper the end. Shape the socket such that the tiller can be moved up and down a little, but has no play from side to side. The tiller may have a pin through the rudderhead, or a lashing to hold it in place. Some people prefer to taper the tiller end and socket—this takes more work—and use a bungee lashing to hold the tiller tightly in the socket.

If your sharpie has a sternpost, the rudder and post should be of the same thickness—this will simplify the hardware manufacture and installation, and you may be able to purchase gudgeons and pintles ready-made from suppliers such as Schaefer or Wilcox-Crittenden.

Engines and Oars

Most sharpies really don't need an engine of any kind, as they row and sail so well. However, if you have to get out of a long, narrow canal that has fluky wind, rowing a large sharpie with her masts up can be quite difficult. A small outboard can be very handy; the problem is where to put it. Few sharpies have a stern that will mount an outboard conveniently. This leaves us with adding a bracket somewhere or building a well. Wells, properly designed and built, are very effective, but they take up a lot of cockpit space and involve a lot of work. If you build a fairly large cruising sharpie and intend to live aboard at times and travel pretty extensively, a well or inboard motor might be the answer. This is particularly true if you intend to travel in the Intracoastal Waterway or similar places.

Because sharpies have such thin sterns, avoid long-shaft outboard motors in the wells of all but very large sharpies (around 50 feet). You will probably have to offset your well to clear skeg and rudder, though you may be able to modify either or both to accommodate a centered well on the large boats.

I prefer teardrop-shaped wells, which allow

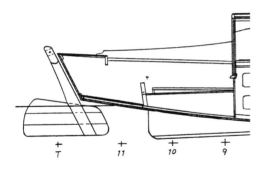

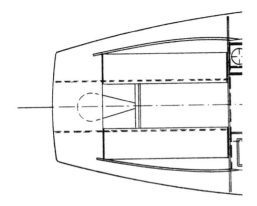

Figure 5-4. Outboard wells.

the outboard to be tilted up in place, but these take a lot of space and work. If you use a small, light motor that can be lifted out, you can make a square or rectangular well. In any case, you will need to save the cutout, add a plywood flange to it, and make it into an aperture plug.

Outboard brackets may be purchased from several manufacturers. They are through-bolted to the transom, and are hinged to lift the motor clear of the water for safety, and to reduce drag under sail. For the sharply raked transoms of some sharpies, modifications might be required. These may involve fabricating an additional wedge-shaped fitting of metal or wood to decrease the mounting angle of the bracket. Do some research before purchasing a bracket and motor.

If you elect to install an inboard, please refer to my book *The New Cold-Molded Boatbuilding, from Lofting to Launching* (International Marine, 1990); there is also a section devoted to outboard wells. One simple option is to use a large, horizontal-shaft lawn mower motor under the bridge deck with a belt drive to the propeller shaft. You can use an idler wheel, centrifugal clutch, or electric clutch (such as used on automotive air conditioner pumps) to disengage the motor—but if so you'll have to get by without reverse. These motors are air cooled, so you will have to leave a large hatch open when running; you will also need an exhaust system and muffler other than the standard ones. You can belt-drive a small automotive alternator to charge your battery, if so desired.

Keep in mind that gasoline is a very dangerous fuel. *Design, build, and operate marine gasoline engines with safety foremost in your mind.*

Oars and sweeps are much simpler. The biggest mistake I see people making is buying short, little oars for their boats—no wonder no one knows how to row anymore! Too many of today's boats don't row worth a damn anyway, and when you add such ridiculously undersized oars to the picture, it can lead to accidents involving loss of life. Perhaps you've seen some poor guy trying to row an inflatable against a strong current. While I

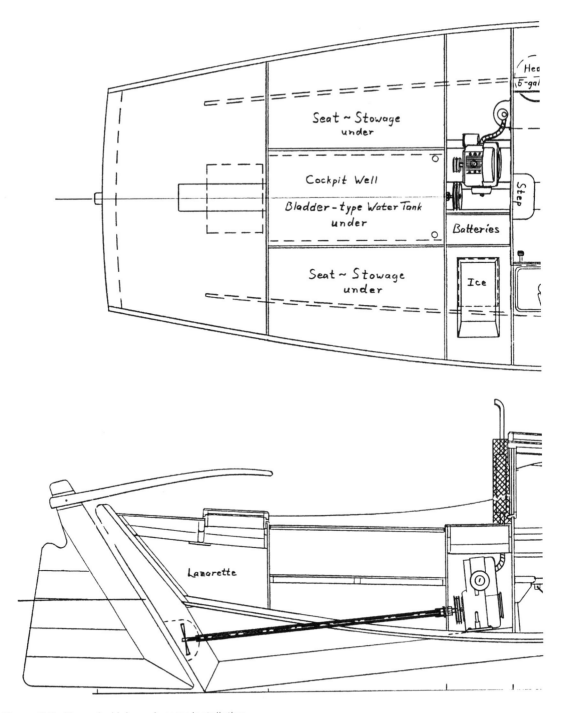

Seat ~ Stowage
under

Cockpit Well

Bladder - type Water Tank
under

Seat ~ Stowage
under

Hea
5-gal

Step

Batteries

Ice

Lazorette

Figure 5-5. Air-cooled inboard motor installation,
showing a Tecumseh OH140 electric-start 14
horsepower motor.

lived in Key West, two people died due directly to this "recipe for disaster."

I find oars shorter than 7 feet long to be ineffective even in 8-foot prams. Since your life may literally depend on good oars, I can't recommend too strongly buying long, strong, well-made oars, leathering them properly, keeping them varnished, oiled, or painted, and installing high-quality oarlocks and sockets. Those chromed "pot metal" cheap oarlocks will break—don't use them. Buy good, bronze oarlocks and sockets, such as those from Wilcox-Crittenden or Perko. I also insist on round oarlocks—I detest the open-topped ones that your oars jump out of when you are rowing out through the surf in a gale. The round ones will stay on your oars, kept there by a thick leather (rawhide) strip at the inboard end of the leather sheath, and you can't lose them.

It is best to sew the sheath on, using a "baseball" stitch; soak the leather first so it stretches tight when it dries out. Nail the thick "keeper" strip in place with bronze ring-shank nails (put the oarlock on *first*), cutting a scarf joint where the ends meet.

Mortise the sockets into the rails or blocks, and use long screws or flathead through-bolts to secure them. Seal the wood, and use bedding compound to prevent rot. Make the mortises and holes fit snugly so the sockets don't work loose.

You can often purchase oar-leathering kits from your marine supplier. If you have trouble finding them, go to your shoemaker, shoe-repair person, or craft shop.

Leave paint and varnish off the handles of your oars—it will make them slippery. An occasional coat of oil, such as Deks-Olje #1 (The Flood Company), will keep the handles from drying out and checking.

At times it is better to scull than row—in a crowded anchorage, in a narrow canal, or among pilings, for example. To scull, a large sharpie requires a fairly long oar—at least 8 to 10 feet. Once you learn to scull, you'll be amazed at how effective it is. It's all in the wrist and elbow, but hard to describe in print; the elbow must lead the side-to-side motion, and the wrist follows.

Location of oarlock sockets in relation to thwarts is critical. In general, the sockets should be 11 inches aft of the thwart's after edge, and 8 or 9 inches higher than the thwart. It also helps to keep the sockets at least 4 feet apart or more, to get oar leverage. There should be a footrest to push against, and nothing directly behind your back, if possible (the centerboard trunk presents a problem—one reason the after trunk post is frequently raked forward).

Finally, to really take advantage of the excellent rowing properties of the sharpie, the masts must come down, presenting the problem of what to do with them when rowing. In general, the masts should lie on each side of the oarsman (or woman), crossing the thwart as low and far outboard as possible to keep them out of the way. If you design a custom interior for your open sharpie, think about this problem during layout and construction. On larger sharpies with cabins, the masts can lie along the housetop, perhaps in a boom crutch or scissors crutch or gallows aft, high enough or perhaps off to one side to clear the oarsman's head.

Cockpits

Cockpits are a difficult part of a boat to design well, and are equally hard to build. A lot of careful thought and planning goes into the cockpit, and if it is not well built in every way, it will leak, rot, and always be a problem. For these reasons and the ones I am about to cite, many bluewater cruising boats (as well as commercial craft) have *no* cockpit at all.

To start with, cockpits generally include a well, or "steering room" in traditional boat talk. A well can, of course, be filled with water. Water has terrific weight—enough to alter the trim and balance of a boat at the least, and to swamp her and sink her at worst. The well must therefore be as small as possible, as high above the waterline as possible, and must be voided of water as rapidly and easily as possible.

Other considerations are comfort, safety, and utility. A good cockpit affords some protection from seas, wind, and spray, provides a comfortable place from which to control the boat or just enjoy the ride, and creates an efficient work area from which the boat's steering and sheeting (at least) can be handled, including cleating, winching, and stowing line. Proportions are critical: A well that is too wide or long is dangerous (you can be thrown across it) and inefficient (controls may be too far apart or in the way of something or someone). Seats that are too narrow or set at

a bad angle are exhausting and uncomfortable. A tiller that sweeps the whole cockpit will always hit someone or cause people to keep moving. And a poorly placed outboard well will take up precious space, assault you with smoke, fumes and bad smells, and make so much noise no one will be able to hear anything else.

And so, good yacht designers spend a lot of time designing cockpits, and good shipwrights spend a lot of time building them well. Here are several guidelines: Make the well small, and no less than 6 inches above the waterline (if possible—this is not possible in some small sharpies). Make the seats wide enough to lie down on—

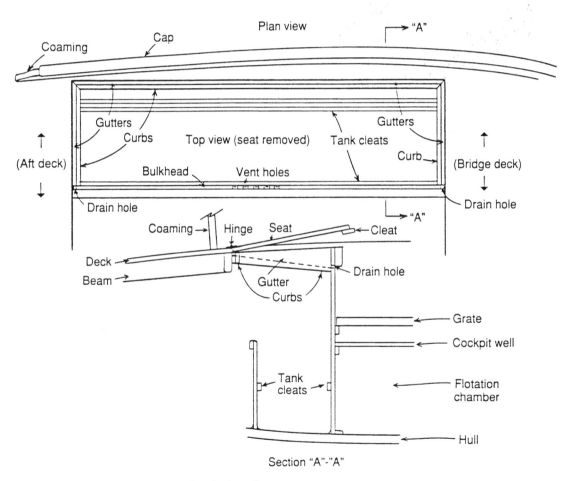

Figure 5-6. Cockpit seat drainage ("tank cleats" support carry-on outboard motor steel fuel tanks).

6 feet 4 inches long and at least 21 inches wide, when possible (this will be immeasurably helpful to seasick crew, and to a tired watch-mate). Make a drop-in panel to cover the well and thus convert the seats into a huge platform for yoga, sleeping, or making love. Make the seats no farther apart than can be reached by your shortest helmsperson's feet from the opposite seat (hanging onto the tiller in a blow requires something solid, high, and not too far away under your feet).

Pitch the well deck at least one degree (usually forward), and provide two large scuppers (drains) at the low end. If the well is large, provide more scuppers; if it is long or has little pitch, provide scuppers at both ends. Make the well waterproof—no leaks. Cross the scupper hoses to the opposite side if the well is wide, to prevent water coming in the lee scupper when heeled well over (wide cockpits can go below the waterline).

Make the well sides (bulkheads) extend down to the hull, and cleat, fasten, and glue (or bed)

them securely. Set the well deck on strong cleats around the perimeter, with strong floors (beams) across; think of the weight of water it must support if you were "pooped." A grate or duckboards on the bottom are a nice addition—they keep your feet dry and provide something to dig your heels into. Make the seat lids as watertight as possible—build them with large perimeter gutters (at least ¾ inches wide and deep)—and hinge them (outboard) so they can't blow away or fall overboard in a knockdown.

Make your cockpit coamings at a comfortable height, so you can rest your elbows on them. On large sharpies, or those with curved coamings, laminate between two and four layers of ¼-inch plywood to form coamings. This may be done in place or on a jig. Fabric/epoxy cover the finished coamings to protect them.

If you make an outboard well, you might pitch the cockpit well deck aft, with scuppers draining into the outboard well instead of forward. But keep the deck *high*, or it may fill with water when motoring or sailing fast. Also,

Figure 5-7. Laminating cockpit coamings.

because cockpit seats are usually higher aft, you will want a grate or duckboards set parallel to the seats for comfort and better standing visibility.

Cabins and Accommodations

There are three basic ways to set up the medium-to-large sharpies: as open boats, with cuddy cabins, or as cruisers with full trunk cabins and self-draining cockpits.

The cuddy cabin can be made as an add-on—almost like a convertible hardtop. To do this, you can deck and fit out the sharpie as an open boat, and make the cuddy to fit over the front- and side-deck coamings, to which it is through-bolted. The back of the cuddy can be left open, bulkheaded to fit snugly to either a bridge deck or thwart (which may be in turn bulkheaded off from the cockpit to make the cabin watertight), or a canvas-and-screen cover can be made to close the back of the cuddy.

Another variation on this theme is the "pop-top," where the roof is either rigid or a fabric-covered frame, with fabric and screen sides. The top, or lid, may be fitted over the deck coamings like a three- or four-sided hatch cover (acting like a flush deck). When anchored, the top is raised—either on halyards to the mastheads, lanyards rigged from the boom, or on "legs" fitted from inside at the corners, essentially becoming a wall tent. Fabric flaps should be made to cover the screened portions of the sides (essential for ventilation), with means provided for securing the flaps in foul weather.

The simplest variation is the boom tent, which hangs under (or over) the boom, forming an awning over the forward portion of the open boat. Zippered curtains with netting can be made for all four sides, turning the open boat into a camp tent. You can lace canvas bunks to eyestraps along the hull and centerboard trunk for comfortable sleeping.

If you build a permanent cabin on your sharpie, it should be low and narrow enough to provide easy, safe access around or over it to the foredeck. Many inexperienced sailors try to rig their boats so they can be "singlehanded" from the cockpit, but I have rarely seen this work well. It is very difficult to raise and lower a large sail effectively from anyplace far away from the mast to which it is attached. I am not saying it cannot be done—just that it rarely works well. Nor can you anchor, weigh anchor, come to a dock and tie up, furl sails, handle jibs, or clear fouled lines forward without quick, easy access to the foredeck.

Side decks need to be wide enough so that they can be negotiated safely and quickly at all times. One feature of modern "Tupperware" sailboats that irks me no end is narrow, obstructed side decks that are nothing less than a foot-mangling obstacle course, blocked by shrouds that are nearly impossible to get past without performing heroic feats of contortionism and acrobatics. To make matters worse, these boats often sail at such ridiculous angles of heel that you can't get down the lee deck at all (it's underwater), and when you come to the shrouds on the weather deck you have little choice but to climb over the lifelines and go around the shrouds, climbing back over the lifelines once you're past them.

One way to deal with all this is to just build a raised deck, and go over the cabin. The thing to avoid here is making a raised deck too high—weight and windage high up will hurt your

Figure 5-8. Removable cuddy cabin.

sharpie's performance, to say nothing of its appearance. I do have a friend, however, with a wonderful (and somewhat grotesque-looking) raised-deck sharpie named, believe it or not, *Hog Fish Lips*. This vessel has a frightfully high (to my eyes) raised flush deck, which comfortably and charmingly accommodates a family of three. *Hog Fish Lips*, only about 30 feet long, was sailed singlehanded from Florida to the Virgin Islands offshore the whole way—a very long beat to windward. Anyone who does not believe sharpies are seaworthy should talk to Chris Morejohn, who designed, built, and sailed *Hog Fish Lips* several thousand miles upon the Atlantic Ocean.

This remarkable vessel notwithstanding, I would still stress keeping cabins and flush decks as low as possible. A number of years ago, my close friend and co-worker Bill Smith built *Lahoma*, an *Egret* replica (Commodore Munroe) from *WoodenBoat* magazine's plans, with a low raised deck. This craft, a 28-foot double-ender with outboard in well, has proved to be a comfortable, safe, fairly fast and weatherly boat. It is great fun to sail her in the Indian River, Florida, where all the Clorox-bottle boats are confined to short-tacking or motoring in the dredged channel while *Lahoma* takes long, graceful tacks from shore to shore and leaves them behind. When they all turn to run back with the wind, *Lahoma* passes them again with centerboard up, running wing-and-wing. This particular raised deck was tastefully designed, though fairly modern in style, and in no way harms the vessel's performance. The raised deck also provides a large, open, well-ventilated interior, even though the headroom is low. A final advantage is that raised decks provide valuable self-righting buoyancy where it is most needed during a knockdown.

On sharpies, hatches should be located on the vessel's centerline and not offset to either side. On large sharpies, this rule may be broken, but not by much. All vessels have a "capsize waterline," and there should be nothing below this waterline, or even close to it on a seagoing vessel, that could sink her. Because sharpies have lim-

Figure 5-9. Bill Smith's *Egret* replica, *Lahoma*, with raised flush deck.

ited headroom, oversize hatches are desirable. The cook will frequently stand in the open hatch (the galley should be right there), and you'll also find this is the most comfortable place to pull on your drawers. Therefore, these oversize hatches should be lightly but strongly built, and their carlins should also be adequate. I like to end my sliding hatch carlins in knees (with handles cut in them), against the after bulkhead to stiffen the coach roof.

"Boxtop" hatches are the easiest to make. They consist of a square frame with a flat or arched top covered with plywood or Lexan (polycarbonate sheet). Make the corners either mitered, half-lapped, or rabbeted. Cut arches on the forward and after top edges, and bevel the sides on top to match the arches. Glue the frame together in place on its coaming, with plastic or waxed paper under the joints. Use fasteners in the corners for strength. After the frame cures,

~The Boxtop Hatch~

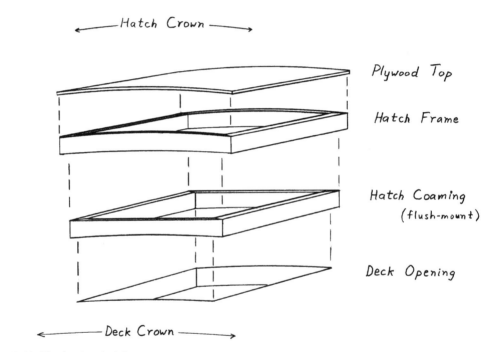

Figure 5-10. The boxtop hatch.

~The Boxtop Hatch~
(surface-mounted coamings)

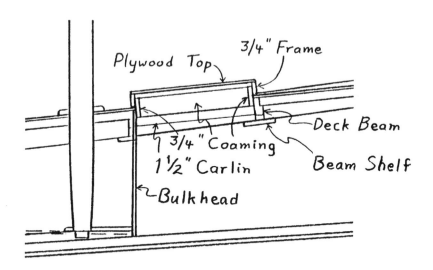

Plywood Top

3/4" Frame

Deck Beam

3/4" Coaming

Beam Shelf

1½" Carlin

Bulkhead

~Three Types of Coamings (cockpit or hatch)~

optional cockpit coaming cove molding (water-stop)

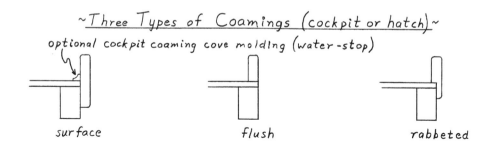

surface · flush · rabbeted

~Five Types of Corners (coaming or hatch frame)~

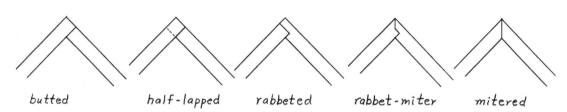

butted · half-lapped · rabbeted · rabbet-miter · mitered

glue and fasten the top in place. On small craft, this may be ¼-inch plywood; for larger craft, use ⅜-inch ply; for big cruising sharpies, laminate two layers of ¼-inch ply. Orient the plywood grain fore-and-aft; curve the plywood across the grain. After curing, trim the edges and ease them, fill holes, sand smooth, and fabric/epoxy-cover the hatch. Make the cloth overlap a little on the corners—this is where you most need strength.

If you cover the frame with Lexan, use plenty of screws—flat or oval heads—about 3 inches on center, and countersink the heads slightly. Bed with 3M 5200, which can be cleaned up with mineral spirits; other solvents will attack the plastic. Don't use inferior plastics, like Plexiglas—they will crack. For hatch skylights under 18 inches square, you can use ¼-inch Lexan; for hatches over that size, you'll need ⅜-inch Lexan or a support in the middle.

Manufactured skylights that are waterproof when dogged down may be placed anywhere, but conventional hatches and hatch skylights, as well as traditional gable skylights, should be located on the centerline.

Accommodations will vary according to your needs and style. In general, keep furniture simple and light. Painted plywood with varnished trim is the norm for home-built boats, and in many ways it's the best. Use the thinnest plywood you can get away with to save weight; cleats and stiffeners of 1 x 2 material can beef up thin panels. Bulkheads should be substantial—½-inch plywood is adequate for all but large sharpies, which should have ⅝- or ¾-inch plywood bulkheads. Bunk tops, countertops, and shelves can be of ¼- or ⅜-inch plywood if backed up by 1 x 2s, or ½-inch plywood if not. Nonstructural and cabinet bulkheads can be as thin as ¼-inch plywood. Interior furniture may be removable if desired. Anchor your furniture to cleats that are secured to the hull, deck, and structural bulkheads with screws and, if permanent, glue. Often, improperly secured furniture will make annoying squeaky noises, or worse, come loose in rough weather.

Get as much light and air into your cabin as possible. Pay particular attention to the galley, head, and bunk areas; in a sharpie, that's the whole boat! Good cross-ventilation is essential. Buy or make a windscoop or two. Small-mesh (no-see-um) screens are also highly desirable for every opening.

A portable two-burner stove is the easiest way to cook in a sharpie. Cassette-Feu makes a good stove with self-contained propane cans; Coleman also makes good stoves of this kind, both in white-gas and propane models. Build a simple counter for the stove, with fiddle-rails to keep it in place, and perhaps a lashing or clamp of some kind.

Your sink can be a basin—plastic or stainless steel (restaurant steam trays are best)—set into a cutout in the countertop. Leave some "finger holes" on each side so you can lift out the tray when full to toss its contents overboard. Seal the plywood edge-grain with epoxy, and try not to store anything under the sink that is easily damaged by water.

Stowage behind bulkheads is best accessed with "stuff-holes." These are much simpler, lighter, and cheaper than drawers or doors. Essentially, stuff-holes are cut-out holes in plywood bulkheads—small enough and high enough above the shelving to keep the contents inside, but large enough and well placed to provide good access. Stowage under bunks generally requires lift-out panels. Cut out sections of your plywood bunks, rounding the corners with a saber saw, and glue and screw 1 x 2 cleats under the edges for the panels to rest on. Make the cleats a little short so dirt doesn't accumulate in the corners, binding the panels or stopping them from lying flush.

Provide line and anchor lockers in your boat, and have good access to them, plus ventilation and some means to evacuate accumulated water and dirt. Watertight bulkheads are a good idea for family boats, those operated by children, and those going cruising. They can be used to isolate compartments (generally at each end of the hull—the line and anchor lockers) to provide flotation in the event of capsizing or swamping. As previously mentioned, another safety device is watertight compartments under the thwarts, which may be foam-filled if so desired, or hollow with sealed access plates for storage.

Iceboxes are a lot of trouble to make, but they are wonderful to have, particularly if you are going cruising. Make your liner of ¼-inch plywood, stoutly glued together and lined with fabric and epoxy. With the liner securely braced in place, pour 2- or 4-pound-density foam around the sides and under the bottom. You can purchase this two-part polyurethane foam from marine suppliers. It must be kept cool until used, when the components are mixed with an electric drill motor and stirring device, and quickly poured in place. You can trim off the overflow with a hacksaw blade and a Surform (like a cheese grater). Allow at least 4 inches of foam around the sides near the top of your icebox, and more lower. Make the lid hollow, and fill it with foam as well. If you'd rather not attempt pouring foam (it is a real fire drill), you can buy sheets or blocks of foam (4-pound-density closed-cell polyurethane is best) and fit them in place. Seal the edges and corners with foam from spraycans, available at your hardware store.

Top-loading iceboxes are much more efficient than front-loading ones, which dump out all the cold when you open the door as well as losing it around the edges. Conventional household refrigerators are an extravagant waste of energy because they are all front loading. Nonperishable food storage is best accomplished in the small boat by means of plastic trays and jars with tight-fitting lids. If you are a serious cruiser, buy the sizes you need before building the galley, and give them all a custom fit. Fruits and most vegetables may be stored in nets hung at their corners from the overhead. On large sharpies, plates, bowls, cups, and glasses (usually plastic) can be stowed on the outboard edges of countertops under the side decks, behind high fiddle rails (with centered cutouts to allow access to plates and bowls).

If you elect to have a water system on your boat, bladder tanks are a reasonable alternative to fitted tanks and integral tanks. Integral tanks must be strongly built and completely watertight. Use cleats on all bulkheads, including internal baffles and lids. Line them with a fabric/epoxy skin and "potable water tank-coating," available from International Paint Company. (You can find much more detail about this in *The New Cold-Molded Boatbuilding*.) Fitted water tanks may be plastic or stainless steel. Some manufactured tanks are available from marine suppliers, but they rarely are the exact size and shape you need. The bladder tanks (available from Vetus and Avon) are great because they conform to odd spaces and are easy to install and plumb. Foot pumps and hand pumps are the obvious alternative to electric ones, and sharpies can't really afford the weight of gravity "day" tanks. For showers, the black-plastic-bag Sunshower is hard to beat on deck; and on cold, rainy days you can always heat a kettle of water to take a spit-bath, crouching in the cabin.

One last item—foam rubber. Buy 3-inch, extra-firm foam for your bunk and settee mattresses. It will seem a little hard at first, but after a few weeks the foam softens a little, and it will give you the healthiest sleeping of your life.

Spars and Rigging

Wooden spars—masts, booms, sprits, yards, gaffs—have what is called "parabolic taper," as opposed to "conic taper." You can see the difference by sighting along the spar: the surface has a convex curve, rather than being a straight line. Structurally, a parabolic-tapered column carries its strength and stiffness higher, or further, than a conic-tapered one.

Sharpie spars have always been made from solid timber—typically, small trees in the case of masts, and for smaller spars square-milled balk-timber cut to one side of the center, or heart, of the tree. This is because timber in smaller sizes that includes the heart often has more structurally weakening knots and is more prone to checking. Large spars include enough of the tree's diameter to get away from the heart, though checking has always been a reality and is acceptable in large masts. Ship masts frequently have checks large enough to slide your hand into—yet these pose little or no structural problem.

The sharpies in this book all have masts small enough that they can usually be "got out" of timbers available at large, commercial lumberyards. In America and Canada, such yards either stock or can order Douglas-fir timbers in sizes up to 12 inches x 12 inches x 32 feet. Most sharpies have masts 30 feet or less, the exceptions being the marconi or "jibheaded" rigs of the large New Haven, North Carolina, and Ohio sharpies.

None of the masts is over 6 inches in diameter; therefore, most of the masts in the book can be cut (got out) from ordered Douglas-fir timbers. The other spars—sprits, booms, bowsprits, and gaffs—can be cut from 4 x 4, 3 x 3, and 2 x 2 stock. This stock should be of high-quality material: architectural grade, number one grade, or number two grade (large stuff); or "clear, heart, vertical grain" in the case of small stuff, in which a large knot might pose a fatal structural problem. In general, wood for spars should be carefully inspected before purchase. Unfortunately, this is not possible if the material is ordered, and refusal of large custom orders will likely make an enemy of your supplier. My solution is usually to buy at least one extra timber in the size for the spar(s) in question, pick the best for the spar or spars, and use the extra timber for bitts, maststeps, stem aprons, blocking, bowsprits—whatever I need. Or I rip some of the timber into smaller stuff for toerails, coamings, carlins, and hatch frames. It never goes to waste.

I advise staying away from spruce. The only acceptable spar-grade spruce is Sitka, which is expensive, virtually unobtainable, and inferior to Douglas-fir in every way except weight. If you have access to large Southern yellow pine timber, it is excellent for spars; however, there are several species classed under the name "Southern yellow pine," and some are drastically inferior for spar material. The wood you use must have long, straight grain, high density of growth rings, small fixed knots (no large loose ones), and should not be oozing large quantities of pitch from large, open pitch pockets (a little is normal).

One excellent alternative to the problem of large mast material is to buy 3 x 6 or 2 x 6 (full-dimension) material and laminate your masts in two or three "slices." Cut long scarfs in the slices to obtain the lengths you need; make these scarfs very long, at least 12 to 1 (the scarfs in 2-inch material should be 24 inches long). For example, a 36-foot mast 6 inches in diameter can be made from *full-dimensioned* 2 x 6 stock using three 20-footers and three 18-footers, the extra 2 lineal feet per "slice" being used up in the scarfs.

First, the scarfs are cut and glued—these must be accurate cuts, and the timber must continue straight on both sides of the scarfs. Then the three slices are "stack laminated": Place the scarf in the middle slice low and the scarfs in the outer slices high in the mast; the outer scarfs should point "down and out." This will require many clamps and a long, straight work area. An alternative to clamps is rope strops (Spanish windlasses). Because rope strops apply pressure only at the edges of square material being bound, it is advisable to rip the corners off your outer slices (the complete lamination will then look like an octagon in section) to create additional pressure points near the centers of the outer slices. This will also give you a head start on shaping the spar.

You can see that there will be a lot of wasted wood in this process. In some cases, it can be recycled as cleat and block stock. Yet another alternative is lay out and cut the taper into the two or three slices before lamination, but this only works for two sides of the spar—the other two sides (through the lamination) will still be full thickness. Still, it is a head start, and gives you dimensions to work to when you start trimming down the full-thickness sides.

In summing up this approach, I recommend cutting out all slices to the correct taper, and cutting the outside corners off the outer slices with a circular saw and ripping guide (set the saw to 45 degrees). Use rope strops (tied loops) and sticks placed every foot along the lamination to clamp it. Lock the end of each stick against the knot of the previous strop. Set the laminations on as many sawhorses (of the same height) as you can muster, and be careful to keep the spar straight. Another way to clamp the laminations is to "spiral wrap" them with 180-pound or stronger nylon twine. Use this method for small and medium spars only: With the slices glued (always apply glue to both mating surfaces) and clamped in position to the sawhorses, start at the butt (large) end with several very tight turns around in one place (to trap the end of the twine), then wrap the spar very tightly with about 3 inches between each wrap. Pull down

Figure 5-11. The spiral wrap for spar lamination.

very hard as you make each wrap, and maintain the tension as you come under and up the other side (someone may have to hold the spar down so you don't lift it off the horses). At the head, again make several tight wraps in one place, and clove-hitch the end off. *Wear leather gloves while doing this.* I have used this clamping method for 20 years with great success (I "invented" it for laminating handrails in place on spiral staircases in California), but I never heard of anyone else using it.

To determine how much corner to cut off in converting a square shape to an octagonal shape, the multiplication factor is 0.2085—that is, the amount you come in from the edge to make your 45-degree cut is 0.2085 (call it 0.21) times the width of the face. Looking at this another way, each octagonal face is equal to approximately five-twelfths (0.417) of the square face before cutting. Use this factor when making any square into an octagon.

In years gone by, sparmakers didn't fuss too much. They knew their work, had good eyes and high craftsmanship, and got out the spars incredibly fast. Using modern power tools and working alone, I can get out as many as six 10- to 20-foot spars a day—that is, rough cut, tapered, octagon cut, and planed round; after that, they still need sanding. The process is as follows.

Let's say we're making double-tapered spars—booms, sprits, gaffs, or yards. Strike a centerline on each side of your timber with a chalk box and line. Lay out the maximum diameter in the middle, and the smallest diameters at each end. Spring a stiff batten the length of the spar through the three points along one edge of one side of the timber. Measure in one-quarter of the length of the spar from each end, and pull the batten towards the edge just a hair; this makes the ends of the spar parabolic, a little fuller than if the curve of the batten were merely the arc of a circle. Make these two additional points the same distance from the centerline; the batten now passes through five points. Trace the curve on the spar, and repeat the process along the

Figure 5-12. Making Masts: (a) lay out;

(b) cutting square;

(c) cutting octagonal;

(d) planed to a "sixteen-agon";

(e) sanded round with truck-irons fitted;

(g) primed for paint.

(f) epoxy sealed, showing butt-tenons;

other edge, and along both edges of the other side of the timber.

Cut along all four lines with your circular saw—if the saw blade reaches all the way through the timber, you obviously don't need to lay out or cut both sides of the timber. Now turn the timber 90 degrees and lay out the same curves on the new-cut face, and again on the opposite new face if necessary, and cut these out. You now have a double-tapered square spar. Measure the widths of the faces every 3 or 4 feet along the spar, and mark each location with the width there. Multiply these amounts by 0.21, and measure those amounts in from the edges

Figure 5-13. Double-tapered octagonal spars (right); rounded spar (left).

at each marked point along two opposite faces of the spar, lay your batten through these points, and trace the lines. Set your circular saw to 45 degrees and carefully cut the corners off, cutting *outside* your lines (closer to the edge).

You now have an octagonal double-tapered spar, and you should feel pretty good about that!

If this is to be a boom, choose which end will have jaws attached, and mark those faces with a crayon—you want to leave them flat to fasten the jaws there. Shape the rest of the spar with a hand or power plane (be very careful with the latter, or you might end up with a very small spar). First knock off the corners of the octagon, forming a sixteen-agon (my Latin fails me). Next, if you have a low-speed body grinder and soft pad, "roll" the edges off with a rocking motion of the grinder using 40- or 60-grit paper, taking care not to "dish out." Or use 40- or 36-grit paper by hand, and just sand the spar smooth. Smaller spars, like sprits made from 2-inch square stock, will have to be hand-sanded. An orbital sander might help here if you don't have a good heart (hand-shaping spars is a hell of a good aerobic workout). I per-sonally love this work—you sweat and grunt and groan and sand like mad until your arm muscles burn, and watch the spar emerge under your hands. Keep your back straight and feet well apart—get the spar up as high as you can, but not so high you can't get body weight behind that sandpaper. I usually hand-sand with 8-inch stick-on disks folded in half so the two-sided grit keeps them from slipping out of my hands. If you have soft hands, wrap your fingers loosely with masking tape. When the spar looks uniformly round and fair, sand it again with 80-grit.

Finish-sand the spars with 120-grit, clean them up, and get some finish on them—paint, spar varnish, epoxy sealer and polyurethane varnish, oil (I like Deks-Olje #1 and #2), whatever you choose. Traditionally, the ends of all spars are painted white so you can see them in the dark.

The process for laying out mast taper is very similar to the above. If you have a taper schedule with your plans, lay out the stations along the mast with their respective dimensions, and trace the curves with a stiff batten. If there is no taper schedule, as is the case with most of the sharpie designs, taper the masts as follows: Lay out the largest diameter of the spar at the partners—deck or thwart level. Taper the mast below, to the shoulder at the step, and lay out the smaller mast tenon below the shoulder (the tenon and corresponding mortise in the mast step will be round and of nearly equal dimensions). Taper the mast from the partners to the masthead by springing a long batten along one edge with a long, gentle, convex curve. (For the first few feet, there will be no taper at all.) When this curve looks good to the eye, trace it on the timber. Lay out equidistant stations along the timber—say, every 3 or 4 feet. Measure the distance in from the edge to the line at each of these stations, and reproduce them along the other edge and along both edges on the other side of the timber. From this point on, proceed to cut out the spar, trace the new sides and cut them, lay out and cut the octagonals, plane and sand, and finish as above.

Most traditional sharpie masts had a slot cut through the mast just below the head, in which was inserted a sheave for the halyard. You can buy replacement 2- and 3-inch-diameter Delrin sheaves at most marine hardware stores, and these will do nicely. Make a brass, bronze, stainless-steel, or aluminum pin, and drill a hole through the mast for it to hold the sheave. Cut the slot as true as possible—if it's uneven, the halyard will jump off the sheave and jam between it and the slot. If this ever happens to you, don't panic and make the jam worse; instead, pull on the opposite end of the halyard while maintaining gentle tension on the other end until the line rides back in the sheave, then keep a little tension on both parts to hold the line in the sheave. This always seems to happen when you are lowering sail in a blow: wind blows the loose end of the halyard off the sheave, and you jam it trying to pull the sail down. If your sheave is a lot larger in diameter than the mast diameter, the halyard will be more prone to jamming. On very small craft, just drill a hole for the halyard and round the openings downward with a file (to reduce friction).

You can also hang blocks on the masts with rope strops, eyebolts and shackles, or heavy-duty eyestraps (the four-hole kind are best). I generally buy all my blocks and rigging hardware from A and B Industries (A.B.I.) in San Rafael, California. Their blocks are teak, bronze, and stainless steel with bronze roller bearings, made in the Orient to American patterns. The price is right and the quality is reasonably good.

I frequently use four-hole eyestraps to mount blocks wherever I need them—on spars, decks, bowsprits, thwarts, and bulkheads. Use long, stainless-steel self-tapping screws (to get maximum thread-holding power at minimum price; wood screws cost more) when fastening eyestraps to spars. Use stainless-steel flathead machine screws with lock-nuts and fender (large) washers to through-bolt the eyestraps to planking or plywood, and make plywood backup blocks if the plywood is thin or if a lot of tension on the strap is anticipated.

Sprit ends are fitted with a "snotter." This is a lanyard spliced tightly around the mast just above the desired sprit height. The snotter passes through a drilled hole in the end of the sprit, and is then tied in a half hitch, using a loop end so it can be pulled out in a hurry, around the sprit end. Traditionally, large sharpies often had a sheave in the sprit end, similar to that described for mastheads, and some very large sharpies made use of a small block-and-tackle to compress the sprit and flatten the sail. Sharpies of all sizes often had a small cleat fastened to the sprit for the snotter.

I often hang sheet blocks and gaff halyard blocks on their respective spars by means of a sling spliced tightly around the spar, passed through the strop of the block, and tied securely to the spar. I use a clove hitch around the spar or sometimes on the sling itself, and I often seize the end of the line so the hitch won't come out. On large vessels I seize a small leather patch between the sling and strop to reduce chafe.

Avoid metal boom bails; this is just part of the 20th-century disease to complicate the world with metal hardware.

If you don't want your sprit or boom to drop to the deck (or on someone's head) when lowering sail, you will want a topping lift. On smaller sharpies, this can be a line spliced tightly around the masthead and made off to the sprit or boom near its after end with a clove hitch. On larger craft with booms you may want a lift on each side of the sail, and you can also splice additional lifts into it in loops under the boom (this doesn't work on sprits) called "lazyjacks." Big-boat topping lifts are usually adjustable through blocks at the masthead or through cheek blocks or dogs with holes drilled in them on each side of the boom. On very large sharpie schooners, the bitter ends of the main-boom topping lifts may be spliced to blocks perhaps 10 feet above the deck, which are incorporated into tackles.

Sprit-rigged sharpie sails were reefed vertically instead of horizontally by lowering the sail and tying the reef nettles to the hoops, lacing lines, or grommets as the sail was hoisted back up. Have your sailmaker install large-enough grommets along the luffs of your sails so you can tie the reef nettles through them along with the lacing line already rove there; or at least install large grommets in the sail luff at the places where the top and bottom of the reef is tied. These grommets, in effect, become the new head and tack of the sail; they are under a lot of strain. The in-between nettles may just be tied around the sail luff for speed and convenience. Boomed sails have conventional "slab" reefing, whereby the halyard(s) is slacked, the sail pulled down with tack and clew reef tackles (I usually leave the first pair, for the first reef, permanently rove), the nettles tied in, and the halyard(s) set back up.

On the small boats (under 20 feet), make up sheets and halyards from ⅜-inch rope, and topping lifts and reef nettles from ¼-inch. On the larger boats, use ½-inch rope for sheets and halyards. I prefer Dacron (long-filament polyester) three-strand rope, which has low stretch, is easy

Figure 5-14 . Finished sharpie spars: (left) for a crabbing skiff, and (right) for a sharpie schooner.

to splice, and remains soft and pliable. For anchor rodes, painters, and docklines, use ⅜-inch or ½-inch three-strand nylon rope, depending on the size of your boat. Splice blocks to spars with ¼-inch rope for small boats and ⅜-inch or ½-inch rope for large ones. Lacing lines can be ³⁄₁₆-inch, ¼-inch, or ⁵⁄₁₆-inch, depending on boat size. Make your reef nettles the same size. Make boom outhauls, reef outhauls, and tack lines from ¼- or ⅜-inch rope; gaff peak and throat lanyards may be the same size or one size smaller.

Figure 5-14 *continued.*

Some of the large sharpie schooners had standing rigging. This consisted of wire rope spliced around the masts aloft and led to turnbuckles or deadeyes and lanyards shackled to chainplates on the hull topsides. The only vessels in this book with standing rigging are the San Juan Islands double-ended sharpie and the Clapham Nonpareil sharpie. These vessels would use ¼-inch, 7 x 7 stainless-steel or galvanized-plow-steel wire rope for stays and shrouds. Optional rigging for the Hampton Flattie is described in Chapter Six.

For more information on standing rigging, and how to build hollow hexagonal masts, please refer to *The New Cold-Molded Boatbuilding*. You can also find much more detailed information there on hatches, skylights, door and drawer construction and interior joinery, inboard diesel installation, plumbing and electrical work than the scope of this book will permit.

Fabric and Finishing

As previously mentioned, I consider polyester cloth to be the best fabric for covering wood, used in conjunction with epoxy. At present, the only mainstream supplier is Defender Industries in New Rochelle, New York, which sells Xynole-polyester cloth in 4.2-ounce thickness about 60 inches wide. This material is a coarse, open-weave scrim of twisted polyester yarns, looking a little like curtain material. It is much stronger for its weight than fiberglass cloth, has better abrasion resistance and peel strength, and is dramatically easier to work with. It doesn't itch, either—you could probably wear it. Because it is slightly flexible, it stretches around compound curves and conforms to odd shapes and corners in ways that fiberglass absolutely cannot do.

Wood surfaces to be covered must be smooth, clean, and dry. Cracks and holes must be filled with epoxy putty (epoxy with Cab-O-Sil and microballoons mixed in), sanded, and cleaned. Stretch the fabric snugly over the area to be covered, and hold it in place with masking tape, pushpins, or staples. Wet out the cloth, starting from the middle, with epoxy using a roller frame with a fuzzy (⅜-inch nap) cover. Apply two or three coats, or "saturate the cloth to rejection"— in other words, fill up all the little holes in the mesh.

In general, large hulls are covered as follows:

each side of the bottom, overlapping the chines; then the keel; then the topsides, again overlapping the chines. To avoid bumps from the previous fabric layer, "feather" the edges with a body grinder and soft pad, or with a sharp block plane. When the decks are finished, cover them with fabric, just overlapping the topsides such that the fabric edge will be under the rubrail.

Use masking tape (good-quality—plastic Fineline, made by 3M, is best) to mark the edges of your cloth, and when covering your decks hang masking paper below the tape to keep dribbles off the topsides. Before the epoxy is totally cured, use a razor knife to cut the fabric along the masking tape, leaving a clean, straight edge. Use this technique wherever you need it, such as where the trunk cabin fabric laps out onto the deck an inch, and where the coach roof fabric overlaps the trunks an inch.

After curing, sand the fabric/epoxy with 40- or 60-grit paper with a soft pad if you have one. To achieve a professional finish on topsides and cabin trunks, you will need to "glaze" and "fair" the sanded surfaces. Glazing and fairing are done very much like sheetrock finishing, and the compound you mix should be very close in consistency to sheetrock gypsum, or spackling compound. Mix Cab-O-Sil and microballoons into epoxy (in a ratio about 30 percent to 70 percent, respectively), and apply it with a putty knife or plastic squeegee. Smooth it out, if necessary, with an 8- or 10-inch-wide sheetrock taping knife. I use a stainless-steel trough for my compound, the kind also made for the sheetrock industry. I also use a 16- or 18-inch stainless-steel knife-edge trowel (the kind with a plastic handle often used by painters doing trim work) for fairing.

Glazing involves troweling on the compound to smooth and fill the surface; fairing involves building up areas to fill low places in a large surface. As you may imagine, this second process can be very complex, requiring a lot of skill. In general, you need not be concerned with it unless you see an obvious flaw in your topsides that troubles you, such as at the taped butt joints. Build them up and sand them smooth until they look right.

Inside corners can benefit greatly from "fillets." Make fillet material from epoxy thickened with Cab-O-Sil and microballoons. Use the same proportions as for the glazing compound, but make the mix thicker so it doesn't sag. Place it in a large Ziploc bag, cut off one corner, and squirt the material along inside corners, such as those along chine logs and at the bases of cabin trunks and toerails, after fabric-covering is complete. Use a tongue depressor, a Popsicle stick, a rubber cake spatula, or a short piece of PVC pipe to form the fillet, and clean up excess with a putty knife. Fillets strengthen joints and keep out moisture, dirt, and insects, besides looking good. They are not essential on most sharpies, but are very useful on large boats that are built to last.

Sand your finished surfaces carefully with 80- and 120-grit paper, looking for fairness. Clean the surface thoroughly, and you are ready for primer.

In the spirit of your sharpie being a family project, built in your garage or backyard, you may not want to bring all these toxic chemicals into your home. There are alternatives, but they don't last as long. One that I have experimented with is using synthetic curtain fabric of a fine mesh (nylon works well) and saturating it with either latex or oil-based paint. An excellent product for this purpose is arabol latex rubber steam-pipe lagging compound. It can be purchased from Doc Freeman's in Seattle, Washington, in 5-gallon pails (Doc's Cov-a-Dek) at a very reasonable price, but I don't know where else to get it. Arabol should be painted over with latex, oil-based, or epoxy paint.

Alternative fabrics are synthetic window screen, open-weave cotton and linen, "Yellowjacket" (polypropylene-coated fiberglass, also available from Doc Freeman's), Dynel, and polypropylene. If you look for alternatives, do some experiments before using them on your boat. You can also use fiberglass or polyester tape and epoxy on your seams to protect joints and end-grain, and just prime and paint the plywood. If you use marine plywood, the boat may last many years, with good maintenance.

There are many kinds of primers and paints on the market these days. I use a lot of Sherwin Williams industrial paint products, to avoid that ol' marine markup. I would also recommend Z-Spar #2 paste glazing compound for filling fine scratches and imperfections, and Z-Spar sanding primer. Polyurethane finishes are the best and most durable—they are also the most toxic, difficult to apply, and expensive. Sherwin Williams Industrial Enamel works very well, as do other high-quality oil-based house paints, particularly urethane-reinforced porch and floor enamels and window and sash paints. Then again, a lot of people just use top-quality exterior latex, and repaint once a year.

I use Sherwin Williams Tile-Clad #2 epoxy paint for primer and interior finishing—white for above the water and Hi-Bild red below. *These products are toxic and must be used with protective clothing, latex gloves, and a respirator.* You can use enamel primers if you prefer, but they won't work below the waterline. Either check your marine supplier for an underwater primer, or just sand your epoxy thoroughly with 80-grit paper and apply bottom paint, reducing the first coat the maximum allowed by the manufacturer. There are also chlorinated rubber primers that work below the waterline, and I have been instructed by one of my industrial paint suppliers to use chlorinated rubber to seal old bottom paint before seasonal recoating.

There are many nonskid compounds available, both as additives and complete paint systems. I prefer fine sand sprinkled into epoxy paint with a large salt shaker (often a coffee can with holes drilled in the plastic lid). Roll a small area with paint, sprinkle the sand in a consistent pattern not quite up to the wet edge of the paint, and continue down the deck. After curing, clean off the loose sand and roll on two more coats of paint. For a professional look, paint all your perimeters first, and mask them off before applying nonskid. If you use contrasting colors, it will look great. You can use latex or oil-based paint instead of epoxy, including the above-mentioned arabol, for this nonskid process. Coach roofs don't really need nonskid. If you leave the texture of the cloth exposed (don't sand it very much— just "skip-sand" to knock off the big bumps), and apply paint, the finish will be coarse enough to keep you from slipping under normal conditions, and it will look like a traditional canvas covering.

Paint decks and coach roofs with light colors; otherwise, your boat will turn into a toaster-oven in the sun. You can get away with dark colors for trunks, toerails, and hull topsides, unless you plan to spend a lot of time in the low latitudes.

Bottom paints are all toxic: Wear protective clothing, gloves, and a respirator whenever handling them. You will always see people, even children, messing around with bottom paint in shorts and nothing else. This is incredibly foolish and self-destructive, when warnings are all over the can. I prefer the vinyl-type bottom paints, such as Interlux Supervinyl antifouling paint. Apply three coats the first year, then haul out once a year to pressure-wash the bottom and add two coats, thinning the first one 10 percent with the recommended solvent (usually xylol). Or apply a reduced coat of chlorinated rubber primer after pressure-washing and one or two full-strength coats of bottom paint. Don't worry a lot about centerboards and trunks—because they don't get much sunlight and because of board movement, very little marine growth takes place. For big cruising sharpies, try to have your yard "hang you in the slings" the last night of your haulout, so you can lower the board and get one good coat on it.

Many small sharpies will be trailered and may not need bottom paint at all. Boats that are in and out of the water can use the vinyl bottom paints, which seem to hold up pretty well to this abuse, but there are other antifouling paints on the market specifically made for intermittent use.

An important thing to remember about paint and varnish work is that cleanliness is of paramount importance. Paint won't adhere well to even the slightest film of dirt, and dirt in the paint or on the paint will ruin its appearance. Sand well between coats, and keep everything clean. Denatured alcohol is the best "wipe-down" solvent, but tack rags are essential, too. Always do two or three wipes; lots of clean, white cotton rags are essential to professional-quality work. Scotch (3M) scuff-pads work well as a substitute for sandpaper between coats of varnish.

Hardware and Fitting Out

Fortunately, sharpies are not hardware intensive. The very minimal hardware used in the original boats was forged by the community's local blacksmith, as already described. In most cases, cleats, chocks, bitts, even centerboard pins were made from hardwood. The Mississippi Yawl even has wooden tholepins instead of oarlocks.

In our day, your boat will need a centerboard pin, rudder hardware (either strap-type gudgeons and pintles or shaft and pipe), a tiller fitting for shaft-hung rudders, cleats and chocks, blocks, shackles, thimbles, eyestraps, oarlocks and sockets, shoulder-eyebolts, and in rare cases, chainplates, turnbuckles, through-hull fittings, and seacocks. If you have a bandsaw or a talent for whittling, you can make your cleats from hardwood.

I have had difficulty finding manufactured strap-type gudgeons and pintles. Pintles are easy, but most gudgeons these days have a flat strap for fastening to a transom instead of a sternpost. On *Mallard*, my crabbing skiff, I bought four Schaefer pintles, cut the pintles off, and drilled $^{11}/_{32}$-inch holes through the remaining $^{1}/_{2}$-inch slugs, through which I used $^{5}/_{16}$-inch bolts and lock-nuts. Your best bet might be to haunt very old marine hardware stores that have dust-covered Wilcox-Crittenden, Perko, and Merriman hardware on some forgotten shelf.

Figure 5-15. Tiller fitting for a shaft-hung rudder.

Certainly, some hardware must be custom made. Use series #304 or #306 stainless-steel and compatible rod, or bronze and brazing rod. This will probably have to be done by a local professional you trust who is familiar with the items you need and already knows how to make them. Tiller hardware can be ordered—but the head of your rudder shaft must be machined to fit it. Have this done *before* you build the rudder around it. For big sharpies, the pipe, or rudder-shaft tube, should have a flange welded to the top at the angle the deck is intersected by the pipe. Drill four holes in the corners of the flange and countersink them for machine screws. Glue the pipe in place with 3M 5200, Bostik or Sikaflex after carefully sealing all holes in the wood with epoxy.

For the large sharpies in Chapter Six that require them, the chainplates should be $^{1}/_{4}$-inch x $1^{1}/_{2}$-inch or $^{3}/_{8}$-inch x 1-inch stainless steel or bronze strap. Drill and counterbore each chainplate for three $^{5}/_{16}$-inch flathead machine screws (stainless steel), and drill $^{7}/_{16}$-inch holes at the tops for shackles. Two of the machine screws should pass through the hull into $^{3}/_{4}$-inch plywood backup blocks; the third passes through the hull and sheer clamp. Use flat washers over fender washers under each locknut. Epoxy seal the holes before installation. The chainplates pass through mortises cut in the back sides of the rubrails and up along the toerails. If the chainplates interfere with the toerails after being bent to the same angle as the shroud lead (this is important), cut away the rail, leaving $^{1}/_{8}$ inch clearance.

For blocks, cleats, chocks, eyestraps (both two- and four-hole type in a variety of sizes), and other miscellaneous hardware including windlasses, steering wheels, and portlights, I use bronze and stainless-steel hardware from A and B Industries (A.B.I.). They usually have everything any size sharpie might need, and quality and prices are good. (No, I don't get a "kickback," but I should!)

For through-hulls and seacocks, I prefer to use all plastic, as I don't like metal fittings in the hull or in the water if I can avoid them. I use heavy-duty Delrin or Marelon through-hull fittings, and PVC/Teflon or Marelon seacocks (the Marelon items, manufactured by Forespar, are incompatible with any but their own products—clever, huh?). The PVC/Teflon ball valves are available at your local plumbing supplier, and because they aren't listed "marine items," they are very inexpensive.

I prefer stainless-steel shackles and thimbles to bronze or galvanized steel, though all three are fine. If you use galvanized shackles (or turnbuckles), keep them well greased with a waterproof grease so they don't rust up. Splice line very tightly to thimbles so they don't "cock" on you—this is a problem particularly with nylon anchor rodes. A.B.I. has good prices on stainless and bronze shackles; avoid paying the high prices charged by retail marine stores if possible. Commercial rigging suppliers—the people who rig cranes and elevators—often have good prices and availability on shackles, thimbles, and turnbuckles, as might surplus stores.

Some of the boats may benefit from ballast, internal trim ballast, or outside metal shoes. Large family cruising sharpies and some racing sharpies may require permanent ballast—inside, outside, or both. Inside ballast must be firmly anchored in place—a loose lead pig can go right through your hull during a capsize. Try to locate ballast as low in the hull as possible, stay away from the ends of the hull (heavy ends will make turning slow, and aggravate pitching motion), and try to stay very close to the hull centerline.

Outside ballast might be lead or steel. Steel plate can be ordered up to 1 inch thick in 4-, 6-

and 12-inch widths, 10 and 20 feet long. Such a plate might be trimmed and have a centerboard slot cut in it for use as a shoe. Drill ½-inch holes in the plate and plug-weld in (from both sides) ½-inch stainless-steel threaded rods (use stainless welding rod of the same series as the threaded rods) in pairs every 18 inches along the shoe. Sandblast or Ospho the shoe as needed, and fabric/epoxy-cover it before and after installation, so that there are at least two layers of cloth under the installed shoe. Bed the shoe to the hull with 3M 5200, Bostik or Sikaflex, and countersink nuts and washers into the keelson plank. After curing and final fabric-covering, remove the nuts and washers (every other pair at a time) and pour epoxy down the boltholes (drilled oversize for this purpose as well as for ease of installation) to eliminate voids. After replacing the nuts and washers, bung the holes. You can make large bungs like this with a hole saw and drill motor. If you have access to one, use a drill press, but remove the pilot bit from the hole saw first.

The only sharpie in this book that requires an outside ballast shoe is the Clapham Nonpareil sharpie. Lead and iron shoes must be cast, and this is a major project. To cast large amounts of lead, I use an old cast-iron bathtub set up on steel I-beams, with a large drainpipe and gate valve. Forms can be made from 2x lumber, tightly screwed together and well braced. Save up all your scrap wood, and build one hell of a fire under the tub with the lead already in it (*never* try to add lead). When the lead is completely molten and the junk floats to the top, open the valve and fill the form. The pipe should aim down the length of the form, and you will need a very hot charcoal fire under the whole length of pipe and valve. Use drag boards to pull the lead into the ends of the form. *Wear protective clothing including boots, heavy clothing, leather gloves and respirator—lead is extremely dangerous!* (I might add that open-air lead casting is now illegal in many states and municipalities.)

For the bolt pattern, drill holes in the bottom of your form, and drive in ½-inch hardwood dowels. Make 1⅛-inch plywood "doughnuts" and nail them down at the base of each dowel for your boltheads (the shoe is cast right-side up); you will have to drill out the charred wood later, but it's a lot easier than drilling lead. Bolt 'er up same as the steel shoe, using ½-inch stainless-steel threaded rods, nuts, and washers.

In the fitting-out process—putting all this stuff together—there are some simple rules to keep in mind: Whenever you drill a hole in wood, drill oversize and seal it with epoxy. If you anticipate "working" of a fastener in a hole, such as a large eyebolt being used as a towing eye, install a PVC pipe bushing in the hole with epoxy before installing the bolt. For ⁷⁄₁₆- and ½-inch bolts, use ½-inch CPVC pipe for bushings.

(You will have to drill out the pipe after curing for ½-inch bolts.) When fastening hardware like padeyes, eyestraps, chainplates, cleats, and chocks to plywood, use a plywood backup block inside, sealed with epoxy. Bed all hardware and fasteners in the hardware with bedding compound such as Dolfinite, silicone, polysulfide, or polyurethane bedding compound. Avoid permanent bedding/adhesives such as 3M 5200 if you anticipate removing the hardware at any time (an alternative is 3M 101). Use large-diameter fender washers, backed up by regular flat washers and locknuts inside the hull.

Now you really have a boat, and all you need is safety equipment and a few creature comforts—and you're ready to sail!

CHAPTER 6
DESIGNS, LOFTING, AND SCANTLINGS

Hydrodynamics and Stability

A brief lesson in hydrodynamics for the layman is in order, to enhance your understanding of the sharpie hull—for its assets as well as its drawbacks.

There are three crucial properties of a body moving through water that profoundly affect its speed: (1) How much water that body has to *displace*—push out of the way—as it moves. (Quantitative.) (2) How far and how hard the body actually pushes on that water, which in turn has to be pulled back into place behind the moving body. (Qualitative.) (3) How much *wetted surface* there is—literally, the area of the body immersed in water—which determines the amount of drag that will be created by the friction of water moving across it. (Quantitative.)

If you look at a variety of different-shaped hulls of approximately the same size, you will begin to understand why sharpies are so fast. They are light, shallow-bodied, and narrow, especially for their size; hence they displace very little water. Their lines are very flat, straight, and fair, having the gentlest curves and flattest sections possible; hence when moving they push and pull water the slightest possible amount. Their fine, slender bodies have minimal wetted surface; hence there is very little friction against the water.

Likewise, there are properties of hull shape that affect *stability*—whether or not a floating body will tip over easily. If you imagine a V in the water, with only its tip immersed, you will readily see that it wants to fall over. In order to keep it from doing so, a compact, heavy weight must be placed in the very bottom of the V to sink it lower in the water and stabilize it. On the other hand, a wide rectangle in the water, much wider than it is high (like a low box), will be very stable and almost impossible to tip over. And if you place the same weight in the center of the box that you placed in the V, the box will sink only a very slight amount; therefore the box shape will float in shallower water than the V carrying the same weight.

The above applies to what is called *initial stability*. As our two floating objects are forced over, some interesting things happen. The V shape can be pushed over very easily in the beginning, but as we push it farther, the high side of the V floats against the water, counteracting the weight in the bottom of the V, which is now off to the side pulling down. If the V were covered over—if it had a deck—and we pushed it over until it became sideways, a large volume of air would be immersed at the corner of the deck and the side of the V, and this contained air, or *flotation*, would be pushing the V back upright. The weight in the bottom of the V would be as far away as possible, pulling down the bottom of the V, or pulling it upright. The weighted V has a powerful *righting moment*.

Now let's do the same thing to the box. As we try to push it over, the lower corner will push up very hard because of its large volume of flotation air. The raised corner will want to settle back down due to its weight, and also due to the weight in the middle of the box that is starting to lift. In the beginning, the box will resist being pushed over with great force. But as we apply more force to make it tip over, there will come a time when it starts to get easier. Let's cover the box—deck it over—as we did the V. When we get the box up on its edge, it will not resist anymore, and finally it will fall over on its deck—upside down. It has no righting moment at all.

What can be said about these two shapes is that the V has very low initial stability and very high *ultimate stability*—it is *self-righting*. The box has extremely high initial stability and no ultimate stability; it is not self-righting.

In terms of boat hulls, you can begin to see the age-old controversy. The deep-V-shaped hulls are *tender*—they heel way over under sail, initially. They also tend to be slow, relatively speaking, because, weight for weight, they push more water farther out of the way and pull it back, and have more wetted surface. The flat-bottomed hulls are *stiff*, they stand up to their sails, which means they present more sail area to the wind, go faster, and don't heel over much. Weight for weight, they move less water a smaller amount and have less wetted surface—and so they are much faster. To keep them from sliding sideways across the water, they have centerboards—underwater vertical planes—which can be immersed or removed as needed, to adjust their wetted surface and *lateral plane* to the ideal for the particular circumstance.

You can see that boat hulls in general are a compromise somewhere between these two extremes of *tender* and *stiff*. The ultimate compromise might seem to be to take the flat-bottomed shape and add a fin under it with a big chunk of streamlined lead attached to the bottom—and that is essentially what most modern racing sailboats are.

The sharpie is one extreme. And sharpies, in their pure form, are not self-righting. They do, however, have great *form stability*—initial stability based on that flat bottom shape—and are very stiff and stable until you mess up. If you push them over beyond a certain point, they capsize. Now, the sides of sharpies are strongly V-shaped—flared—and this adds a lot of *reserve stability*. With some ballast in the very bottom, or in a shoe outside the hull, they start to have some of the properties of the V shape. And because their wooden masts float, sharpies float on their sides when capsized and don't turn upside down, like the box did. (Aluminum masts, however, would fill up with water and completely invert the boat.) Some sharpies are self-righting—particularly the Clapham Nonpareil sharpies, with their slight V-bottoms and outside ballast. Some raised-deck sharpie designs (like *Hog Fish Lips*) are also self-righting, even with minimal ballast.

Lofting

I have made all the lines and construction drawings of the sharpies as simple and systematized as possible. I have drawn very few stations, and wherever possible I located the stations where bulkheads are needed in construction. Drawing so few stations is not common practice today, but during the period when the sharpies were built and sailed, it was. Often craft of all sizes were formed with little more than a center mold, stem, transom, and keelson. The "wisdom of the wood" determined much of the hull shape as longitudinals—planks, ribbands, or chine logs—were sprung into place in contact with only the stem, center mold, and stern. As demonstrated in Chapter Two, the hull shape of the sharpie was frequently determined by springing the side planking around a center mold. The boatwright may have then wedged a stick between the planks forward, near the sheer, to put some flare in the topsides there.

The key to getting fair and accurate hulls with

very few molds is in using good-quality, straight-grained wood for longitudinals. It is important that scarfs in longitudinals and scarfs or butt blocks in plywood planking be straight, such that when you sight down the wood, there is no deformation.

Refer to your plans, to the page labeled "Lines." The *body plan* is the drawing to the left of the page, and this is all you need to loft. On the right-hand portion of the page is a drawing of the hull in profile (above), and a drawing of half the hull, viewed from below (below). On the profile drawing there are two horizontal straight lines. The upper one is the designed waterline, or *load waterline* (LWL), representing the plane of the surface of the water at which the hull will float when properly loaded, ballasted, and trimmed. The lower line is the arbitrary *base-line*, used as a reference from which to measure points in the hull above. In the designs in this book, the baseline is typically located at the deepest part of the hull, usually the bottom tip of the skeg.

In the lines drawing, the *sheerline* (upper edge of the hull side planking) and *chine line* (bottom edge of the hull side joined to the bottom plank-ing) are drawn. In the profile drawing you will also see lines representing the toerail and rubrail, and perhaps the wale, but these lines are not shown in either the bottom view or the body plan, because they would clutter the drawings and are not used in the lofting. Other lines seen in the profile representing coamings, houses, and various details are likewise not shown in all the views. In hulls with deadrise, or V-shaped bot-toms, a third sweeping line shows in the profile just below the chine line. This represents the joint where the bottom planking meets the keel or skeg.

The vertical lines on the profile and bottom view (also called plan view) represent the *design stations*. They are numbered along the baseline, and the measurements between them are shown beneath the baseline. These design stations, turned sideways, are what you see when you look

at the body plan, and they are what you will loft. The two horizontal lines are still the load water-line and baseline. The vertical line that divides the body plan in half is the *centerline*. The right side of the body plan shows the forward half of the hull, and the left side shows the stern half. In most cases I drew the design station that best represents the middle, or biggest section of the hull (called the *midship section*) on both sides, so that you may better see what the hull would look like from each end. The sheer and chine lines are seen on end, as if the hull were trans-parent. The lowest lines represent the keel or skeg.

The line along the stem, on the profile, plan view, and body plan represents the forward edge of the side planking, and also the joint between apron (inner stem) and outer stem.

Now look at your *table of offsets* (offsets for 15 of the following 16 designs appear in Appendix I, Tables of Offsets for Adapted Sharpie Designs). This is a graph of all the points on the body plan. The top half consists of "heights from baseline"; these are the heights of the points on the body plan above the baseline. Along the top of the table are the numbered design stations, including the stem and transom. Along the right edge are the *longitudinals*—sheer, chine, and keel top, if the hull has dead-rise. The bottom half of the table contains *half-breadths*—these are the distances out from the centerline to the same points listed in the "heights." Thus, each point in each design sta-tion, representing the intersection of longitudi-nals with that station, has an address, or location, consisting of a height above the baseline and a half-breadth out from the centerline. The lines drawn between these points on the body plan represent the outside of the hull planking at that station.

Loft the design stations full-size on a sheet of clean, flat plywood. The left-hand edge of your plywood represents the centerline—the vertical line of the design body plan. The bottom edge, or edge close to you, is the baseline. Loft all the stations on one side, to the right of the center-line, unlike the body plan in the design. Make sure the side and bottom of your plywood sheet are at right angles to each other.

Use two tape measures, one hooked on the centerline (to measure the half-breadths) and one hooked on the baseline (to measure heights), to locate the points on your lofting. First draw the waterline (LWL) on your lofting. This is usually equal to the draft of your boat. Measure up from the baseline the amount of draft (use the LWL height if there is one on your table of off-sets), and draw a line across the lofting parallel to the base. As you make mold frames and bulk-heads, it is vital that you record the waterline and centerline on them to use in aligning the hull frame.

Next draw the *stem line*—equal to half the thickness of your outer stem (1¼ inches or 1¾ inches for most of the designs in this book)—alongside and parallel to the centerline. Then locate the points of each design station, using one tape for the half-breadth measurement and the other for the height. Keep your tapes perpendicular to the edge, or your measurement will be inaccurate. Draw the point where the tapes cross, and number it for the station. Circle your points for visual clarity. When the points for a station are lofted, connect them with a good straightedge; one line represents the outside of the hull side planking, and the other (parallel to the base and LWL unless there is dead-rise) represents the outside of the bottom planking.

When the stations are lofted, make mold-frames and bulkheads by subtracting the thickness of the planking (and false butt blocks, if used) from your lines, and placing the edges of the mold-frames and bulkheads at these sub-tracted locations. You can subtract the planking and draw the actual perimeters of frames and bulkheads right on the lofting if you want to, or make a plywood "gauge" or two with cut-out notches equal to the plank thicknesses. These gauges are called "angels." To use them, place the notch on the loft line and place the frame lum-ber at the end of the angel. Since half of your mold-frames and bulkheads will extend beyond the left edge of your lofting table, set a sawhorse (or a helper) there to support them. As mentioned earlier, bulkheads can be lofted right on the plywood stock from which they will be made. It won't hurt to do your lofting first, how-ever, to get used to the process and to see what the boat's design stations look like full size.

Use plywood gussets to hold the corners of the mold-frames together—or you can just over-lap them. To lay out the bulkheads, draw a centerline and waterline on the plywood and actually loft the station on both sides of the cen-terline and up and down from the waterline, tak-ing careful measurements off the lofting. *Remember to subtract the planking.* As mentioned in Chapter Four, I spring a little curve into the bottoms of my bulkheads to make the hull bot-tom stronger—just ¼ inch or so (½ inch for the big sharpies).

From this point, refer back to Chapter Four for instructions on building your strongback and setting up mold-frames and bulkheads.

There is one more item that needs to be addressed again: the shape of side planking. The easiest way to determine it is to temporarily spring a sheer clamp and a chine log into place on your molds (set up on the strongback) and spring a sheet of plywood around the side, trac-ing the clamp and log onto the plywood. The bottom of the plank (along the chine log) will often be nearly a straight line, whereas the sheer-line might describe a wild S curve. If you use this method, mark the ends of the plywood on the clamp and log where the butt block will be placed, and *make sure you cut the end of the next piece of plywood to those marks.* Or overlap one piece of planking over the other slightly, trace that, and cut it. In any case, cut your planking oversize and trim it in place.

In some cases the clamp and log are difficult to spring into place and keep there. You can use battens of a slightly smaller size and fasten them to the stem and stern just to trace the side plank, taking them off when finished. Or you can just spring plywood around the frame, mark where the plywood crosses each station (top and bottom), lay the plywood out flat (inside up) and spring a batten through the points, trace, and cut oversize. When you have the planking for one side cut out, spring it back on the frame and make sure it fits; then trace and cut the other side using the first as a template. At that point you are ready to butt-block the planking sections together.

Some designs include scale drawings of "expanded" side planking, often imposed on rectangles representing 4 x 8 sheets of plywood. If you are fortunate enough to have these, lay out the drawings full size on your side-plank plywood stock and cut them out slightly oversize. The layout process will be like lofting, though you may have to "pick up" dimensions from the drawings with dividers and a scale. Use a good batten to "connect the dots" of your transferred dimensions.

After adapting and designing all these incredible boats, I find myself wishing I could build every one of them and sail them for the rest of my life!

Designs

For sharpies to sail their best, they should be heeled over until their chines present a shallow V to the water. Because they are narrow, shallow-bodied, and have long, straight lines and little or no ballast, they are very fast boats. But they do require basic skill and common sense in their handling, and *they can be capsized*. As mentioned elsewhere, sharpie proportions are very sensitive. Attempts to change their highly evolved proportions by more than incremental amounts virtually always result in inferior performance. Sharpies are easy to build but hard to design.

Virtually all existing traditional sharpie design information comes from, or at least through, Howard I. Chapelle. Chapelle was probably America's most industrious historian of marine

architecture, ship models, and designs; he created the catalogue of the National Watercraft Collection for the National Museum of History and Technology in Washington, D.C. This catalogue of information, plans, drawings, photographs, and ship models is one of the finest on Earth. Chapelle was a big fan of sharpies, and he collected every scrap of information he could find about their history, design, and use. He published his findings in various publications, several of which were quoted from in Chapters One and Two and are listed in the bibliography of this book.

The wealth of information Chapelle organized includes the lines drawings, construction plans, and sail plans of many traditional sharpies, both fishing vessels and yachts. Chapelle was a talented naval architect in his own right and was inspired to design sharpie yachts himself, based on the traditional types. Several of these are published in his book *American Sailing Craft* and in *Good Boats* by Roger C. Taylor.

Over the years, I have collected designs of sharpies from various sources, studied them, designed several based on what I learned, built, and sailed them. I believe the qualities of the type are unique, and are ultimately suited to the home builder and to protected water and coastal sailing. The abilities of sharpies in adverse wind and sea conditions are well documented but require good seamanship and experience to be fully exploited. There are those among us, myself included, who would sail a carefully designed, well-built sharpie around the world.

The designs in this chapter are closely based on various traditional types documented primarily by Chapelle and his associates. Often Chapelle would hear of the remains of a sharpie and have a reliable naval architect or historian take the lines off the vessel. Because the methods of taking off lines varied, and because the drawings were often more of an historical nature than those prepared for modern construction methods, I have redrawn the examples chosen for this book.

Another consideration for redrawing—one that I have agonized over—is that the original boats were built specifically to carry large weights of oysters, fish, or cargo, and were designed, built, and rigged for their industry. Because the designs included here are intended to be used as yachts and built of much lighter materials, I have very carefully and subtly altered the designs appropriately. In many cases, this involved modifying the bottoms of the hulls by shifting the rocker slightly forward, decreasing the depth of body aft, and deepening the stern—essentially, lightening displacement and flattening the run. Both these modifications are conducive to increased speed and weatherliness. In a few cases I increased topsides flare slightly, and in some hulls I shifted the center of buoyancy slightly.

Because modern sailcloth and running rigging are lighter than traditional materials, I have left the rigs mostly unaltered, other than making some simplifications.

In many cases I drew smaller versions of the boats than the models I worked from, believing that most home builders will prefer them. Chapelle gives size ranges for each sharpie type, and I simply worked toward the small ends of the ranges. Hence, the boats shown are all historic types, of sizes that were once common and in extensive use—they are authentic. Modifications are subtle.

Sharpies are high-performance boats, even by modern standards, and they require basic skill and care in handling. As stated, *the boats can be capsized*, like almost all small craft, *and most are not self-righting*. For family use, I strongly recommend incorporating flotation in the hulls, in the form of foam-filled compartments or watertight bulkheads with centerline latch-down hatches. The cruising sharpies should have self-draining cockpits if possible, particularly if they are going offshore. Ballast may also be used to bring the boats down to their designed waterlines; this can include internal ballast, water ballast, and in some cases, external metal shoes.

Engines can be incorporated in the designs, but they are redundant in any but large sharpies,

and questionable in those. Chapter Five discusses inboard engine installation, outboard wells, and brackets. These boats row, scull, sail, and maneuver so well that I hope you will consider leaving their beautiful lines and functions unsullied by the noise and stink of engines. The weight and drag of outboards, propellers, apertures, and wells will certainly injure the sharpie's sailing ability, as well as taking room away from something else.

Strictly speaking, sharpies under 20 feet or so should be called skiffs, but we needn't belabor the distinction. The following designs range in size from the 14-foot Flatiron skiff to the 38-foot Clapham Nonpareil sharpie. More small sharpies are included because few home builders are likely to jump into a big-boat project. All the designs are credited to their sources for comparison, should you wish to study the originals. As stated above, some of the designs are smaller than the models they are based on, and many are the smallest of the historical type, to keep them within the means of the home builder.

I have drawn fewer design stations than convention dictates, because our interest here is not historical duplication, but rather ease of construction. This keeps lofting simple, and molds and bulkheads are deliberately represented by the design stations for simplicity. *Length overall* (LOA) refers to the length of the hull "between perpendiculars"—dashed lines on the drawings. Lines are drawn to the outside of the planking.

14-foot Cape Cod Oystering Sharpie (Flatiron Skiff)

LOA—14 feet 1 inch; beam—4 feet 3 inches; draft—9 inches.

Typical of skiffs all over southern New England and Long Island Sound, this model was used through the last four decades of the 19th century. This is an excellent small craft—a fine example of a boat easy and efficient to row, a good performer under sail, and reliable in all weather. The sail is powerful and large for the hull's size and weight, and the centerboard, skeg, and rudder provide a large and balanced lateral plane.

The model is utterly simple, yet contains all the detail and components of larger craft. This is an excellent first boat for the amateur builder. The finished product will display great beauty and style as well as performance and utility. In Chapelle's words (*American Small Sailing Craft*):

> The very high-tucked stern, giving a shallow much-raked transom, was popular in working skiffs because it allowed heavy loads to be carried without forming a drag by immersing the transom....even when loaded they kept the stem nearly clear of the water....the skiffs usually had a beam not much exceeding one-third the total length, and, due to flare, the bottom width was only about one fourth the length. The small beam

was the result of the widespread belief that a wide, shallow boat would lose way in tacking in a sea, and when paying off on a new tack would fall off so much that it would be in danger of an upset if the main sheet were not slacked away a great deal.

The model for this design came from Chapelle's *American Small Sailing Craft*, Figure 36. My version is considerably smaller—14 feet instead of 18, with a modified stern as explained earlier.

Construction Notes
Scantlings for longitudinals: Keelson—1 x 4; chine logs, sheer clamps, inwales, and centerboard trunk cleats—1 x 2; trunk logs—2 x 2; thwart risers—½ inch x 1¼ inch; rubrails—1-

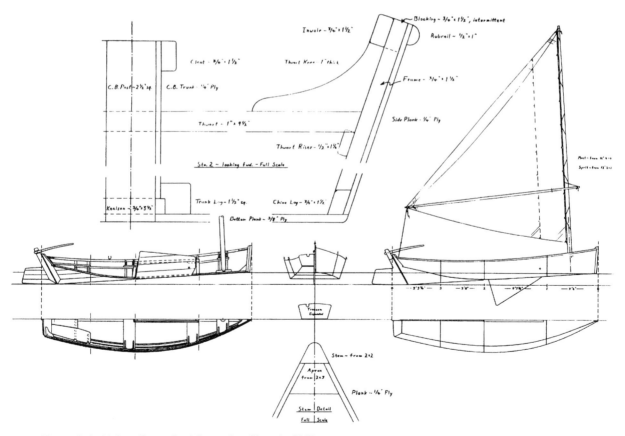

Figure 6-1. 14-foot Cape Cod Oystering Sharpie Skiff.

inch half-round. Make the apron from a 2 x 3, and the stem from a 2 x 2. Scantlings for planking: Sides—¼-inch plywood; bottom—⅜-inch plywood; centerboard trunk—¼- or ⅜-inch plywood; transom—¾-inch plywood, with ¾-inch cleats along sides and bottom.

Side frames (1 x 2) are placed in pairs only where needed: outboard of thwarts where thwart knees are placed, and outboard of the stern sheets. I have drawn these frames and knees set in from the edges of the thwarts; they may also be placed flush to the edges (set the knees in ½ inch). Hanging knees support the side extensions of the stern sheets; these are upside-down versions of thwart knees. An athwartships beam spans between the after side frames to support the width of the stern sheets; this beam is usually cut to a fanciful curve according to the builder's taste. The after end of the stern sheets rests on the bottom transom cleat, which should be beveled to the angle of the stern sheets (paint it first, and use bedding compound to prevent rot here). The thwarts and knees may be thinner than 1 inch: If you use white pine, make them 1 inch thick; if yellow pine or Douglas-fir, make them ⅞ inch thick; if you use plywood, mahogany, or another hardwood, they may be ¾ inch thick. Make the stern sheets from ¾-inch stock (softwood) or ⁹⁄₁₆-inch (hardwood).

The more common method shown in this book for supporting the thwarts is to install plywood "hull stiffeners" the same thickness or one size thicker than the hull topsides, cut equal in width to the thwarts. Install a cleat below the thwart for it to rest on, and install one or two thwart knees above. The drawings for this skiff are intended to supply a more traditional alternative.

Place 1 x 2 filler blocks between the hull sides and inwale as needed to stiffen the structure, approximately every foot or so (never block this slot solidly). Make the breasthook and stern knees from 1-inch stock and fasten them securely, using bedding compound.

Always align grain diagonally across knees, for strength and to prevent cracking. If you can find wood with curved grain, from branches or roots, so much the better. Just make sure it is well cured.

Make the mast from a 16-foot 4 x 4, finished to 3½ inches at the thwart, 2½ inches at the shoulder, and 1½ inches at the head. Make the tenon 1½ inches, and make the step from a 2 x 4. Make the sprit from a 12-foot 2 x 2, finished to 1½ inches tapering at both ends to 1 inch. Drill a second snotter hole in the sprit where shown, to be used when the sail is reefed. Make the centerboard posts from 3 x 3's. Make the rudder, centerboard, and skeg from 1½-inch stock covered with ¼-inch plywood; or the skeg may be laminated from 2½-inch stock.

15-foot Mississippi Yawl River Skiff

LOA—15 feet 1½ inches; beam—4 feet 8 inches; draft—5¼ inches.

This unusual craft is halfway between dory and skiff. This model, which I modified for this book, will be surprisingly weatherly and seaworthy as well as capable of carrying heavy loads. The easily driven hull rows extremely easily and rapidly, and needs no more sail than shown. The craft may seem a little tender compared with the beamier sharpie skiffs, but the narrow bottom that causes this is responsible also for the craft's speed and seaworthiness. In *American Small Sailing Craft*, Chapelle states:

> This boat was in use as early as 1845 and appears to have been developed in its present form as a river steamer's service and lifeboat. This led to the development of a wide stern, to permit carrying heavy line ashore without depressing the stern so much that the boat would be in a dangerous or unhandy trim. This was accomplished by twisting the side plank sharply, as the stern is approached, so that here the boat is quite wide at gunwale, but narrow on the bottom.

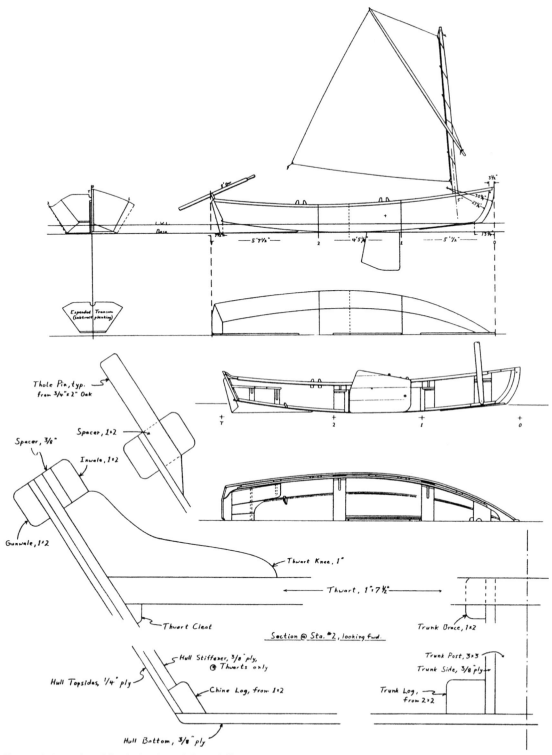

Thole Pin, typ.
from 3/4" x 2" Oak

Spacer, 1×2

Spacer, 3/8"

Inwale, 1×2

Gunwale, 1×2

Thwart Knee, 1"

Thwart, 1'-7½"

Trunk Brace, 1×2

Thwart Cleat

Section @ Sta. #2, looking fwd.

Trunk Post, 3×3

Trunk Side, 3/8" ply

Hull Stiffener, 3/8" ply,
@ Thwarts only

Hull Topsides, 1/4" ply

Chine Log, from 1×2

Trunk Log,
from 2×2

Hull Bottom, 3/8" ply

Expanded Transom
(subtract planking)

Figure 6-2. 15-foot Mississippi yawl river skiff.

An interesting feature is the gunwale and inwale angle, which was maintained at right angles to the hull sides right back to the transom, accounting for the angular and handsome transom shape. This boat will make an excellent workboat, fisherman, and yacht tender. Those of you who have rowed out large anchors and chain in the stern of a tender (especially in an emergency) will love this boat; she has the ability to carry a lot of weight and remain easily driven. She'll also make an excellent camp boat.

This vessel is steered with an oar. If you prefer to have a rudder and tiller, make them like those shown for the Maryland Crabbing Skiff (Figure 6-6) or the Eastern Shore Stick-up Skiff (Figure 6-3). My inspirations were Figures 34 and 35 from *American Small Sailing Craft*.

Construction Notes

Scantlings for longitudinals: Chine logs, inwale, gunwale, and trunk brace—1 x 2. Make the curved stem apron from a 3 x 8, and the outer stem from a 3 x 10 (or from laminates). Make the knees, thwarts, and transom from 1-inch stock. Make the stern sheets from ¾-inch stock. The breasthook and stern knees may be made from 1-inch solid stock, or laminated from four layers of ¼-inch plywood or two layers of ½-inch plywood. The transom may be made from 1-inch stock or ¾-inch plywood, with 1 x 2 cleats around the perimeter. Get the mast out of a 4 x 4 and sprit from a 2 x 2, finished to the same dimensions as those of the previous boat (Figure 6-1).

16-foot Eastern Shore Stick-up Skiff (Flattie)

LOA—16 feet 2 inches; beam—5 feet; draft— 12½ inches.

This is the "flattie" model of this skiff—there was also a V-bottomed version similar to the modified sharpie of Figure 6-4. The model shown has deadrise in the stern and represents a transitional type between the pure flat-bottomed sharpie and the deadrise, or V-bottomed, skiff (small craft) and skipjacks and bateaux (large

craft). Another of this type is represented in Figure 6-8, the Chesapeake Flattie. Figure 6-4, the Modified Sharpie Skiff, is an example of the next stage of evolution on the Chesapeake. In the words of Chapelle (*American Small Sailing Craft*):

> The model of the Chesapeake flattie was apparently created in an effort to produce a wide sharpie that would sail well. A wide, flat-bottomed hull is often slow when loaded, and, when paying off on a new tack, the boat falls off badly before gathering headway. This may lead to a knockdown or capsize in a fresh breeze, if the handling is careless or slow. Someone had made the discovery that deadrise aft helped such craft, and so the cheap but efficient flattie model developed.
>
> The use of deadrise in the flattie seems to have been confined to the Bay and to boats turned out by one northern builder, Clapham. [Thomas Clapham; see Figure 6-16.]
>
> These stick-up rigged flattie skiffs were highly regarded [on the Bay] and did not go wholly out of use until the motorboat drove sail out. The skiffs were particularly approved of for weatherliness in a fresh wind, and some were said to be able to go to windward in strong winds under the stick-up sail alone, which seems impossible theoretically.

The source for this vessel is Figure 113, *American Small Sailing Craft*.

Construction Notes

Scantlings for longitudinals: Keel plank—1 x 4; chine logs, sheer clamps, trunk cleat, and deck carlins—1 x 2. Make the apron and stem from 3 x 4 stock (cut the apron bevels orienting the stock "on the flat"—it is wider than deep). Scantlings for planking: Hull sides—⅜-inch plywood; bottom—½-inch plywood; decks—¼-inch plywood; centerboard trunk—½-inch plywood; transom—two laminations of ½-inch plywood with 1 x 2 cleats around the perimeter (except the exposed top).

Place side deck support knees, made from

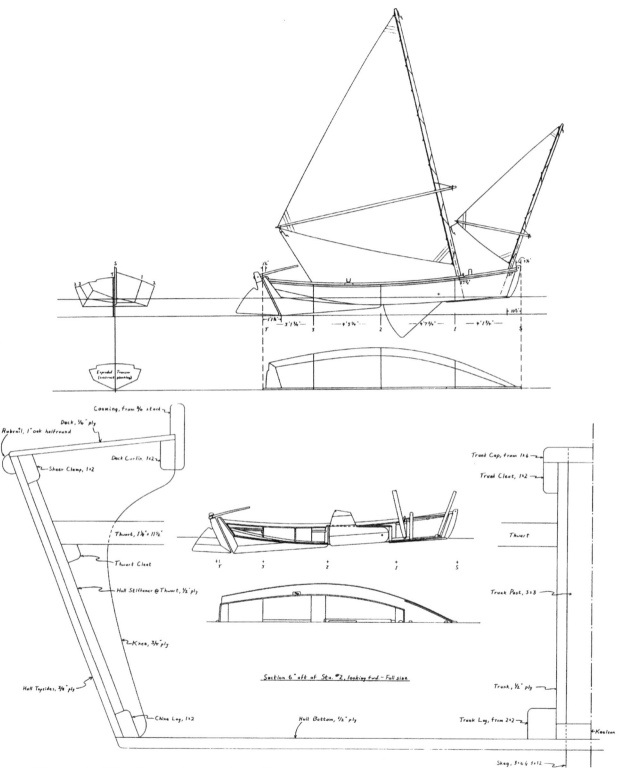

Figure 6-3. 16-foot Eastern Shore stick-up skiff.

¾-inch plywood, about 24 inches apart. Fore deck stiffener—1 x 4. Deck crown—¼-inch per foot; make deck beams flat on the bottom and crowned on top. Thwarts are ⅝ inch thick; stern sheet platform—½-inch plywood.

Cut the coamings from wide stock by laying the stock in place along the deck carlin and tracing the bottom of the carlin on the stock. Cut along the line and reproduce a parallel line above by the desired coaming height, and cut that. After shaping and fitting the ends, install the coamings. Rabbet the forward inner ends of the side coamings for the forward coaming. If you have a table saw, rabbet the bottom outer edges of the coamings to lock over the deck.

Make the mast from an 18-foot 4 x 4, finished to 3⅜ inches at the partner, 1½ inches at the head, and 2½ inches at the foot, with a 1¾-inch tenon. Make the stick-up from an 11-foot 3 x 3, finished to 2¼ inches at the partner, 1¼ inches at the head, and 2 inches at the foot, with a 1½-inch tenon. Make the sprit from 2 x 2 stock, finished to 1½ inches tapered to 1 inch ends; make the stick-up sprit ¼ inch smaller in proportion.

If you like this model, but cannot live with the "stick-up," adapt the "balance jib" shown in Figure 6-6 (Maryland crabbing skiff). Either rig

the jib from the stem head or incorporate a short plank bowsprit (about one foot long). Make your jib similar in shape (to Figure 6-6) but a little smaller.

18-foot Modified Sharpie Skiff (Chesapeake)

LOA—17 feet 10 inches; beam—5 feet 6 inches; draft—15 inches.

This excellent small craft represents the highest stage of evolution of the sharpie into the deadrise skiff. The type is very close to the Nonpareil sharpies developed by Thomas Clapham (see Figure 6-16). Just prior to this modified sharpie skiff was the flattie type (Figure 6-3), with deadrise (V) in the stern only; the types that followed were the skipjack and bateau.

A good example of a modern boat of this type is the Lightning class. The model shown is moderate, neither a burdensome workboat nor a flat-out racer. For this boat you might make a removable cuddy to fit around the coaming, and canvas bunks could be laced to strap-eyes in the hull and centerboard trunk, thus converting her to a "pocket-cruiser." The source for this boat is Figure 115, *American Small Sailing Craft*.

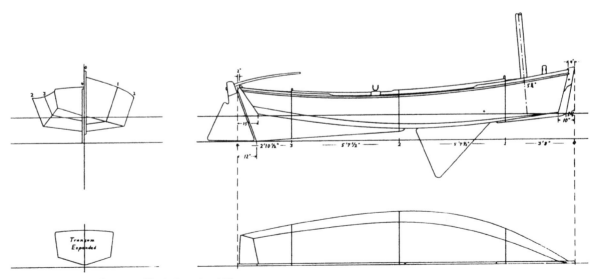

Figure 6-4. 18-foot modified sharpie skiff.

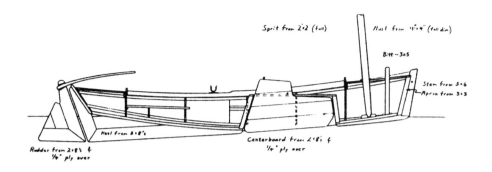

Sprit from 2×2 (full)

Mast from 4"×4" (full dim.)

Bitt ~ 3×5

Stem from 3×6

Apron from 3×3

Keel from 3×8's

Rudder from 2×8's &
¼" ply over

Centerboard from 2×8's &
¼" ply over

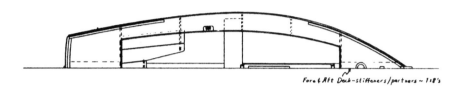

Fore & Aft Deck-stiffeners/partners ~ 1×8's

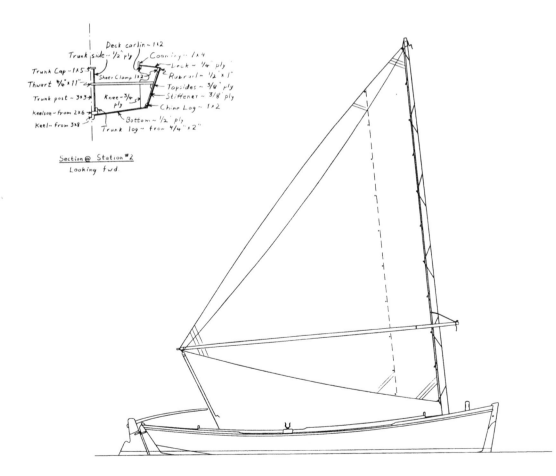

Deck carlin ~ 1×2

Trunk side ~ ½" ply

Coaming ~ 1×4

Deck ~ ¼ ply

Trunk Cap ~ 1×5.5

Sheer Clamp 1×2

Rubrail ~ ½"×1"

Thwart ¾"×11"

Topsides ~ ⅜" ply

Trunk post ~ 3×3

Knee ~ ¾ ply

Stiffener ~ ⅜ ply

Keelson ~ from 2×6

Chine Log ~ 1×2

Keel ~ from 3×8

Bottom ~ ½ ply

Trunk log ~ from 4/4"×2"

Section @ Station #2
Looking fwd.

Construction Notes

Scantlings for longitudinals: Keelson—2 x 6; chine logs, sheer clamps, deck carlins—1 x 2; rubrails—1-inch half-round. Make the keelson from a 2 x 6, with beveled edges for the bottom planking. Strike two chalklines on the bottom of the keelson 2½ inches apart (1¼ inches from the centerline on each side) and bevel outboard from these lines. Fit the bottom planking from these lines out, and fit the keel forefoot, centerboard slot, and skeg between. Make the apron from a 3 x 3, and the stem from a 3 x 6. Scantlings for planking: Sides—⅜-inch plywood; bottom—½-inch plywood; deck—¼-inch plywood; transom—two laminations of ½-inch plywood with 1 x 2 cleats; trunk—½-inch plywood.

The deck crown is ½ inch per foot. There are no deck beams. Install 1 x 8 deck stiffeners on the centerline both forward and aft; pierce the forward one for mast and bitt. Make the mast-step from a 2 x 6. Make the centerboard trunk posts from 3 x 3s, and the trunk logs from ⁴⁄₄-inch x 2-inch stock. Make the rudder and centerboard from 2 x 8 stock covered with ¼-inch plywood. Make the forefoot keel from a 3 x 4 and the skeg from 3 x 8 stock. Get the mast out of a 20-foot full-dimensioned 4 x 4, finished to 3⅞ inches at the partner, 1½ inches at the head and 3 inches at the foot with a 2-inch tenon. Make the sprit from a 14-foot full-dimensioned 2 x 2, finished to 1⅞ inch tapered at both ends to 1¼ inch. Make the oarlock socket bases from 2-inch x 3-inch x 6-inch white oak or locust.

19-foot Small Ohio Sharpie.

LOA—19 feet 5½ inches; beam—5 feet 8 inches; draft—6 ¾ inches.

This craft is essentially a half-size version of the Ohio pound-net boat shown in Figure 6-15. The Great Lakes sharpies varied greatly in size, shape, and proportion, being built by both professionals and amateurs without plans or, frequently, models. Chapelle mentions that the Ohio boats were known to be built as small as 20

feet, and may have been sloop-rigged. I found this model very attractive, and felt that its proportions were excellent for a craft around 20 feet, noting that the 36-footer shown in *American Small Sailing Craft* (Figure 47) was very beamy and heavy for a sharpie of that size. In scaling down, one typically increases beam, depth, rocker, freeboard, underbody plane, weight and sail area. This particular hull, simply reduced without changing its proportions, happens to be very well proportioned in comparison to other regional sharpies in the 20-foot size range. Hence in the down-scaling process, a hull that is slightly burdensome becomes quite light and streamlined. I did raise the freeboard (this was fairly essential), which consequentially increased the beam ratio; I also flattened the run and lowered the stern slightly to alter the model from workboat to yacht. She will still, however, carry 1,000 pounds in cargo, fish, oysters, passengers—or camping gear. I designed and built a modified version for myself, adding arc-deadrise (curve instead of V) to the stern, higher freeboard, and adapting the Florida sharpie rig for the boat, which I named *Gato Negro*. I also decked the hull like the Chesapeake or New Haven boats, including a bridge deck instead of thwart to step the mizzenmast through. I placed about 100 pounds of lead sheet in her bottom as ballast, and I would recommend using twice that, unless you are carrying something heavy and low in the boat. *Gato Negro* carried seven or eight people comfortably and still performed well.

I found the boat to be quite fast and weatherly, and as perfectly balanced as any I have ever sailed. I spent idyllic days sailing her on the flats of the Florida Keys, slipping along in scant inches of water, steering by shifting my weight slightly while sitting on the bridge deck without tending sheets or tiller! I must say that of all the boats I have built and owned, *Gato Negro* is the only one that could be steered like that.

I took *Gato Negro* to Maine one summer and sailed her around Camden on Penobscot Bay, and out on Megunticook Lake, where she attracted so much attention that she finally got written up in *The Camden Herald.* Sharpies seem to be strangers to Downeasters—though I did find a lovely little round-sterned plank-on-frame sharpie in neighboring Rockport, built by a graduate of the Rockport Apprenticeshop. When I told him my sharpie was built of plywood and epoxy, he wouldn't talk to me anymore.

The version presented here is more traditional and both lighter and finer than *Gato Negro*, which was intended as a work boat. I have drawn two rigs for the model: one is a sprit-rigged cat ketch, with spar dimensions the same as *Gato Negro*'s, and the other is my reconstruction of a sloop-rigged pound-net boat, which I imagine may resemble the rig used in the small Ohio sharpies. Either rig will prove powerful and exciting, as this sharpie has the beam to carry more

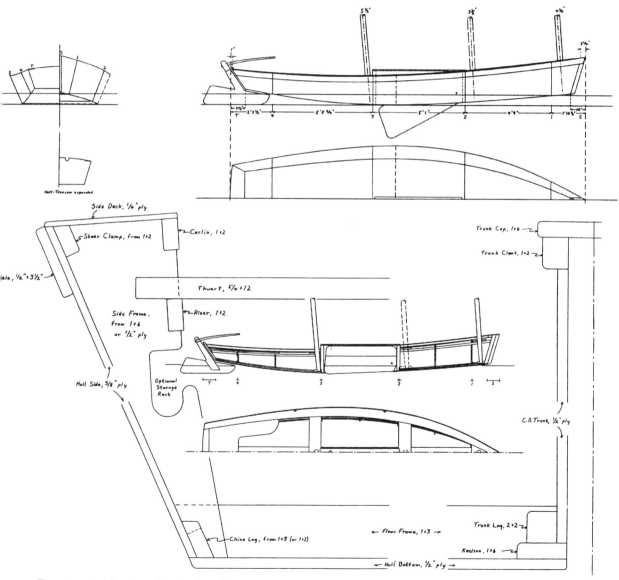

Figure 6-5. 19-foot small Ohio sharpie.

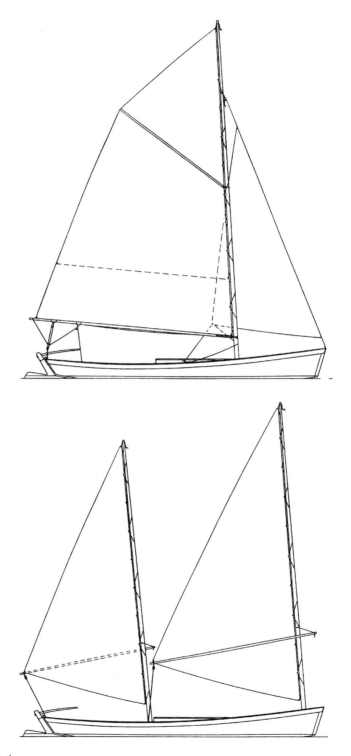

Figure 6-5 *continued.*

sail than the others in her size range. This particular boat is also very simple to build, and represents an excellent model for the beginner. The sources for this boat are from Figures 47 and 48 in *American Small Sailing Craft*, text from the same, and from a photo from The National Watercraft Collection (see Figure 1-12).

Construction Notes

Longitudinal scantlings: keelson—1 x 8; chine logs, sheer clamps, deck carlins—1 x 2. Make the apron from a 3 x 3, and the stem from a 3 x 3. Plank scantlings: sides—3/8-inch ply; bottom—1/2-inch ply; deck—1/4-inch ply; transom—two laminations 1/2-inch ply with 1 x 2 cleats; trunk—1/2-inch ply. The side decks rise 1/2 inch at the carlins. This hull has four permanent frames: make the bottoms (floors) from 1 x 3's and the sides from 1 x 6's or 1/2-inch plywood. Make three extra pairs of side frames to support the side decks as shown. Notch the side frames for carlins and thwart risers. Make the breast hook from a 2 x 4 block, crowned on top and notched to receive the carlin-ends. There are no deck beams. Make the mast steps from 2 x 6's and the thwarts and stern sheets from full-one-inch stock (support them from the adjacent side frames). Make the centerboard trunk posts from 3 x 3's, and the trunk logs from 2 x 2's. Make the rudder and centerboard from 2 x 8 and 2 x 6 stock covered with 1/4-inch plywood. Make the wales from 1/2-inch x 3 1/2-inch solid stock or plywood. Get the mast(s) out of 4 x 4's (20 feet, 22 feet; 24 feet for the sloop), finished to 3 3/8 inches at the partner, 1 1/4 inches at the head and 2 1/2 inches at the foot (no tenon). Make the sprits from 2 x 2's, finished to 1 1/2 inch tapered at both ends to 1 1/8 inch. If you like, hole the forward thwart and add the extra mast step beneath so that you can step either your main or mizzenmasts there to sail as a sloop in very windy weather. This may sound like a strange way to reef, but it's how many of the sharpies did it! If you opt for the sloop rig, the spar that looks like a captive gaff was traditionally two oak or ash battens bolted or riveted

through the sail—a modern alternative is 1/2-inch PVC pipe in a batten pocket with a spruce or fir core inside the aft three-fifths of the batten (heat the ends with a heat gun or boiling water and flatten them with a clamp). Seize the forward end of the batten to a mast hoop (this could be a 1-inch segment of 4-inch PVC pipe).

20-foot Maryland Crabbing Skiff

LOA—19 feet 6 inches; beam—4 feet 6 inches; draft—6 1/2 inches.

As stated much earlier, I first fell in love with these unique craft when I discovered the beautiful drawings of them in the back room of Marmaduke's Pub in Eastport, Maryland. I found several additional sources for my own designs of crabbing skiffs in an old issue of *WoodenBoat* magazine, in *American Small Sailing Craft* (Figure 37), and in Chapelle's excellent booklet on crabbing skiffs published by the Chesapeake Bay Small Craft Museum.

I designed and built a 17 1/2-foot boat, *Mallard*, of which several photos appear in this book. Because the type is very small for its size, I include here my 20-foot design of a Maryland Crabbing Skiff, which is a little roomier.

The boats are very fast and weatherly, and handle somewhat differently than anything I have ever sailed. *Mallard* has lee helm in light air (it helps to keep the centerboard all the way down) but develops very slight weather helm (desirable) in more wind. When the boat is overpowered, the jib is taken in, and she balances and handles perfectly under mainsail alone. Being so long and narrow, the boat is slow to turn; to maneuver in tight spaces, the centerboard must be down. Even so, I found *Mallard* difficult to turn and dock in the very narrow canal where she was berthed, and because the wind blows straight up the canal, I have twice found myself horribly tangled in the mangroves at the lee end. I also rammed the cement seawall trying to round up to my dock, leaving a big dent in the end of the bowsprit.

In short, *Mallard*, and perhaps crabbing skiffs in general, are very sensitive, fast vessels that require a higher level of consciousness and skill to handle than many of the other vessels shown here, particularly in tight spaces. But once in open water, the craft are like greased lightning. It's not so much that they lack responsiveness as that they are long (it's quite far from the centerboard to the rudder), need room to turn in, and are so damn fast

that you *really* have to think ahead.

The "balance" jib is another unusual feature: The boom is fixed by a lanyard between about one-quarter and two-fifths of the way aft (depending on the design), which supplies tension to both the luff and leech of the jib. Therefore, the sheet need only position the sail (not pull down on it), and it is effective off the wind, which no other jib or even staysail is. The jib is a pivoting semi-rigid airfoil,

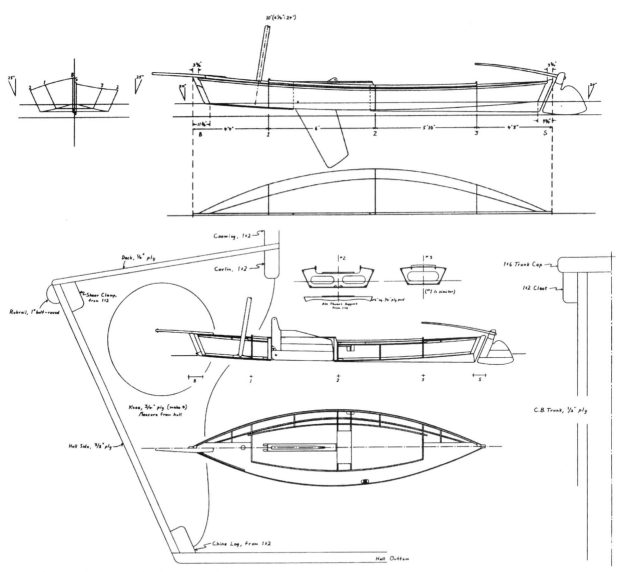

Figure 6-6. 20-foot Maryland crabbing skiff.

whose shape, once adjusted by the lanyard location, is good for all wind conditions. The bowsprit is shorter than it would otherwise need to be, and there is no forestay. You know, those 19th-century fishermen were pretty clever fellows.

Construction Notes

Longitudinal scantlings: (no keelson); chine logs, sheer clamps, deck carlins and coamings—1 x 2. Make both aprons from 3 x 4's on the flat, and the stem and stern post from 3 x 4's. Plank scantlings: sides—⅜-inch ply; bottom—½-inch ply; deck—¼-inch ply; trunk—½-inch ply; bulkheads and deck stiffeners—¾-inch ply. Deck crown is ½ inch per foot. Make deck beams from ¾-inch ply, flat on the bottom and crowned on top—notch them for the longitudinal deck stiffeners. Centerboard trunk posts are 3 x 3's; trunk logs are from 2 x 2 stock. Make the centerboard and rudder from 2 x 6 and 2 x 8 stock covered with ¼-inch ply. Get the mast out of a 20-foot

4 x 4, finished to 3½ inches at the partner, 1¼ inches at the head, and 2¾ inches at the foot with a 2-inch tenon. Make the maststep from a 2 x 4 with a ¾-inch ply cap. Make the sprit and balance boom from 2 x 2 stock finished to 1½ inches at the centers, tapered to 1⅛ inches at the ends. Make the bowsprit from a 4-foot 2 x 8. Notch the stem head ¾ inches into the bowsprit, and fasten the sprit to the deck with four ¼-inch carriage bolts. Make the thwart seat from ¾-inch plywood, 11½ inches x 26 inches. Make the gripe from a 1 x 3 and the skeg from a 3 x 8. Make four ¾-inch plywood knees to support the side decks between bulkheads. Make the centerboard trunk cap from a 1 x 6 with a long open slot tapered at the end to match the top of the centerboard. Shape the centerboard core more like a daggerboard—this unique board acts like a centerboard halfway down, and like a daggerboard (high-aspect-ratio raked foil) all the way down. It is the most powerful and effective board I have ever used, and I highly recommend adapt-

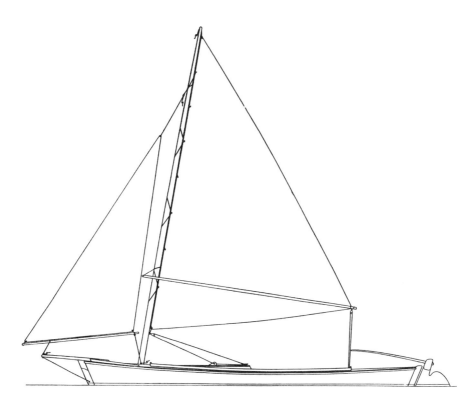

ing the type for other small craft, as well as for larger racing boats. Make the rubrails from 1-inch half-round hardwood.

22-foot Cedar Keys Sharpie

LOA—21 feet 10 inches; beam—5 feet 8 inches; draft—11½ inches.

I was first attracted to this design for the rig, which I have adapted and used on many vessels, including the Exuma 52 schooner *Sarah*, Exuma 44 cat-schooner *Teresa*, and 19-foot sharpie *Gato Negro*. Full-length battens are very useful devices in creating good sail shape, and have been known and used for centuries. In sharpies, the battens frequently consisted of two thin oak strips riveted or bolted through the sail, one on each side. Instead, I sew on reinforced batten pockets, and use PVC pipe for battens, with octagonal wood cores inserted inside the after 60

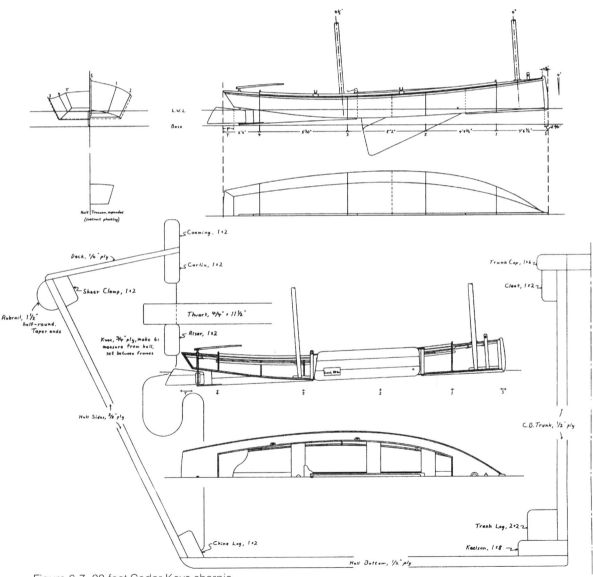

Figure 6-7. 22-foot Cedar Keys sharpie.

percent of the pipes to stiffen them. I dip the pipe ends in boiling water for one minute or heat them with a heat gun and clamp 2 x 4 blocks on each side to flatten the ends. This allows the ends to fit snugly in the batten pockets, as well as allowing a long taper to be made at the forward batten ends to induce additional camber. I also duct-tape the forward batten ends to prevent chafe. I drill ¼-inch holes in the aft batten ends (which protrude from the leach 2 to 4 inches depending on boat size) for the tension lacings (battens must be placed under tension). Unless the sail has dramatic draft, the forward ends of the batten present no problem; they stay in line with the luff of the sail. One reason for this is the extreme flexibility of the PVC pipe—fiberglass and wooden battens don't work as well.

The hull model for this boat—Figure 45 from *American Small Sailing Craft*—is somewhat odd,

and makes an interesting contrast to the other sharpies. It has rather a lot of beam forward, compensated by very shallow draft forward, and narrower beam aft by way of the after mast, with deep rocker at the same point. The stem rakes aft slightly, and the transom seems a little steep. In redrawing the model for this book, I altered the lines slightly to balance these design elements more harmoniously, without eliminating them and the character they represent. (Chapelle described the model as somewhat crude, so I felt justified in altering it.) In other aspects—beam, flare and sheer—I like the model. The figure from Chapelle is of a much larger boat (32 feet), and he states that the type was often smaller (18 to 22 feet). Since no drawings exist of the smaller, more common models, I can only speculate what they were like; this drawing represents that speculation. It is also interesting to note that

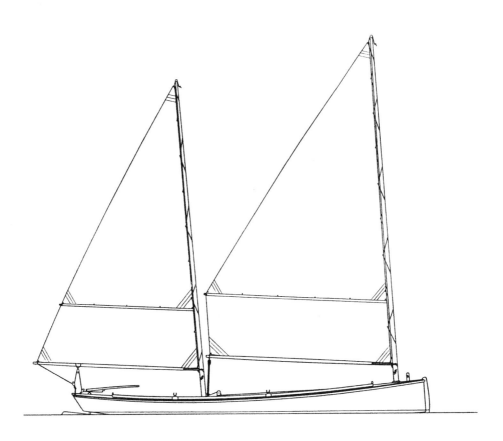

the lines were taken off a hulk at Cedar Keys, Florida, in 1928 by Larry Huntington, at the direction of Ralph Munroe.

Because the Cedar Keys sharpie has more beam and displacement than other similar-sized sharpies, I feel this craft would make an excellent camp boat and family pocket cruiser for her size, yet will also perform very well, being stiffer than her peers and faster off the wind.

Construction Notes

Longitudinal scantlings: chine logs, sheer clamps, deck carlins and coamings—1 x 2; keelson—1 x 8. Make the apron from a 3 x 4 on the flat, and the stem from a 3 x 4 on edge. Plank scantlings: sides—⅜-inch ply; bottom—½-inch ply; deck —¼-inch ply; trunk—½-inch ply; bulkheads, side deck knees and deck stiffeners—¾-inch ply. Make the transom from ¾ inch plywood with 1 x 2 cleats. Deck crown is ½ inch per foot. Make deck beams from ¾-inch ply or 1 x 4's, flat on the bottom and crowned on top—notch them for the longitudinal deck carlins and thwart risers. Centerboard trunk posts are 3 x 3's; trunk logs are from 2 x 2 stock. Make the centerboard from 2 x 8 stock covered with ¼-inch ply. Get the masts out of 22- and 20-foot 4 x 4's. Finish the main to 3½ inches at the partner, 1½ inches at the head, and 2½ inches at the foot (no tenon); finish the mizzen to 3¼ inches at the partners, 1¼ inches at the head and 2½ inches at the foot. Make the maststeps from 2 x 6's. Make the booms from 3 x 3 stock: finish the main to 2½ inches at the center tapered to 1¾ inches at the ends; finish the mizzen to 2¼ inches at the center tapered to 1½ inches at the ends. Make the thwarts from ⁴⁄₄-inch x 11½-inch stock. Make the gripe from a 3 x 3 and the skeg from 3 x 6 stock. Make six ¾-inch plywood knees to support the side decks between bulkheads. Make the centerboard trunk cap from a 1 x 6 with a long open slot for the top of the centerboard. Make six 6-inch-long ¾-inch plywood beam shelves (a pair for each deck beam) and fasten these under the sheer clamp. Make the

rubrails from 1½-inch half-round hardwood; taper the ends to 1-inch half-round if desired. Make the rudder shaft from ¾-inch stainless steel with ¼-inch x 1½-inch tangs welded fore and aft, and the gudgeon from ¼-inch x 1-inch stainless steel strap bent around and welded to a 1-inch segment of ¾-inch pipe with ¼-inch x 1-inch stock welded along the bottom (inset). Epoxy or polyurethane in place a length of ¾-inch pipe from deck to hull bottom in which to install the rudder shaft, set at an angle of ½ degree. Make the rudder core from 1 x 8 stock slotted to fit over the tangs on the shaft, planed to a foil shape, and covered with ⅜-inch plywood.

Use ⅜-inch line and blocks for halyards and sheets. Slot the mast heads for halyards and install sheaves. Use one double and three single blocks for the main sheet, placing one single block on each side of the main thwart to fairlead the sheet ends aft to the helmsman and one single block on the centerline (use padeyes for all these) facing athwartships. Use three single blocks for the mizzen sheet as shown.

24-foot Chesapeake Flattie

LOA—24 feet 2 inches; beam—7 feet 9 inches; draft—2 feet ½ inch.

Proportionately, this is the largest boat presented in this book. Featuring the maximum beam ratio successfully used in the sharpie type, she is a "big little boat" and will make an excellent, safe, and comfortable pocket cruiser. She has a different character than the other craft, being a gaff-rigged cutter, and her large skeg gives her a deeper draft than even the largest "true" sharpies. While this model is not as fast or weatherly in comparison to some of the more extreme types, she is easier and less critical to handle, making her an excellent family cruiser.

Also known as the Hampton Flattie, this type was very popular on the Bay through the last quarter of the 19th century, and varied in size from 16 to 30 feet in length, according to C. P. Kunhardt, who wrote about the type in *Forest and Stream* and *Small Yachts*. Chapelle, in his research, found a hulk near Elliot, Maryland, on the Chesapeake in 1940–41, and made plans from it (Figure 112 in *American Small Sailing Craft*). These craft were used for oystering and crabbing until at least 1910, and lend themselves well to being used as small yachts. The original working models had a small cuddy forward, which I simply expanded aft in creating a pocket cruiser. These boats were called "handscrapers," as they dredged oysters using small manual winches. I have explained the theories and development of the hull shape in Chapter One and in the description of the Eastern Shore Stick-up Skiff (Figure 6-3).

Construction Notes
Scantlings for longitudinals: Keelson—2 x 8; chine logs and carlins—2 x 3; sheer clamps—1 x 3. Make the step apron from a 3 x 6 on the flat and the stem from a 3 x 6 on edge. Scantlings for planking: Sides—½-inch plywood; bottom—⅝-inch plywood; transom—two laminations of ⅝-inch plywood with 1 x 2 cleats; decks—⅜-inch plywood; coach roofs—¼-inch plywood; hatch tops—⅜-inch plywood; cabin trunks and cockpit coaming—⅝-inch plywood; bulkheads—½-inch plywood; centerboard trunk—½-inch plywood.

Make the centerboard trunk posts from 3 x 3's. Install a 3-inch sheave in a slot at the top of the after centerboard post, and cut a groove in the back of the centerboard for the lanyard to lie in (see Figure 6-8). Use plywood or a plank, ¾ inch x 10 inches, for the mast partner, and ¾ inch by 8 inches for the bitt partner. Make the mast-step from a 3 x 8.

Make the mast from a 24-foot 6 x 6, finished 5 inches at the partner, tapering to 4 inches at the step, 4½ inches at the gaff and 3 inches at the head; make the tenon 3 inches. Make the boom from a 4 x 4 finished to 3 inches, tapered at each end to 2 inches, and the gaff from a 3 x 3 finished 2½ inches, tapered at each end to 1¾ inches.

Shrouds and forestay are optional. Make them from ³⁄₁₆-inch wire rope if desired, set up with ⅜-inch jaw-and-eye turnbuckles shackled to ¼-inch x 1-inch chainplates bolted to the hull with 3 (each) ⁵⁄₁₆-inch flathead machine screws. The forestay chainplate is formed to wrap over the stemhead 6 inches fore-and-aft, with a tang welded on top for the shackle pin.

The hatches in Figure 6-8 are drawn with mating rabbets cut in 1½-inch coamings and hatch frames as an alternative to the boxtop hatches shown elsewhere. These are harder to make, and require a table saw. If a small inboard engine is used, install a hatch over it.

Make the rudder and centerboard cores from

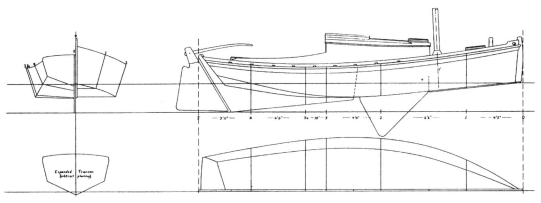

Figure 6-8. 24-foot Cheasapeake flattie

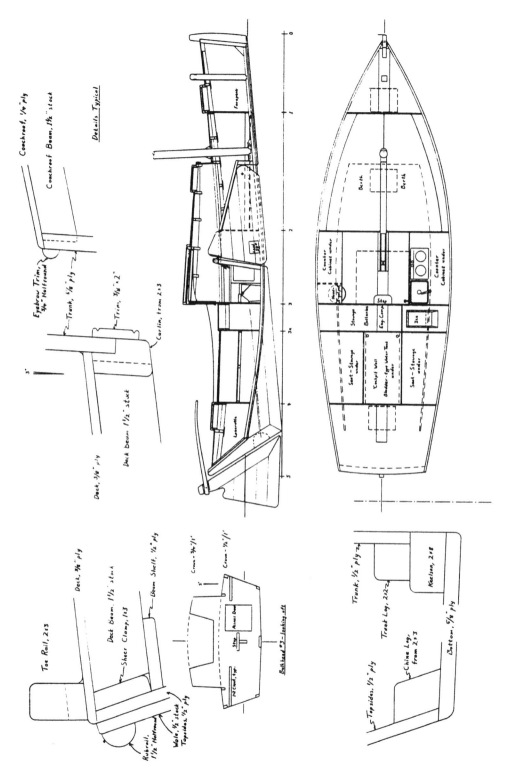

Figure 6-8 continued.

2 x 8 stock covered with ⅜-inch plywood; you can also make the skeg/keel this way or stack-laminate it from 3 x 8 stock. Make the bow gripe from ¾-inch x 2½-inch oak. You may also want to use an oak shoe on the skeg bottom (finish it to the same dimensions). Deck beams are 1½ inch x 3 inches, tapered at the ends to 2½ inches; coach roof beams are 1½ inch x 1¾ inch, tapered at the ends to 1½ inches. Make the toerail from 2 x 3 stock, and laminate a layer on top at each side of the bow for the hawse holes. Make the hawses from brass pipe, set angled down and forward (use a hole saw with a long pilot bit to drill the angled holes); cut the pipe ¼-inch long both inside and out, and peen the ends over with a ball-peen hammer. Be sure to use bedding compound.

25-foot Maryland Fishing Sharpie

LOA—25 feet 1½ inches; beam—7 feet; draft—1 foot 7 ¾ inches.

This craft, based on a model from *Paper 25*, is one of the most beautiful I have ever seen. She is also the only sharpie I have seen that used a daggerboard.

The Chesapeake Bay sharpies had many unusual features. The cockpit in the model runs almost the length of the hull, and the forward and after decks are very short. For simplicity, the

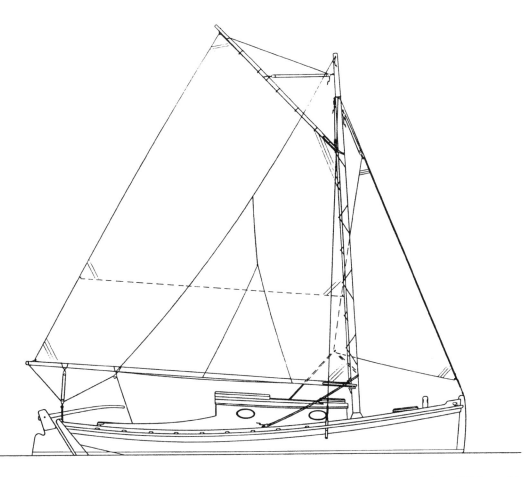

coamings forward are tied directly to the bitt. The mast steps are hinged aft so that the masts may be easily stepped by setting their tenons in the steps, standing them up in place, and clamping them to strong thwarts with metal clamps.

The toerail runs aft only, with none forward at all, and there are three pairs of large rowing-socket blocks, indicating that the boat was frequently rowed, probably with her masts down.

When rigged for sailing, the after sail is

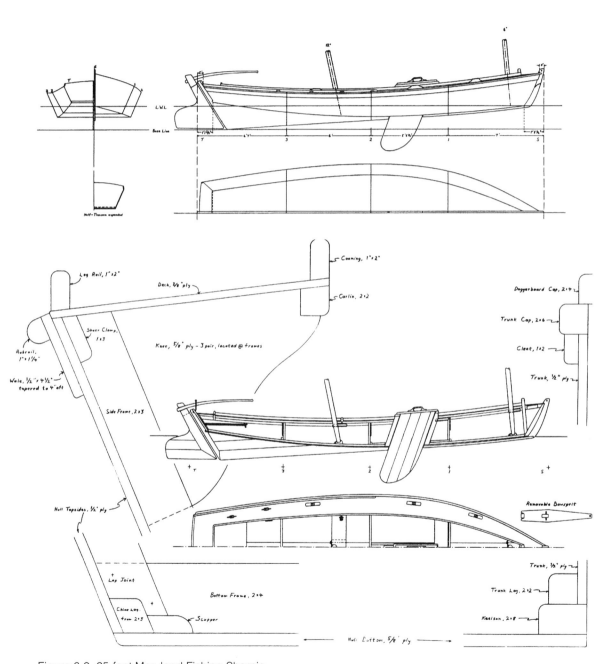

Figure 6-9. 25-foot Maryland Fishing Sharpie.

sheeted to a large, high traveler, under which passes the tiller. A bowsprit is used in conjunction with a "balance" jib for light air, and this whole arrangement is removable. Evidently (the original drawing is poor) the bowsprit was a plank type that fit right over the high stemhead, through which there is a hole for a pin to lock the bowsprit in place, there being no bobstay. One can only presume that the aft end of the bowsprit was forked to lock onto the bitt (this is how I have drawn it)—altogether an ingenious arrangement.

The hull is relatively beamy and deep for a sharpie, and recommends itself as a pocket cruiser, particularly since the daggerboard is more compact than a centerboard in the cabin. For this reason I recommend a convertible trunk, to be used as an option or a permanent addition. The foredeck will also need a cover of some kind that allows the mast to pass through, and consideration must be made for the dagger-

board to come up. A simple canvas-and-netting camp cabin might be the answer.

This is a beautiful and unique sharpie, and I would love to build and own one myself. The design has many unique features, and I like the jib in the sail plan very much. I think this sharpie might be the ideal family camp boat. She is also one of the simplest of all the sharpies to build, has a particularly roomy cockpit, and would make an excellent workboat. There is a photograph of the type in Chapter One, Figure 1-8.

Construction Notes
Scantlings for longitudinals are: keelson—2 x 8; chine logs—from 2 x 3's; sheer clamps—1 x 3's, carlins—2 x 2's; wales—from ½ inch x 4½ inch tapering to 4 inches aft; rubrails—1 inch by 1¼ inch; coamings and log rail—1 inch x 2¼ inch (sprung into place); trunk posts—3 x 4; trunk logs—2 x 2. Make the apron from 3 x 4 stock; make the outer stem from 3 x 8 stock

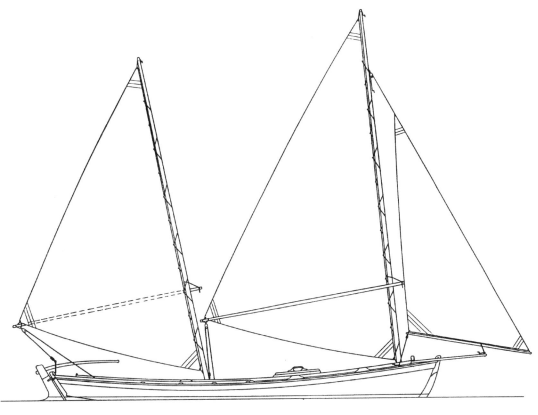

square above and beveled below. Scantlings for planking are: hull sides—½-inch plywood; hull bottom—⅝-inch plywood; transom—two laminations of ⅝-inch plywood; daggerboard trunk—½-inch plywood; deck—⅜-inch plywood. Make the side-deck support knees from ⅝-inch plywood.

Make the three frames from 2 x 3's for the sides and 2 x 4's for the bottoms, notched for sheer clamps, chine logs, keelson and scuppers (at all bottom corners). Cut a ¾-inch crown on the bottom of frame #2 and ⅜-inch crowns on the bottoms of frames #1 and #3 to add strength. Lap the frame sides to the bottoms and glue and fasten with two ¼-inch carriage bolts (at "+" on plans). Set up the frames and transom on a strongback, and support the apron with the keelson before laying up chine logs and sheer clamps. Take care to align the stem on the centerline at the correct height and angle.

Make the daggerboard and rudder from 2 x 8 stock, shaped and covered with ⅜-inch plywood. Laminate three layers of ½-inch ply cut to the shape of the daggerboard handle with the bases extending down into to slots cut in the daggerboard cap (2 x 4). Securely fasten the cap to the daggerboard with adhesives and long screws. As the daggerboard is unballasted a lanyard must be used, rove through eyes on each side of the trunk cap (2 x 6) to hold it down. Make the gripe (bow skid) from a 2 x 3, and the skeg from stack-laminated 3 x 8 stock or from 2 x 8 stock sheathed with ⅜-inch plywood. Make rudder cheeks from ⅝-inch plywood and the tiller from 2 x 6 hardwood stock.

Make the two deckbeams from 2 x 4 stock, flat on the bottom, crowned ½-inch per foot. Make the breasthook from a 3 x 4. Notch the side-deck knees for the sheer clamps and deck carlins—make three pair (all different) and fasten them to the frames. Make the bitt from a 3 x 4.

Get the mainmast from a 24-foot 4 x 4, the mizzen from a 22-foot 4 x 4, and the sprits from 3 x 3 stock. Taper the spars similarly to those for

the Cedar Keys Sharpie (Figure 6-7). Make the jib boom from a 3 x 3 (finished 2½ inches tapered to 1¾ inches at the ends) and the bowsprit from a 2 x 10 (see Figure 6-9). Use double blocks on the sprit ends, a single block on the traveler aft and another fixed to the forward side of the mizzenmast for sheets. The two ends of the mizzen sheet lead to deck cleats port and starboard; the two ends of the main sheet lead through blocks port and starboard on the middle thwart aft to cleats inside the coaming, and the two ends of the jib sheet lead through deck eyes aft to deck cleats port and starboard. Thus all three sheets are double-ended and can be tended from either side of the cockpit.

Make the tumbling maststeps from 7½-inch-wide blocks 6 inches long, with ½-inch ply plates on top and on both sides. Fasten the side plates to the keelson, and use a ⅜-inch bolt for the pivot pin. Keep the pin tight so the tumbling step will receive the mast butt without falling down. Make the thwarts from 2 x 12 stock, with ½-inch ply partners under the mast thwarts. Cut ⅜-inch-square troughs under the thwarts (shown by dashed lines) and glue in ⅜-inch stainless steel all-thread with the ends protruding aft for the mast brackets and wingnuts. The plywood partners will encapsulate the all-thread. Bury nuts on the forward ends of the all-thread just inside the thwart edges. When you cut out the thwarts and partners for the masts (watch the angle of the mizzen!), save the pieces and glue/screw them to the mast brackets. Use ¼-inch x 2-inch stainless steel bar stock 12 inches long for the brackets with over-size holes drilled to fit the all-thread.

27-foot New Haven Sharpie (Round Stern)

LOA—27 feet 10 inches; beam—6 feet; draft—8¾ inches.

Of all the boats in this book, this one probably epitomizes the sharpie. I also feel that this is the most beautiful and fine-lined of all the craft, having excellent proportions and form. The model for my drawing is Figure 39 from *American Small Sailing Craft*; I did not alter the original form in any way, except for minor details of construction.

The model is a late version of the one-man, or 100-bushel boat, as they commonly appeared in the late 1880s and early '90s. According to Chapelle, the masts for these boats were spruce; they were commonly unstepped and stepped to pass under bridges. How one man did this alone is not explained; I have a little trouble imagining him just grabbing and unstepping a 27-foot mast. Apparently this was possible only in the earlier and smaller boats such as this one. In Chapter Seven, I explain using the sprit as a gin pole for stepping masts.

Chapelle states that this particular model (taken from an abandoned hull in 1932 at New Haven) represents the most highly developed type of one-man sharpie. He also notes that her stern was slightly lower than on the earlier models, giving her a better shape for yachting and racing.

I moved the after thwart forward slightly, gave the rudder a little more area on top (I found it helped on *Gato Negro*), and drew the mast at 26 feet instead of 27. I also drew the forward bulkhead at full height, instead of stopping it at the thwart—this simplifies construction, as the bulkhead is used as a design station. In conjunction with the half-bulkhead just aft, a watertight box is formed under the thwart/step which can be used as a locker, or for flotation.

The traditional craft carried only one sail, with the mast raked very slightly—only ½ degree. I drew in an optional "balance" jib, borrowed from the Chesapeake, to be used as a light-air sail. I would recommend raking the mast somewhat more, to 5 degrees, if you opt to use this sail—otherwise, the vessel will very likely have lee helm in light air. Another possibility is to shorten the mast height and shift the centerboard trunk forward until the forward post is against the forward bulkhead, effectively converting the rig to a sloop.

Because the hull is very narrow and fine, it will be very easily driven, and probably needs no alteration of rig. I would only recommend the balance jib if you live in an area of notoriously light air, or if you intend to race the boat. I also think this hull would scale up very nicely, to 50 or 60 feet, for use as an island cruising yacht. I would then rig her as a yawl, with a shorter, raked mainmast, a "stemhead" jib (on a stay), shrouds and backstay, and a moderate-sized mizzenmast with a sprit- or lug-rigged mizzen sail; or perhaps a rig resembling that of Clapham's Roslyn Yawls (see Figure 6-16).

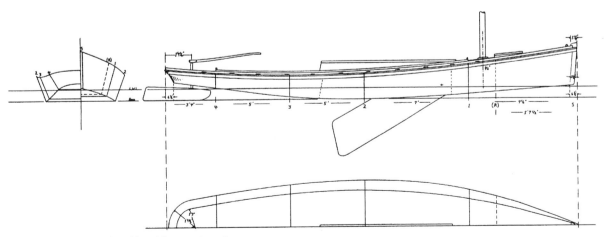

Figure 6-10. 27-foot New Haven sharpie.

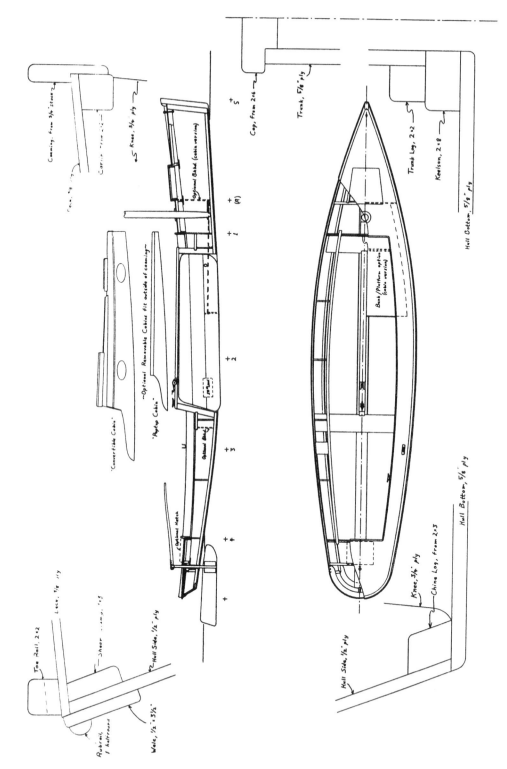

Figure 6-10 *continued.*

Construction Notes

Scantlings for longitudinals: Keelson—2 x 8; chine logs—from 2 x 3s; sheer clamps—1 x 3; carlins—2 x 2; wales—from ½ inch x 5½ inch; rubrails—1-inch half-round; coamings—¾ inch x 3½ inch (sawn from wider stock); trunk logs—2 x 2. Make the apron and stem from 4 x 4 stock; taper the outer stem to follow as closely as possible the planking angle coming into the bow, to bring the stem to a fairly fine point. Scantlings for planking: Hull sides—½-inch plywood; hull bottom—⅝-inch plywood; stern—four laminations of ⅛-inch doorskin (veneer grain vertical) with the first two layers butted to

side planks over a cleat, and the second two layers landed in a 2-inch-wide rabbet in the side planks; centerboard trunk—⅝-inch plywood with a butt block forward overlapping the pin location for strength; deck—⅜-inch plywood; hatch tops—⅜-inch plywood.

Make the side-deck support knees from ¾-inch plywood; they can be curved inboard (cut away) or run straight from the deck carlins down to the chine logs. Save your doorskin cutoffs from laminating the stern and use them to make the curved after segment of the wale; use the same rabbeting technique for the outer two layers.

Cut the deck beams from 2 x 6 stock, 2¾

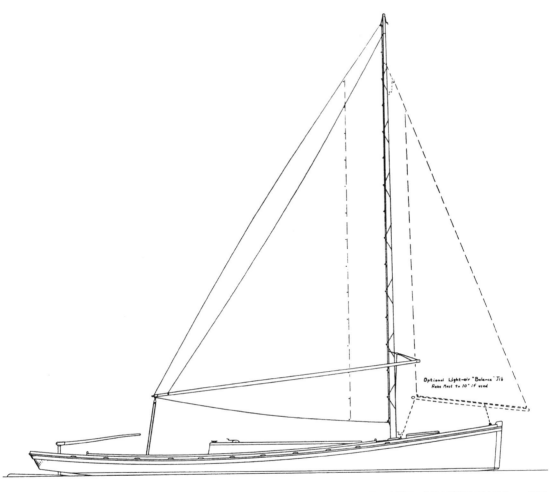

inches high at the centerline tapered to 2½ inches at the ends; the deck crown is ½ inch per foot. Make the centerboard trunk posts from 3 x 3 stock. Because the centerboard is longer than 8 feet, the ¼-inch plywood skins will have a butt joint; cut this butt at a 45-degree angle (short scarf), and locate it forward. Make the rudder from a 2 x 12 (or edge-glued 2 x 6 stock), slotted to fit over the ¼-inch x 3-inch tangs welded to the 1½-inch rudderpost, and cover with ¼-inch plywood skins. Make the thwarts from 2 x 12s and the bulkheads from ½-inch plywood.

Get the mast out of a 26-foot 6 x 6, finished to 4½ inches at the partners, 1½ inches at the head, and 3½ inches at the foot, with a 2½-inch tenon. Make the sprit from a 16-foot 3 x 3, finished to 2½ inches tapered to 1½ inches at the ends. Install a small sheave in a slot at the forward sprit end for the ⅜-inch snotter line. Use a corresponding ⅜-inch block with becket seized to the mast to make up the snotter tackle—make the line long enough to slack it for the reef-points.

If you make the "pop-top" cover, make the sides and roof from ¼-inch plywood over beams spaced every 16 inches made from 1 x 4 stock, crowned ½ inch per foot. Make the beams 2 inches high in the middle, tapered to 1 inch at the ends, and cut a notch in the middle for the beams to fit onto the centerboard trunk cap. Make small plywood knees for the after corners of the top, to stiffen the side-to-top joints. The whole top should act as a cover, fitting snugly in place, and lashed down (outside or inside) at the four corners. Use two lanyards to lift the pop-top to the sprit, with plastic, canvas, or screened sides fitted from the top to the coamings. The top should be lifted high enough to provide sitting headroom on the bunks.

If you make a convertible or permanent trunk cabin, make the sides from ½-inch plywood, and the coach roof from ¼-inch plywood. Make the beams from 1½-inch stock, cut to a crown of 1 ⅛ inches per foot, finished 2 inches at the centers tapered to 1½ inches at the ends. Build an after

bulkhead to fit snugly to the thwart, which should have a bulkhead under it to make the cabin watertight from the cockpit. Even without a self-draining cockpit, the sharpie set up in this manner, with the house firmly bolted and sealed with bedding or foam weather-stripping, should be quite safe and seaworthy enough for coastal hops alongshore in settled weather.

Set up as a pocket cruiser, the cabin should have the V-berths shown on the starboard side of the construction plan. These bunks will require elimination of the forward thwart and bulkheads. Build a strong floor timber at the front of the centerboard trunk from two layers of ¾-inch x 4½-inch stock, such that the after layers butt against the trunk and the forward layer spans it. Anchor the bunk tops firmly to the trunk; the bunks and the floor timber will take most of the side loading of the giant centerboard, and they must be *strong*. Build the new forward bulkhead (optional) at Station A.

I would add some ballast to this vessel, between 500 and 1,000 pounds, to taste (and safety). Keep the ballast in the lowest part of the hull as close to the centerline as possible, and anchor it in place with dogs, beams, floors, or lashings.

I think you will find this craft to be an exceptionally fast and weatherly sailer, and I have to say that she might be my first choice to build and own of all the sharpies in this book. I cannot imagine a finer way to gunkhole around the Florida Keys, Long Island Sound, Great South Bay, or the rich and various sounds of the Carolinas.

28-foot Munroe *Egret* Double-ended Sharpie Yacht

LOA—27 feet 10¾ inches; beam—7 feet 6 inches; draft—10 inches.

Commodore Munroe's *Egret* is truly in a class by herself. She is widely acknowledged to be the most seaworthy of all sharpies, and I personally believe she is. I won't go on too much about her here, but rather refer the reader to Chapters One and Seven, where I have given several of the Commodore's wonderful stories about her. Munroe described *Egret* as a "sharpie lifeboat," referring to her double-ended shape and seaworthy design features. *Egret*'s midship section represents a healthy cross between dory and sharpie: her narrow bottom is a little deeper—and her topsides are more flaring and higher—than the average sharpie. The design is an excellent compromise between the two types, combining properties of both. Cruising yachts designed along the lines of the *Egret* could be built in larger sizes; such vessels might be the simplest and least expensive possible seaworthy yachts.

No original lines exist for *Egret*, the originals having been lost in the hurricane of 1926. Joel White, with help from D.W. Dillon, Jon Wilson, and Maynard Bray, designed an *Egret* for *WoodenBoat* magazine, working from old photographs, descriptions, and a rumored half model. From these excellent drawings, numerous reproductions have been made, including Bill Smith's highly modified *Lahoma* in Fort Pierce, Florida. These craft perform very well, and seem to exhibit all the qualities of the original *Egret*, so we may assume that the *WoodenBoat* lines are at least an excellent interpretation of the original.

I humbly present here my own version of *Egret*, having fretted considerably over whether or not to request permission to use *WoodenBoat*'s design. Finally I decided to draw my own version largely to present the lines and construction (for plywood) in the same format used for the other designs. There are also minor differences between my interpretation of the old photographs and those of *WoodenBoat*'s highly qualified personnel. Munroe used three different rigs for *Egret*, and I chose to use the fully battened sail version. I worked from six old photographs, and, judging from rig and deck details, I assume *WoodenBoat*'s designers had access to the same or more, including the photo in Chapter One (Figure 1-17), which I suspect has not been previously published.

After sailing many times in Bill Smith's *Lahoma*, I trusted my instinct to ever so slightly flatten *Egret*'s run and lift the base of her stem. I drew the stem and stern posts nearly straight at the rabbett (joint between apron and outer stem) to simplify construction, and because I suspect the originals may have been so made. I also used the rudder shape I prefer for sharpies.

Lest I give the impression of "second guessing" *WoodenBoat*'s excellent research and designing, let me state clearly here that I consider

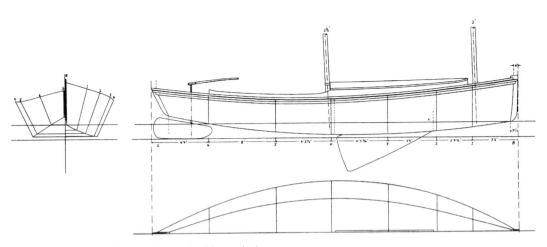

Figure 6-11. 28-foot Munroe *Egret* double-ended sharpie yacht.

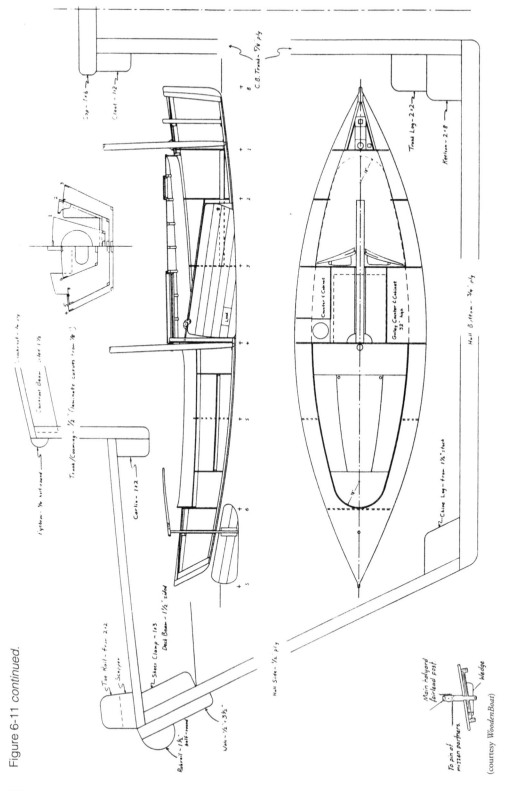

Figure 6-11 continued.

(courtesy WoodenBoat)

WoodenBoat's design to be historically more accurate than mine. I present this version strictly as my own interpretation of *Egret*, for simplified plywood construction. For those interested in historical accuracy and traditional construction, I recommend buying *WoodenBoat*'s excellent plans.

Construction Notes

Scantlings for longitudinals are: keelson—2 x 8; chine logs—from 2 x 3's (cut to parallelogram section); sheer clamps—1 x 3; trunk or coaming carlins—from 1 x 2's; deck stiffeners—1 x 8

forward and aft (¾-inch plywood OK); toe-rails—2 x 2; wales—½ inch x 3½ inch; rub rails—1½-inch half-round white oak. Make the stem apron and sternpost from 4 x 4 stock faced to 2½ inches with planking on, the stem from a 3 x 6 and the outer sternpost from a 3 x 4. Plank scantlings are: hull sides—½-inch ply; hull bottom—¾-inch ply; deck—⅜-inch ply; coaming and cabin trunk—½-inch ply with step-scarfed ⅛-inch doorskins laminated to the fore-and-aft curved sections; centerboard trunk—⅝-inch ply; coach roof—¼-inch ply.

This boat is designed to be built on six bulk-

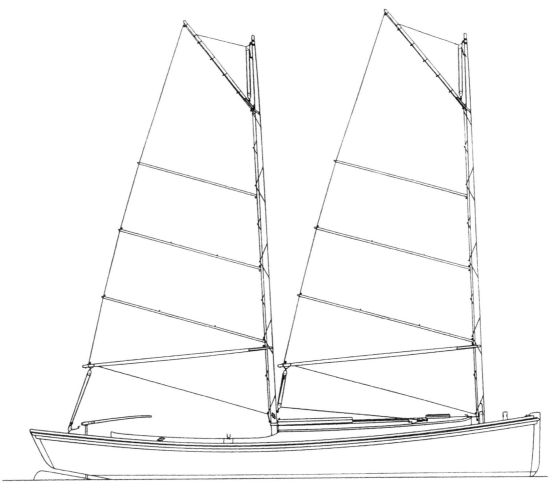

Figure 6-11 *continued.*

heads located at the design stations. Make the bulkheads from ½-inch plywood as shown in the plans. Bulkhead #2 has sides made from 1 x 2 stock fastened to plywood portions above and below so as not to interfere greatly with the bunk platform and mattress. Note that bulkhead #3 is asymmetrical: the portside vertical portion is 19 ½ inches from the centerline, whereas the starboard vertical portion is 17 inches from the centerline. The vertical edges define the location of the fore-and-aft cabinet faces, which can be ⅜-inch plywood with oval "stuff-holes" cut in them accessing shelves behind. Bulkhead #5 has port and starboard companionways, both of which are edged for drop doors, leaving a center portion to be attached to the centerboard trunk post and mast bracket. A large sliding hatch covers all. The original *Egret* had similar twin openings, but no hatch at all: you had to crawl inside on your hands and knees. In setting up, place bulkheads 1-3 aft of the design stations and place bulkheads 4-6 forward of the stations.

Deck beams are 1½-inches thick by 3 inches, tapered at the ends to 2½ inches; coach roof beams are 1½ square, tapered at the ends to 1 inch. Deck crown is ½ inch per foot; Coach roof crown is 1 inch per foot. Centerboard trunk posts are 3 x 3's; make the centerboard and rudder cores from 2 x 6 stock covered with one lamination each side of ⅜-inch ply. Take care that the finished (fabric-covered) thickness of the centerboard does not exceed 2¼ inches.

Make the curved trunk and coaming ends from ⅛-inch doorskins, step-scarfed into the trunks and coamings in the same manner described for building round sterns in Chapter Four. Use a plywood frame for the top, and reinforce the deck edge from beneath with ½-inch ply. Extend the cockpit well bulkheads down to the hull. Make hinged cockpit seats (at the coamings) to access the large stowage compartments beneath. Make the aft cockpit seat removable to access the lazarette. Please refer to Chapter Five for details on cockpit wells or to *The New Cold-Molded Boatbuilding* for more

extensive details. An optional outboard well could be installed between the after cockpit well bulkhead (which would become the outboard transom) and station six; if so, extend the tiller forward.

Make the masts from 24-foot full-dimension 4 x 4's (cut the main to 23 feet 7½ inches), finished 3⅞ inches at the partners tapered to 2½-inches at the foot (1¾-inch round mortises), 3 inches at the gaff jaws and 1¾ inches at the head. Make the sprit booms from 3 x 3 stock, finished 2¼ inches in the middle tapering to 1½ inches at the ends. Make the gaffs from 3 x 3 stock finished 2 inches in the middle tapering to 1¼inches at the ends. If you want to, make the mizzen gaff and sprit ⅛ inch smaller in all diameters—they will look more proportional.

The rudder shaft is 1¼-inch stainless steel with ¼-inch x 2-inch tangs welded on fore and aft. Make the rudder bushing from 1¼-inch pipe, glued in place with 3M 5200, Bostik, or Sikaflex.

Heavy weights, such as ballast, tanks, and batteries should be located under the bridge deck. Make access doors from the cabin, incorporating the quarter-circle steps as handles; the steps rest on cleats on the centerboard trunk. If you install an inboard engine, build a hatch above it. A horizontal-shaft lawnmower motor could be offset to one side with a belt drive to the propeller shaft. An outboard well can be made in the aft end of the cockpit, as stated above. A secure plug must be made for the well, to be used when sailing, and a partial plug (behind the lower unit) may be required when motoring to keep out back wash.

This boat will need some ballast. It can be lead, iron, water, cruising stores or some combination of these. The amount should be between 500 and 1,000 pounds, placed in the absolute lowest part of the hull possible, as close to the centerline as possible. For safe family cruising, I would suggest placing 1,000 pounds of lead under the bridge deck and at the aft end of the V-berths, or under the cabinets, as needed to trim the hull, with stores on board and motor, anchors, etc. in place. Lash or block the lead firmly so it cannot move. Bladder tanks are recommended for fresh water, located under the bridge deck, cabinets, or berths. You can also use jerry jugs under the bridge deck.

The *Egret* had minimal sitting headroom. In the original design there were no hatches, and the cockpit was open to the hull and cabin—essentially an open boat with a cuddy. If you wish to use the boat as a pocket cruiser, you may want to raise the height of the coachroof 2 to 4 inches (no more). A shelf-top stove and basin can be installed on the starboard countertop. I would use a 6-inch-deep stainless steel steam tray for the basin, set down into the countertop with fingerholes at the sides to lift the basin out and toss its contents overboard. The head can be a 5-gallon pan under a wood seat to port. If this sounds primitive, remember that it's much more sophisticated than the original was.

The rig has some unusual features. Munroe used jaws on his sprits instead of mast snotters, and seized the sprits to grommets in the sail luffs. When lowering sail, the whole works came down on deck and was lashed in place—very compact and in keeping with lifeboat priorities. He also used full-length battens in one suit of sails (but not in another). Make these from ½-inch PVC pipe with spruce or fir cores in the aft 60 percent, and flatten the ends. Use ½-inch line for halyards and sheets. Munroe used a vertical post to starboard of the mainmast with a sheave set in a slot at its head, through which he led his main halyard aft to the cockpit. In my design I lead the main halyard to a cleat on the starboard side of the mizzen mast, and the mizzen halyard to a cleat on the port side of the mast. Similarly, I have led the main sheet (by way of a return block on the coachroof forward) to a cleat on the starboard cockpit coaming and the mizzen sheet to a cleat on the port side coaming. For the halyard blocks, mainsheet block, and tack downhauls I show ⅜-inch lag-eyebolts set in the masts. Dismantle the blocks (*not aloft*) and reeve their

strops through the eyebolts, reassemble and screw the eyebolts into the masts. This eliminates the need of twist shackles. Seize twine tightly around the mastheads immediately above and below the halyard block eyebolts aloft. The gaff throat blocks are also shown permanently stropped onto eyebolts, but these cannot be lageyes as they could pull out; use standard eyebolts with large washers under the gaffs. Gaff peak and throat pennants may be rove through paired holes in the gaff-ends and jaws; sprit-boom outhauls may be likewise rove through paired holes. Make the mizzen mast band from ¼- x 1½-inch stainless steel formed around the mast and forward along each side of the centerboard trunk post and through-bolt it there with a ½-inch bolt. Place an oak saddle between the mast and post to hold the mast in its proper location.

33-foot North Carolina Sharpie
LOA—32 feet 10 inches; beam—8 feet 4 inches; draft—10 ¾ inches.

After the New Haven sharpie was introduced at Beaufort in 1874 by George C. Ives, sharpies were built locally for use all through the very shallow Carolina Sounds. The type that evolved was slightly beamier than the New Haven model, with a very raked transom stern, but it retained the fine lines and low freeboard. The Carolina sharpies carried an incredible amount of sail, and often used vertical clubs at the after sprit ends to crowd on even more canvas. In the sail plan I have drawn here, I eliminated these clubs, to make the boat safer and more manageable for family cruising. If you are a raving maniac, the way these 19th-century Carolina oystermen must have been, and want all that canvas, refer to my models for this boat: Figure 44 in *American Small Sailing Craft*, and Figures 6 and 9 in *Paper 25*.

These boats often worked in "the fierce gales that swept the Carolina Sounds in the fall and spring," and so were very able craft under adverse conditions. The Sounds are protected from the sea by continuous barrier islands, and are mostly long, narrow, shallow bodies of water. Large seas do not build up in them, but short, steep chop does, which takes a lot of power to drive through. Large sharpies with powerful sail plans and skilled handlers are probably ideally suited to this abuse, and should be sailed heeled over, as stated previously, to present the V of the leeward chine log to the chop.

I have drawn this boat as a pocket cruiser, doubting that anyone would be prone to build so large an open boat. If I am wrong, build her without the trunk: Make a low coaming in its place, eliminate the cockpit well, lower the thwart and stern sheet assembly 2 inches, and build a platform aft at waterline height for the helmsman to stand on (end the platform 2 feet from the thwart). Some of the smaller boats had a broken toerail—essentially missing a section outboard of the straight part of the coaming.

The boat is rather small inside, having only about 3 feet 6 inches headroom, and would not be a likely candidate for long-term liveaboard use. She is, however, trailerable on U.S. federal highways, having a beam of 8 feet 4 inches (8 feet 6 inches is the limit). I think the masts can be stepped by two strong adults (they were, traditionally), but a simple A-frame can be jury-rigged using the sprits for the shorthanded sailor. This is an excellent camp boat or pocket cruiser,

and I would sail her to the Bahamas in good weather.

Construction Notes

Scantlings for longitudinals: Keelson—2 x 6; chine logs—from 2 x 3s (cut to parallelogram section); sheer clamps—1 x 3; trunk or coaming carlins—from 2 x 3s; deck stiffeners—1 x 10 forward, 1 x 6 aft; toerails—2 x 3; rubrails —1½-inch half-round white oak. Make the apron from a 4 x 4, and the stem from a 4 x 6. Scantlings for planking: Hull sides—½-inch plywood; hull bottom—¾-inch plywood; transom—two laminations of ¾-inch plywood with ¾-inch perimeter cleats; deck—⅜-inch plywood; cabin trunks—¾-inch plywood; centerboard trunk—two laminations of ⅜-inch plywood or ¾-inch plywood with butt blocks at forward end, extended 3 inches forward of the pin (the trunk is longer than 8 feet); coach roof—¼-inch plywood.

Deck beams are 1½ inches thick by 3 inches, tapered at the ends to 2½ inches; coach-roof beams are 1½ x 2 inches, tapered at the ends to 1½ inches. Deck crown is ⅜ inch per foot; coach-roof crown is ¾ inch per foot. Centerboard trunk posts are 4 x 4's; make the centerboard and rudder cores from 2 x 8 stock covered with two laminations *on each side* of ⅜-inch plywood (stagger the butts on the centerboard,

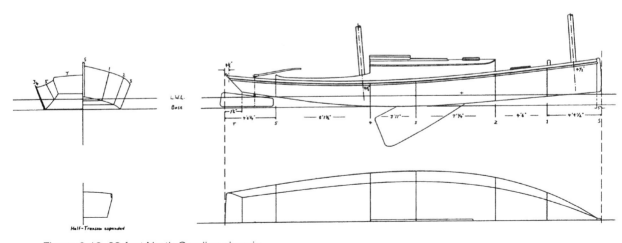

Figure 6-12. 33-foot North Carolina sharpie.

Figure 6-12 continued.

which is longer than 8 feet). Take care that the finished (fabric-covered) thickness of the centerboard does not exceed 3⅛ inches.

Make the curved trunk and coaming corners from ⅛-inch doorskins, step-scarfed into the trunks and coamings in the same manner described for building round sterns in Chapter Four. Use a plywood frame for the top, and reinforce the deck edge from beneath with ¾-inch plywood. If you build the open boat, or wish to varnish your coamings, laminate the corners from ⅛-inch solid stock or steam-bend them in place. Extend the cockpit-well bulkheads down to the hull. Curved corners are really optional here; you could make the bulkhead corners square and cut the seat tops to the curve shown. Make hinged cockpit seats (dashed lines) to access the large stowage compartments beneath, including the area just aft. Please refer to Chapter Five for details on cockpit wells, or to *The New Cold-Molded Boatbuilding* for more extensive details.

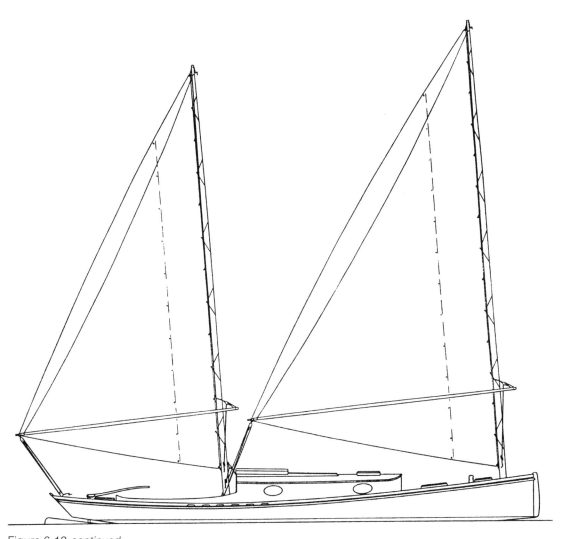

Figure 6-12 *continued.*

Make the mainmast from a 32-foot 6 x 6, finished 5½ inches at the partners to 4 inches at the step and 1½ inches at the head. Make the mizzenmast from a 30-foot 6 x 6, finished to 5 inches at the partners, tapered the same as the mainmast. Make the tenons 2½ inches in diameter; make the steps from 2 x 6's capped with ¾-inch plywood. Make the sprits from 18- and 15-foot 3 x 3 stock, finished 2½ inches in the middle tapering to 1½ inches at the ends.

The rudder shaft is 1½-inch stainless steel with ¼-inch x 3-inch tangs welded on forward and aft. Make the rudder bushing from 1½-inch pipe, glued in place with 3M 5200, Bostick, or Sikaflex.

Heavy weights, such as ballast, tanks, and batteries, should be located under the bridge deck. Make access doors from the cabin, incorporating the quarter-circle steps as handles; the steps rest on cleats on the centerboard trunk. If you install an inboard engine, build a hatch above it. A 7½-horsepower horizontal-shaft lawn mower motor could be offset to one side with a belt drive to the propeller shaft. An outboard well can be made in the after end of the cockpit, shown by the dashed lines. A secure plug must be made for the well, to be used when sailing, and a partial plug (behind the lower unit) will be required when motoring to keep out backwash.

This boat will need some ballast. This can be lead, iron, water, cruising stores, or some combination of these. The amount should be between 500 and 2,000 pounds, placed in the absolute lowest part of the hull possible, as close to the centerline as possible. For safe family cruising, I would suggest placing 1,000 pounds of lead under the bridge deck and at the after end of the V-berths (or under the cabinets) as needed to trim the hull, with stores on board and motor, anchors, etc. in place. *Lash or block the lead firmly so it cannot move!* Bladder tanks are recommended for fresh water, located under the bridge deck, settees, or berths. You can also use jerry jugs under the bridge deck.

Make the settees such that the cushion tops are at the waterline (3 inches lower than the bunk cushion tops). This will give you minimal sitting headroom. If you are tall, you may have to raise the height of the coach roof 1 inch (no more). Make the back cushions from 1-inch foam, covered and Velcroed to the seat backs. Make the seat backs from ⅜-inch plywood, with "stuff-holes" (see Chapter Five) to access stowage behind the settees.

35-foot New Haven Sharpie

LOA—35 feet 6 inches; beam—7 feet 6 inches; draft—9½ inches.

This is the quintessential sharpie, and represents the highest evolution of the type, at least in New Haven, where it all began. The big two-man sharpies really defined the sharpie, historically, and most of the other regional types may be seen as interpretations and adaptions. The 35-foot boats were also the fastest of the sharpies, and were raced very competitively, to the point where flat-out racing machines evolved from them. These big hot rods are known to have reached speeds around 20 knots, putting them nearly in a class with today's racing multihulls. It is most impressive to know that all this happened long before the invention of fiberglass, epoxy, plywood, nylon, Dacron, and carbon fiber. It almost scares me to think of how fast a 35-foot racing sharpie built with modern methods and materials would go.

As background for the model presented here, I used the four big New Haven sharpies from Chapelle's *American Small Sailing Craft*, and Figure 3 from Chapelle's *Paper 25* (see Chapter Two of this book, Figure 2-11). I tried to combine the best elements of these models to create a contemporary cruising sharpie that is completely representative of the type. She is the "queen of our fleet."

Construction Notes

Scantlings for longitudinals are: keelson—2 x 8; chine logs—from 2 x 3's; sheer clamps—2 x 4, carlins—2 x 2; wales—from ½ inch x 4 inch; rubrails—1½-inch half-round; coamings—⅝ inch, laminate curved ends from 5 layers of ⅛-inch door skin (veneer grain vertical); trunk logs—2 x 2. Make the apron from 4 x 4 and stem from 4 x 6 stock; taper the outer stem to follow as closely as possible the planking angle coming into the bow, to bring the stem face to ¾ inch. Scantlings for planking are: hull sides—⅝-inch plywood; hull bottom—1 inch: use two opposite diagonal layers of ½-inch plywood (full sheets); stern—five laminations of ⅛-inch door skin (veneer grain vertical) with first two layers butted to side planks over a cleat, second two layers landed in a 2-inch-wide rabbet in the side planks and fifth layer landed in a 1-inch rabbet; centerboard trunk—½-inch plywood with the forward 3 feet double-thickness overlapping the butt joint of the first layer by one foot; deck—⅜-inch ply; hatch tops—⅜-inch ply; coach roof—¼-inch ply. Save your doorskin cutoffs from laminating the stern and use them to make the curved aft segment of the wale (minus one layer); use the same rabbeting technique for the outer two layers.

Cut the deck beams from 2 x stock, 3½-inches high; crown is ½ inch per foot. Cut the coach roof beams from 2 x stock; 1¾ inches high at the centerline tapering to 1½ inches at the ends. Make the centerboard trunk posts from 3 x 4 stock on the flat. Because the centerboard is longer than 8 feet, the ⅜-inch plywood skins will

have a butt joint; cut this butt at a 45-degree angle (short scarf), and locate it forward. Make the rudder and centerboard core from 2 x 8 stock; slot the rudder ends to fit over the ¼-inch x 3-inch tangs welded to the 1½-inch rudder post, and cover with ⅜-inch plywood skins. Make sure the centerboard finishes out (including fabric covering) to no more than 2¼ inches. The lifting eye for the centerboard is a ¼-inch x 3-inch stainless steel plate set into a slot in the top-most plank, with a scallop cut in the plank to expose a hole in the plate for the centerboard pennant. Fasten this plate with several large screws, bolts, or pins.

Make the bulkheads, on which the hull is built, from ⅝-inch plywood. When setting the bulkheads on the strongback, place #'s 1-3 aft of the station lines and #'s 4-7 forward of station lines. Note that bulkhead #3 is open on the top and bottom to allow unimpeded traffic through the hull; during construction, connect the halves with scrap. Make a floor timber from two layers of ¾-inch ply (or use a 2 x 6) and attach it firmly to the forward centerboard trunk post.

Make mast partners and deck stiffeners from 1 x 8's or ¾-inch ply. Make ¾-inch plywood "donuts" to reinforce the deck from above; line the partners with greased rawhide or teflon. Use ¾-inch ply over the keelson plank for mast partners; make pivot rings from ⅛-inch brass plate (or Teflon) fastened to the steps and mast bases. Get the mainmast out of a 35-foot 6 x 6 (you

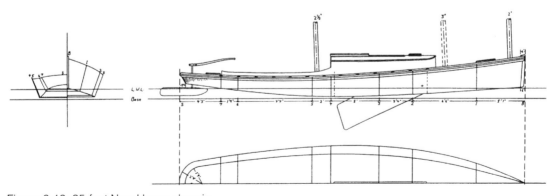

Figure 6-13. 35-foot New Haven sharpie.

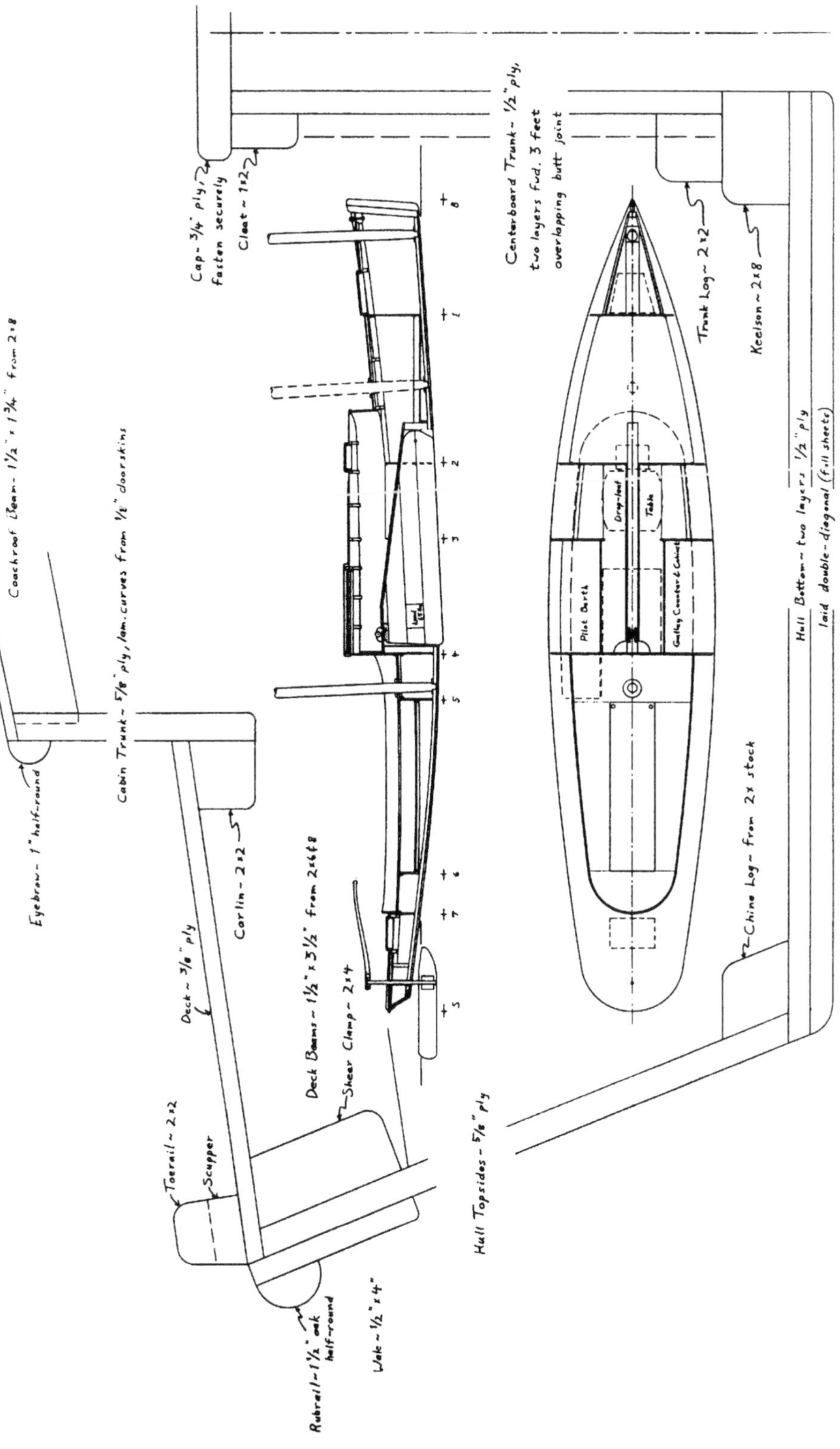

Figure 6-13 continued.

Coachroof ~ 1/4" ply

Coachroof Beam ~ 1 1/2" x 1 3/4" from 2x8

Cap ~ 3/4" ply, fasten securely

Cleat ~ 1x2

Centerboard Trunk ~ 1/2" ply, two layers fwd. 3 feet overlapping butt joint

Trunk Log ~ 2x2

Keelson ~ 2x8

Eyebrow ~ 1" half-round

Cabin Trunk ~ 5/8" ply, lam. curves from 1/8" doorskins

Carlin ~ 2x2

Deck ~ 3/8" ply

Deck Beams ~ 1 1/2" x 3 1/2" from 2x6x8

Shear Clamp ~ 2x4

Hull Topsides ~ 5/8" ply

Hull Bottom ~ two layers 1/2" ply laid double-diagonal (fill sheets)

Chine Log ~ from 2x stock

Plos Berth

Table

Dry-pack

Galley Counter & Cabinet

Toerail ~ 2x2

Scupper

Rubrail ~ 1 1/2" oak half-round

Wale ~ 1/2" x 4"

may have to laminate scarfed 2 x 6 stock), finished to 5½ inches at the partners, 1¾ inches at the head and 4¼ inches at the foot, with a 2¾-inch tenon. Get the mizzen from a 33-foot stick finished similarly, but 5¼ inches at the partners. Make the sprits from a 20-foot and an 18-foot 6-inch 3 x 3, finished to 3 inches tapered to 2 inches at the forward ends, 1½ inches aft at the shoulders and 1 inch aft. Finish the mizzen sprit 2¾ inches at the middle. Install a small sheave in a slot at the forward sprit end for the ⅜-inch snotter line. Use a corresponding ⅜-inch block

with becket seized to the mast to make up the snotter tackle—make the line long enough to slack it for the reef points. Also drop a sling down to the sprit from a rope grommet fixed to the mast by a strap eye to support the sprit. Make the sling loose so the sprit can slide forward when reefing. Use ½-inch line for the sheets and halyards.

When framing the cockpit well, extend the well-side bulkheads down to the hull. Fasten drain cleats around the coaming for the cockpit seats. If desired, an outboard well can be placed

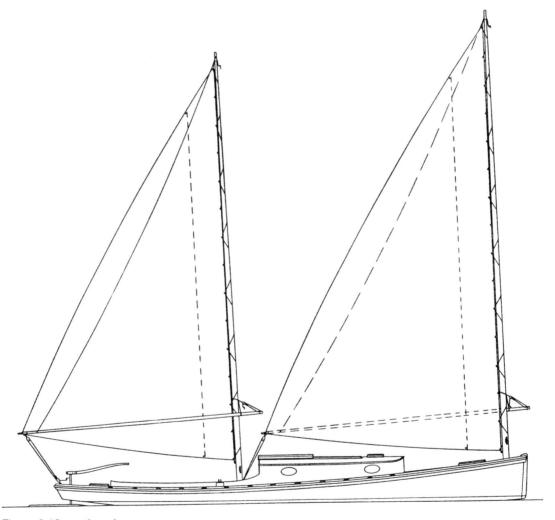

Figure 6-13 *continued*.

in the aft cockpit under what would be the stern sheets.

Ballast is essential in this vessel, between 1,000 and 2,000 pounds, to taste (and safety). Keep the ballast in the lowest part of the hull as close to the centerline as possible, and anchor it in place with dogs, beams, floors or lashings.

One last thing. If you build this sharpie, be prepared for one of the the most awesome sailing experiences of your life. Be sure to read the various accounts scattered through this book on safety and handling of these big sharpies, and make your first shakedowns in light air.

36-foot San Juan Island Double-ended Sharpie

LOA—36 feet 4 inches; beam—9 feet 10 inches; draft—1 foot 11½ inches.

This is the largest of the three known double-ended sharpie types. You can see the model I started from in Chapter One of this book, Figure 1-20, reproduced from *American Small Sailing Craft* (Figure 46). The type was used at San Juan Island in the halibut fishery there. Chapelle describes her as "a double-ended gaff-schooner sharpie of rather good model, but heavily built and ballasted and not intended for great speed." I believe the model lends itself perfectly as a modest cruising vessel for coastal waters, island hopping and extensive gunkhol-ing—there could scarcely be one better for the money, labor, and material that would go into building her. I gave the hull a slightly narrower bottom and slightly less rocker to lighten displacement, increase speed, and add flare to the topsides. I left the sheer, rig and other proportions as they were, and designed a cruising deck and interior plan. The gaff schooner sail plan of this boat makes her powerful, versatile, safe in a much wider spectrum of weather conditions than some of the marconi-rigged models, and guarantees that she will knock the socks right off everyone who sees her. There's nothing as pretty as a little gaff-rigged schooner with the right proportions, and this one has them.

Construction Notes

Longitudinal scantlings are: keelson—2 x 10; chine logs—from 2 x 4's (cut to parallelogram section); sheer clamps—2 x 3; trunk carlins—from 2 x 3's; toerails—from 2 x 6 (tapered); rub rails —from 2 x 2 white oak. Make the apron from a 4 x 6, the sternpost from a 4 x 4 and the stem from a 4 x 8. Plank scantlings are: hull sides—¾-inch ply; hull bottom—two layers of ½-inch ply (stagger butts 2 feet; grind joints hollow and tape-reinforce inside and out); deck— ½-inch ply; cabin trunks—¾-inch ply; centerboard trunk—¾-inch ply with butt blocks at forward end, extended 3-inches aft of the pin for reinforcement; coach roof—⅜-inch ply.

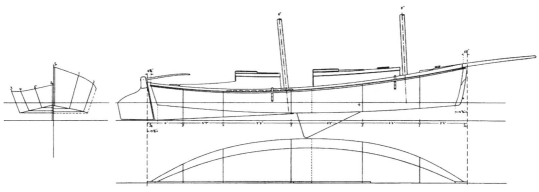

Figure 6-14. 36-foot San Juan Island double-ended sharpie.

Deck beams are 2½-inches thick by 2¾-inches, tapered at the ends to 2¼ inches; coach roof beams are 1½- x 2½-inches, tapered at the ends to 2 inches. Deck crown is ½-inch per foot; coach-roof crown is ¾-inch per foot. Centerboard trunk posts are 4 x 4's; make the centerboard and rudder cores from 2 x 8 stock covered with two laminations each side of ⅜-inch ply (stagger the butts on the centerboard, which is longer than 8 feet). Take care that the finished (fabric-covered) thickness of the centerboard does not exceed 3⅛ inches. Make the skeg and outer sternpost from 4 x 8 stock. Laminate the curved cockpit coamings from three layers of ¼-inch plywood.

Extend the cockpit well bulkheads down to the hull. Make hinged cockpit seats (dashed lines) to access the large stowage compartments beneath. Please refer to Chapter Five for details on cockpit wells or to *The New Cold-Molded Boatbuilding* for more extensive details. A small diesel may be installed under the bridge deck if so desired; locate the transmission under the cockpit well. This will necessitate bulkheading the forward end of the bridge deck area and adding access hatches for the diesel compartment to the bridge deck and well (to get at the transmission and stuffing box). Another option is to eliminate the bridge deck, extending the fore-and-aft cockpit well bulkheads forward to the trunk cabin, and build a box to cover the diesel. Make the forward end of the box open and butt it to the aft trunk bulkhead, which would extend from coach roof to hull. An outboard motor would be a simpler option, mounted on a stout bracket fixed to the hull aft. I would make a wood yoke from a 4 x 6 that spans the deck just aft of the lazarette hatch, cut to the contour of

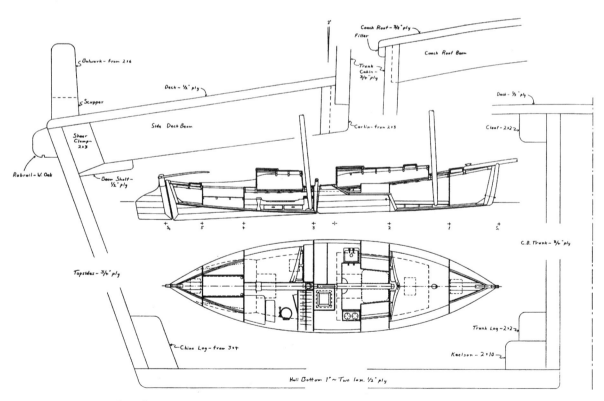

Figure 6-14 *continued.*

the deck and passing through the log rails to extend outboard 12 inches on both sides. This would allow a long-shaft "sailboat motor" such as a Yamaha or Honda to be carried on either side of the stern. You could thereby even carry twin outboards if you anticipate long stretches of river or waterway cruising.

Make the mainmast from a 28-foot 6 x 6 cut to 26 feet 9½ inches; make the foremast from a 26-foot 6 x 6 cut to 25 feet 9 inches. Diameters for both masts are 6 inches at the partners tapered to 4 inches at the foot (make the tenons 3 inches by 2 inches deep), 5 inches at the gaff jaws, 3½ inches at the truck shoulder, 3 inches at the truck (make the stainless steel trucks from 2-inch segments of 3-inch I.D. pipe with double-welded ¼ inch x 1½ inch tangs) and 3 inches at the head. Make the maststeps from 4 x 8's capped with ¾-inch ply. Make the booms from 4 x 4's and the gaffs from 3 x 3's. Taper the booms from 3½ inches in the middle to 2½ inches at the ends; taper the gaffs from 2½ inches in the middle to 1¾ inches at the ends. Lengths are:

fore boom—12 feet 11 inches; main boom—18 feet; fore gaff—12 feet; main gaff—12 feet. Make the bowsprit from three laminations of 2 x 12, weighted between two sawhorses during curing to achieve the curve shown. Taper the bowsprit to 3 inches thick by 4 inches wide at the outer end, and 4 inches thick by 8 inches wide at the inner end. Leave the sprit 11½ inches wide at the stem head, and mortise the top of the stem into the bottom of the sprit. Through-bolt the sprit to the deck with 6⅜-inch bolts; make reinforcing straps from ⅛- x 1½-inch flat stock to span each pair of bolts under the deck. Countersink and bung the bolt heads. Make the sprit iron from ¼-inch x 2-inch flat stock wrapped around the end of the sprit and pass a ½-inch eyebolt through the strap and sprit end. Use an eye nut under this fitting to attach the upper bobstay end, and use a long ½-inch eyebolt to pierce the stem for the lower end of the bobstay. Make the jib club from a 3 x 3 10 feet 6 inches long. Taper it from 2½ inches in the middle to 1¾ inches at the ends.

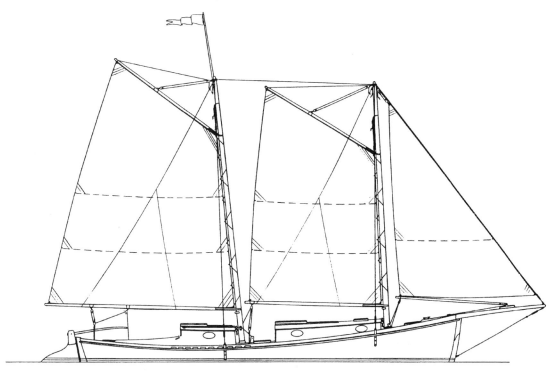

Make the jib club car and tracks as follows: form the two parallel tracks from ½-inch round stock. Bend the ends 90 degrees, weld heavy washers to lie on the bowsprit, and thread the ends such that the nuts and washers will be recessed in the sprit bottom. Make the car from two 3-inch segments of ½-inch pipe welded to a 3-inch-square piece of ⅜-inch flat stock. Make the club straps from ¼-inch x 1½-inch flat stock, 12 inches long, welded to a rectangular slug 1 inch aft of the forward end with a 5/16-inch gap between them. The aft ends of the straps are screwed to the forward end of the club, which is tapered and flattened to fit between the straps; the forward ends are drilled for a ⅜-inch bolt, forming a jaw (the straps are bent at the slug so the sides are parallel forward and tapered apart aft). Weld a ¼-inch x 1-inch tang to a 2-inch segment of ½-inch pipe to form the gooseneck. Drill the tang for the ⅜-inch bolt to fit the club-strap jaw, and bolt the pipe to the car platform with a ½-inch bolt. Before bending the round stock for the tracks, slide the car in place.

Make the chainplates from ⅜-inch x 1½-inch flat stock, bolted to the hull with three ⅜-inch flathead machine screws. Add a ¾-inch plywood backing block inside the hull, and a ⅛-inch x 1½-inch backing plate for the nuts. Use lock nuts. Make the boom travelers from ⅝-inch round stock. Bend the ends to pass through the deck, and weld heavy washers above the deck, to the correct angle to account for crown. Thread the ends for ⅝-inch locknuts. Back up the deck from underneath as for chainplates. Because the travelers are unusually high (to clear the tiller and centerboard pennant), weld 10-inch sections of ½-inch round stock diagonally inside the corners of the travelers to reinforce them; these will also act as stops. Make the fore traveler 12 inches high (above deck) and the main traveler 14 inches high. The jib won't need a traveler: fix two padeyes to the deck (reinforced underneath) 12 inches forward of the cabin corners. Splice the sheet end to the port padeye and shackle a block to the starboard one; fairlead the

sheet back to a cleat on the cockpit coaming.

Ballast can be lead, iron, water, cruising stores, or some combination of these. The total amount should be about 2,500 pounds, placed in the absolute lowest part of the hull and as close to the centerline as possible. For safe family cruising, I would suggest placing 1,500 pounds of lead under the center deck on each side of the centerboard trunk. Use more as needed to trim the hull, with stores on board and motor, anchors, etc., in place. Lash or block the lead firmly so it cannot move. Bladder tanks are recommended for fresh water, located under the center deck, bridge deck, settees or berths.

A large ice box is shown in the plan, accessed through the center deck. Make the liner from ¼-inch plywood and finish it with epoxy and polyester cloth. Make an insulated box-top hatch to cover the deck opening. Pour closed-cell polyurethane foam in place around the liner before decking over. *Lead ballast must be in place first.* The cook, standing in the open hatch, will find the ice hold convenient to use since the deck is nearly countertop height. This ice hold will keep block ice for a good two weeks in the tropics, and will hold all the perishable food and drink a crew of six will need for that period.

Make the settee and berth cushions from 3-inch foam. Make the back cushions from 1-inch foam, covered and Velcroed to the seat backs. Make the seat backs from ⅜-inch ply, with "stuff-holes" to access stowage behind the settees.

After studying my final drawings, I would recommend moving the galley countertops inboard about 6 to 8 inches, both to make them easier to reach and to keep the sink from filling on the starboard tack. Note that in any case the sink through-hull should be closed when not in use and when sailing for safety. The cook should be able to comfortably work the galley while sitting on the centerboard trunk.

Sheets and halyards are ½-inch; topping lifts are ⅜-inch; lazyjacks (spliced into the lifts) are ¼-inch. The jib downhaul and mast lacings are ¼-inch. Reef tackle is ⅜-inch. Use ½-inch nylon and ⁵⁄₁₆-inch chain for the anchor rodes. I would recommend bow rollers on each side of the bow sprit.

36-foot Ohio Pound-Net Boat (Great Lakes Sharpie)

LOA—35 feet 8 inches; beam—10 feet 2 inches; draft—14 inches.

This is one of my favorite sharpie models, primarily for the hull, but the rig certainly is outrageous and unique. While not as seaworthy as the preceding design, this model is about as large and heavy, and will make an excellent small cruiser for the same kind of use. She will be fast, especially off the wind, and her huge sail plan will drive her past all other cruising sailboats as if they were standing still. Her weak point will be driving to windward in a sea or steep chop, and care must be taken in bringing her about in those conditions, as her large, very raked rudder will stop her dead in the water if put over too fast or too hard (see Chapelle's comments in Chapter One). The model is derived from Figures 47 and 48 of *American Small Sailing Craft*.

The rig is unique among sharpies. It was the rig of choice of the Great Lakes fishermen, particularly in Ohio, for their pound-net boats, regardless of hull type. The battens are doubled oak strips, similar to those used by the Cedar Keys sharpies, riveted or bolted together on both sides of the sail. The effect is that of a gaff-rigger with topsails set. I would advise caution using this rig, as it carries, in effect, its light-air sails all the time. The reefs shown are deep, and I expect they were used more frequently than those on other rigs. The hull is quite beamy for a sharpie, and fairly deep of body, indicating that the vessels were heavy and stiff, and stood up to their sails. I have modified the model very slightly to make her a yacht, by altering the amount of rocker in the bottom, depth of stern, and center of buoyancy, for the reasons given at the beginning of this chapter. I tamed her rig very slightly, in the interest of safety, and because her weight and contents are considerably lighter than those of the original. The vessel is still very powerful, and when built with modern materials and methods, will undoubtedly out perform her ancestor. She will need substantial ballast to bring her down to her lines, and a skeg might be advisable for cruising (I would build her without it and consider adding it later). I would start with 1,500 pounds of ballast, and expect that you might easily need twice that weight. If the boat is cruised, water tanks will provide some ballast, along with engine, batteries and other gear.

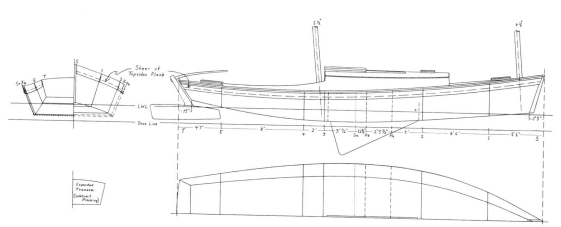

Figure 6-15. 36-foot Ohio pound-net boat (Great Lakes sharpie).

Construction Notes

Longitudinal scantlings are: keelson—2 x 8; chine logs—from 2 x 4's (cut to parallelogram section); sheer clamps—1 x 6; beam shelves—2 x 2; trunk carlins—from 2 x 3's; toe rails—from 2 x 3's; rub rails—1½-inch white oak. Make the apron from a 4 x 4 (face to 2⅛-inches before planking), and the stem from a 4 x 6 (face width ¾-inch). Plank scantlings are: hull sides—⅝-inch ply; hull bottom—two layers of ⅝-inch ply (lay full sheets athwartship or double diagonal); grind joints hollow and tape-reinforce inside and out); deck—½-inch ply; cabin trunks—⅝-inch ply; centerboard trunk—⅝-inch ply doubled forward and extended 6 inches aft of the butt joint for the inner layer; coach roof—⅜-inch ply.

Deck beams are 1½ inches thick by 3½ inches high; coach-roof beams are 1½- x 2½ inches. Deck crown is ½-inch per foot; coach-roof crown is ¾ inch per foot. Centerboard trunk posts are 4 x 4's; make the centerboard and rudder cores from 2 x 10 stock; cover the centerboard with two layers each side of ⅜-inch ply (stagger the butts); cover the rudder with ½-inch ply. Take care that the finished (fabric-covered) thickness of the centerboard does not exceed 3⅛ inches. Make the rudderpost from 2 x 8 hardwood and the tiller cheeks from ⅝-inch ply.

Extend the cockpit well bulkheads down to the hull. Make hinged cockpit seats (dashed lines) to access the large stowage compartments beneath. Please refer to Chapter Five for details on cockpit wells or to *The New Cold-Molded Boatbuilding* for more extensive details. A small diesel may be installed at the forward end of the cockpit. This will require construction of a box cover extending aft of the bridge deck, and will necessitate bulkheading the forward end of the bridge deck

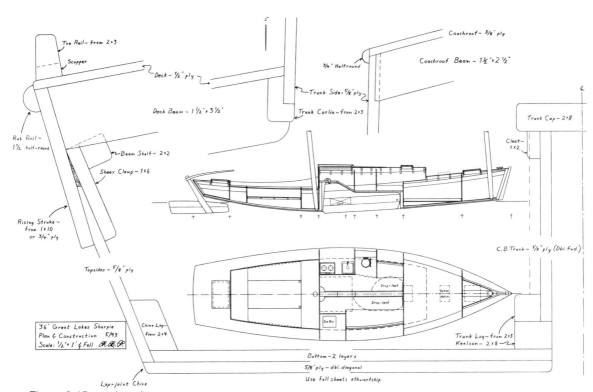

Figure 6-15 *continued.*

area and adding an access hatch for the diesel compartment to the bridge deck. An outboard well can be made at the aft end of the cockpit, but a much longer tiller will be required as well as a different main-sheet fall. The last option is to mount an outboard bracket on the transom. In any case, I would add oarlock blocks and sockets on the outsides of the cockpit coamings so that you can row sitting on the bridge deck.

Make the mainmast 42 feet; make the foremast 40 feet. I would laminate the masts from full-dimension 3 x 6 clear, heart, vertical-grain Douglas-fir. Scarf the mast halves from the longest planks you can find; make the scarfs 30 inches long and stagger them side to side at least

4 feet apart. Cut V-shaped troughs in your finished halves with a circular saw; make these cuts 1½ inches on each face such that you will have 1½ inch square hollows inside your finished masts. Taper these hollows smaller aloft, and terminate them 4 feet from the mast heads and 3 feet above the mast partners. To do this: lay out the cuts with battens on each side of a center-line such that they taper together at the above-named places, and adjust the depth of your circular saw as you make the cuts from zero to 1½ inches and back to zero. Practice on a piece of scrap first. The hollow masts will be stronger and lighter than solid ones. Another option is to build the hollow hexagonal masts described in

The New Cold-Molded Boatbuilding. Taper the mainmast as follows: 3 inches at the tenon; 4 inches at the base; 6 inches at the partners; 5 inches at the "gaff" batten; 2½ inches at the halyard sheave; 1¾ inches above the shoulder (the topping lift spliced eye rides here); 1½ inches at the top. Make the mizzenmast ⅛ inch smaller at all points except below deck. Cut the mast mortises (3-inch) into the keelson plank and lay a ⅝-inch plywood cap, cut to capture the 4-inch mast base.

Make the booms from 4 x 4s, 18 feet and 16 feet. Taper the main boom from 3½ inches in the middle to 2½ inches at the ends; taper the mizzen boom from 3¼ inches in the middle to 2¼ inches at the ends.

Make the mizzen boom traveler from ½-inch round stock. Bend the ends to pass through the deck, and weld heavy washers above the deck, to the correct angle to account for crown. Thread the ends for ½-inch locknuts. Back up the deck from underneath with ⅝-inch ply and fender washers. The main sheets are doubled (one each side) to blocks mounted on each side of the coach roof. Fasten diamond padeyes to ⅝-inch ply backup blocks spanning the distance between the two adjacent coachroof beams using ¼-inch stainless steel flathead machine screws (four each). You can use this twin-sheet arrangement to vang the mainsail flat (take out the twist), or to spill wind in a puff. This is how the original Ohio sharpies were rigged.

Make the "gaff" battens from ½ x 1½-inch white oak. Plane a little taper (take off about ⅛ inch) into the forward third of the battens to build some draft control into the sail. Rivet or through-bolt the battens to both sides of the sails using large roves or washers to prevent splitting. Seize the forward ends of the battens to mast hoops or parrel beads (wooden beads strung on #6 copper wire) by means of grommets installed in the sail luff immediately above and below the batten ends. As repulsive as it may sound, ideal mast hoops can be made from 8-inch PVC pipe

cut into 2-inch rings—sand the edges so they don't chafe masts or sails.

Ballast can be lead, iron, water, cruising stores or some combination of these. The total amount should be about 2,500 pounds, placed in the absolute lowest part of the hull possible, as close to the centerline as possible. For safe family cruising, I would suggest placing 1,500 pounds of lead under the aft end of the double berth and under the bridge deck. Use more as needed to trim the hull, with stores on board and motor, anchors, etc., in place. Lash or block the lead firmly so it cannot move. Bladder tanks are recommended for fresh water, located under the cockpit well, bridge deck, settees or berths.

Make the settee and berth cushions from 3-inch foam. Make the back cushions from 1-inch foam, covered and Velcroed to the seat backs. Make the seat backs from ⅜-inch ply, with "stuff-holes" to access stowage behind the settees.

Sheets and halyards are ½-inch; topping lifts are ⅜-inch. The mast lacings are ¼-inch. Reef tackle is ⅜-inch. Use ½-inch nylon and ⁵⁄₁₆-inch chain for the anchor rodes. Make the ½-inch centerboard pennant off to a cleat on the mizzen mast. I would recommend devising a way to hold the masts in the boat if you plan to sail offshore. This may be accomplished by driving wedges around the partners or screwing lag-eye bolts into the masts and keelson and tying them tightly together. Sharpies will "snap roll" in short beam seas, creating enough centripetal force to literally throw their masts out. I don't see this as a potential problem in any of the other boats but this one.

38-foot Clapham Nonpareil Sharpie Yacht
LOA—38 feet; beam—8 feet 8 inches; draft—2 feet 1 inch.

This is Thomas Clapham's Roslyn yawl *Minocqua*. As explained near the end of Chapter One, Clapham developed the Nonpareil sharpie in the late 19th century in Roslyn, Long Island,

New York. The drawing I have traced is from *Yachting* magazine, December 1938.

Minocqua has classic sharpie form and proportions with a deadrise, or V bottom, and an outside keel with integrated iron ballast. Another interesting feature of the design is that two possible centerboard alternatives are shown: one for use with the outside ballast keel, and the other (in dashed lines) for hulls with no keel or shoe, using solely inside ballast.

Evidently no detailed plans remain for *Minocqua*. I have been communicating with Mr. Gordon Hurley (in possesion of Clapham's surviving work), who supplied the excellent photograph of *Minocqua* in Chapter One (Figure 1-21). Judging by the drawing style, I am certain that the *Yachting* plan was made by Chapelle, and that it and possibly others may still exist in his estate or in the Library of Congress collection.

I have reproduced the plan of *Minocqua* as faithfully as I could, knowing that the small, aging drawings from a 55-year-old magazine, consequently enlarged on a photocopier and traced, can only be a close approximation of the originals. This notwithstanding, I feel that the drawings shown here are good, and would yield a vessel of unique quality and ability, and I would not hesitate to build from them. They represent the highest evolution of the sharpie type, catching it just as it evolved into the modern V-bottomed craft of the 20th century. None of the vessels presented in this book is intended for museum-quality historical replicas—they are intended to produce practical, economical, and beautiful sharpies for amateur builders to build, sail, and enjoy. I present these drawings of *Minocqua* in that same spirit.

The *Yachting* article was written by Clapham's son, who had considerable experience sailing his father's yachts as well as a thorough understanding of design, construction, and handling of sailing vessels. The younger Clapham said the following about his father's designs:

If so good a yacht as, say, *Ducat* or *Minocqua* can be produced at a greatly reduced cost as compared with the conventional type, it seems too bad to have such a worth while model forgotten. Knowing how thoroughly my father worked to develop the sharpie type of yacht to bring it as near to perfection as possible, and having helped to build and sail them, both as a boy and also when much older, I doubt that even today *Ducat* and *Minocqua* could be much improved upon for a safe, fast and comfortable cruising yacht, particularly when low cost of construction is an important item. I do not know of any model easier or less costly to build.

I heartily agree with this statement, and feel that it is even more true today than in 1938. Frameless construction, modern adhesives, deck screws and plywood make construction of sharpies, including V-bottomed Nonpareil models like this one, about as easy as boatbuilding is ever likely to get.

As quoted in Chapter One, Clapham designed the Roslyn yawl rig for singlehanded sailing. I like the rig, and feel it is well adapted to the sharpie hull in particular (it will not work so well on heavier hulls or beamier, deeper shapes). *Minocqua* is well within the means of the home builder, and with outside ballast she probably is the most seaworthy of all sharpies, on par with Munroe's *Egret*.

In 1911, Thomas F. Day, founder, editor, and publisher of *The Rudder*, America's first true yachting magazine, sailed a 25-foot, gaff-rigged yawl, *Sea Bird*, across the Atlantic. *Sea Bird* had a hard-chined, V-bottomed hull which can be seen as a direct descendant of *Minocqua* and the Nonpareil sharpies. *Sea Bird* was designed and built with a centerboard, which was later removed and replaced by a keel. T. F. Day initiated the design, which then went to an eminent naval architect of the time, Charles D. Mower. But the most fascinating thing for us is that the plans were then submitted to none other than Larry Huntington of Long Island, to be cri-

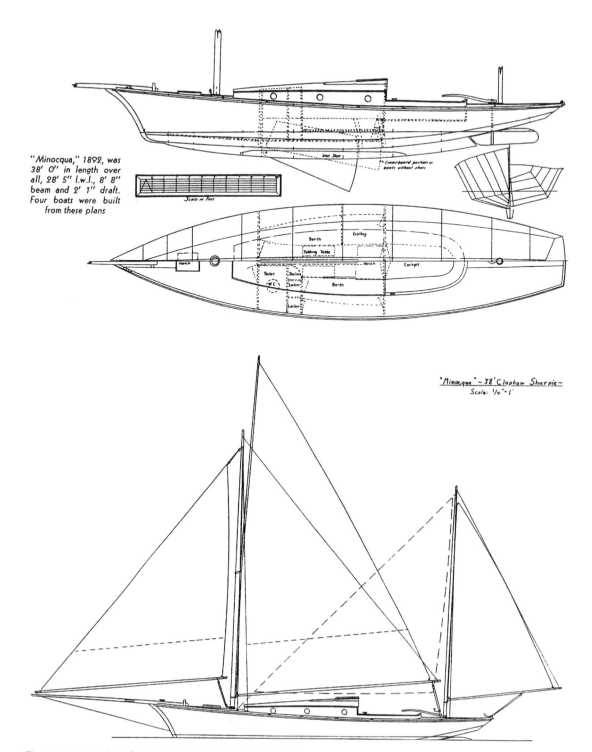

"Minocqua," 1892, was 38' 0" in length over all, 28' 5" l.w.l., 8' 8" beam and 2' 1" draft. Four boats were built from these plans

Scale in Feet

Berth   Galley

Folding Table

Hatch   Cockpit

Toilet

Locker   Berth

Locker

Hatch

Iron Shoe

Centerboard position in boats without shoes

"Minocqua" ~ 38' Clapham Sharpie~
Scale: 1/4" = 1'

Figure 6-16. 38-foot Clapham Nonpareil sharpie yacht.

tiqued and modified by him. Huntington, lest you have forgotten, was a contemporary of Clapham, who also designed and built modified sharpies with both arc and V bottoms. Huntington's suggestions were incorporated into the design, whereupon he developed the construction details and specifications and built the boat.

I mention this to illustrate that a direct descendent of the Nonpareil sharpie, and a very close one at that, with a rig similar to *Minocqua*'s, crossed the Atlantic Ocean in 1911. The trip was a somewhat difficult one due to atypical weather that year, and the little yawl did incredibly well. In Day's words: "If the voyage of *Sea Bird* has accomplished nothing else, it has done much to prove that size has nothing to do with a vessel's seaworthiness...." As a result of this voyage, home builders built and sailed many replicas of *Sea Bird*, new designs were made and sailed based on her model, and the survivors are still cruised extensively today (in the late 1970s, three friends of mine sailed a *Sea Bird* yawl from Half Moon Bay, California, to Hawaii and back).

For extensive long-range cruising, I would alter *Minocqua*'s headsail arrangement. Her rig is plainly intended for sailing Long Island waters, where reefing that huge jib might be practicable. That long bowsprit should also be clipped a little for a cruiser, though I would retain the self-tending boomed jib. In practice, reef nettles would not be tied in all the way out to the tack of that sail, and a permanent reef tack downhaul would be left roved. When hauled down to the reefpoints (you must slack the clew outhaul first), the reef clew would be made off to the boom (I would use a pair of thumb cleats on each side of the boom to tie off around), and a few reef nettles tied around the boom, as can be safely reached. The other alternative is modern roller reefing.

I have not included construction drawings or construction notes for *Minocqua* because of space limitations. Any reader interested in building this vessel should contact me at Parker Marine Enterprises for full construction plans.

CHAPTER 7
SAILING, HANDLING, AND MAINTENANCE

In the 19th century, long before the development of marine engines, men's livelihoods and very lives depended on the performance of their craft. They could not motor home in a calm, motor off a lee shore, or arrange their schedules to their own desires. Departures and arrivals were primarily dictated by the tides and wind, and activities were very attuned to the cycles of nature. Commercial fishing craft were highly evolved in each locality to perform ultimately under local conditions, and work practices were likewise shaped by seasonal demands of commerce and the availability of fish.

Sharpies are not typical of other traditional or contemporary sailing craft. They occupy a unique niche both in history and in the world of sailing. Sharpies are fast, responsive, and generally require more skill and attention than many other craft. This is less true of the skiffs—sharpies under 20 feet in length—than for the larger boats, some of which may be considered radical.

Sharpies performed best heeled over to present their chine to the water when driving to windward, and as upright as possible when running off the wind, when the hulls would plane to very high speeds. This is why their proportions and shapes are so critical. They also had to perform well both unladen and heavily laden—a real design challenge.

Masts and Rigging

Howard Chapelle was well educated in the handling practices of sharpies; the following dramatic descriptions (the first paragraph is from *American Sailing Craft*, the second from *American Small Sailing Craft*) vividly illustrate just how unique sharpies are in their handling. *These valuable insights must be thoroughly understood for their critical educational value by those of us who sail sharpies today:*

> The two-masted sharpie, of the New Haven type, is sailed like a centerboard sloop with a large jib, the foresail taking the place of the jib. In strong breezes it is best to ease a sharpie by slacking the fore sheet, rather than by the sudden easing of the helm, as the stern slews around so fast on the helm that water may come aboard or the boat may trip and capsize. In careful hands there is no danger, however. Heavy rigs, well stayed, make the small sharpie unsafe. The working sharpies will be dismasted before they can capsize, which is one of the reasons why no shrouds are used. Their light, limber spars permit the wind to spill out when the boat is heavily pressed. The whip of these spars seems to help their sailing, as is the case with so many light hulls.
>
> The two-masted sharpies were always built with three mast steps....In summer weather the two masts were carried; in fall, winter and spring,

one mast was carried.... In strong winds the helm was never put down without slacking the fore sheet, as the stern might go under and trip the boat, causing her to capsize. Due to the lack of a skeg, and the powerful turning effect of the balanced rudder used in these boats, they would turn in a very short radius, in fact under certain conditions in their own length. The working sharpie, with two sails, was fast, handy, and surprisingly seaworthy, but required a skillful hand at the helm.

Please note that spar proportions and flexibility, as well as the absence of shrouds, are critical to safety; avoid any urge to alter these factors in your own sharpie. Aluminum masts, in particular, could pose a danger, whereas carbon-fiber masts should not, as long as they are as flexible as traditional wooden spars.

Chapelle wrote that "it was possible for a strong and active man to shift the masts from one step to the other afloat...." I have done this on my small sharpies, and am filled with wonder at the thought of 19th-century fishermen handling the 27-foot spars of the 28-foot New Haven craft. Yet they evidently did so, somewhat routinely, to get under bridges. For those of us who are not the "iron men" of old, I would recommend using your sprit as a "gin pole" to step and unstep large masts: Tie the middle of a line to the after end of your sprit so that the two ends of the line are long enough to reach some points aft and outboard of the mast partners, such as spring-line cleats or scuppers in the toerails. Tie the topping lift forward (leaving the end tied to the sprit) to a point near the stemhead—a cleat, bitt, bowsprit, towing ring, or painter. If you don't have a topping lift, tie the painter to the sprit end. Step the forward end of the sprit just forward of or just beside the mast partner. When you set up the three "stays," keep the gin pole perpendicular to the deck. It helps to place a rubber or carpet pad under the pole end to keep it from slipping or getting scratched. If for some

reason the pole meets the deck at an angle, tie a line or lines to it, going uphill, to keep it from kicking out under load. Use your mainsheet tackle to hoist the mast to the sprit end. Take a length of rope about 6 feet long, pass one end through the strop of your sheet block, double the line, and secure it to the mast with a series of tight clove hitches. Your lifting point on the mast must be low enough to allow the foot of the mast to enter the hole in the deck, although you can lift the mast up slightly to achieve this. It won't much matter if the lifting point leaves the mast a little top-heavy—you will be able to maneuver it because the tackle will have most of the weight. Lift her up, get the mast in the hole, and lower away gently, guiding the mast tenon to the step mortise. You may have to shimmy up the mast a few feet on big sharpies to retrieve the sling and block.

Rudder Options

Rudder types played an interesting role in handling, as did the presence or absence of a skeg. The vertical-shaft counterbalanced rudder of the New Haven boats required a whole different manner of handling than the transom-hung counterbalanced rudder of the Great Lakes boats, as described by Chapelle in *American Small Sailing Craft*:

> The weight carried by the Lake sharpies was probably great enough to overcome the drag of the balanced rudder, set at so sharp a rake. In a light sharpie, such a rudder put over hard would make an ideal brake, rather than a steering fin. The balance rudder must be put over slowly, in any case, but when the post is on a rake the greatest caution is required in handling it in light weather or the boat will go into irons.

I found that the traditional horizontal-plank sharpie rudders are awkward at best, as steering devices. Modern rudders on shoal-draft boats are generally of higher-aspect ratio (they stick down farther). Typically they have a blade set between cheeks on a pivot pin, much like a centerboard in a trunk. If you want to modify your rudder to a modern type, it must "kick up" like the type I have described, or you will lose your shoal-water and beaching abilities. There is also no way to easily counterbalance a kick-up rudder, other than to hinge the after part of the blade between the plywood sides of the forward part (see Figure 7-1b). A shock cord, or bungee cord, is typically used to hold the blade down, yet allow it to kick up upon hitting bottom.

What I have been doing is adding a shallow triangular segment above the after part of the rudder (Figure 7-1a), to increase its area. This works either with the rudder all the way up (the triangle makes use of the stern wave), or with the rudder lowered, in those shaft-hung rudders with adjustable pin holes. You may recall an earlier description of this: All the New Haven boats had holes and pins in the rudder shaft to allow the rudder to be lowered in deep water. This is particularly vital in seas or chop when the boat is moving slowly—under such circumstances the rudder may lift clear of the water as the boat pitches, losing steerage. I used these holes and pins in *Gato Negro*, which has a New Haven–type rudder, and found the arrangement effective even in the steep wind chop of Hawk Channel along the Florida Keys. Finally, keep in mind Chapelle's warning about putting the rudder over too hard or fast—disaster can result.

Skegs and Centerboards

Besides allowing the wind to spill, the absence of shrouds also played a unique role in how the oyster-tonging sharpies were handled on the oyster beds. Chapelle wrote in *Paper 25*:

> Because there was no standing rigging and the masts revolved, the sheets could be let go when the boat was running downwind, so that the sails would swing forward. In this way the power of the rig could be reduced without the bother of

reefing or furling. Sometimes, when the wind was light, tonging was performed while the boat drifted slowly downwind with sails fluttering. The tonger, standing on the side deck or on the stern, could tong or "nip" oysters from a thin bed without having to pole or row the sharpie.

The utility of mast placement in the big New Haven sharpies enabled the rig and hull to balance under different seasonal conditions. This paragraph, also from *Paper 25*, illustrates how the centerboard and absence of a skeg were used to maneuver the boats:

> The unstayed masts of the sharpie were flexible and in heavy weather spilled some wind, relieving the heeling moment of the sails to some degree. In summer the 35- to 36-foot boats carried both masts, but in winter, or in squally weather, it was usual to leave the mainmast [after mast] ashore and step the foremast in the hole just forward of the bulkhead at the centerboard case,

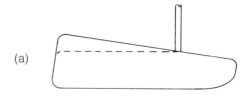

(a)

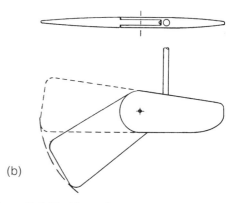

(b)

Figure 7-1. Rudder options.

thereby balancing the rig in relation to the centerboard. New Haven sharpies usually had excellent balance, and tongers could sail them into a slip, drop the board so that it touched bottom, and, using the large rudders, bring the boats into the wind by spinning them almost within their length. This could be done because there was no skeg. When sharpies had skegs, as they did in some localities, they were not so sensitive as the New Haven boats. If a sharpie had a skeg, it was possible to use one sail without shifting the mast, but at a great sacrifice in general maneuverability.

You can see the two schools of thought on skegs, and how they affected performance. Another factor involving skegs is performance off the wind, and this particularly affects yachts: Vessels with skegs will have better *directional stability*—they will track straighter with less attention to the helm—whereas vessels without skegs will be more responsive, slightly faster (less wetted surface), and considerably more demanding of attention on the helm. Hence, skegs benefit cruisers and compromise flat-out racers.

The centerboard is a very useful device, but it must be understood. In general, the board is left down when beating to windward, is left down only partially (perhaps 25 percent) when reaching, and is pulled all the way up (or nearly so) when running. The board must be down a little to provide steerage, particularly under power, or when rowing with the mast(s) in place. In very shallow water, it is common to drop the board right into the bottom to obtain steerage. This is obviously hard on the board, and you can see why it must be strong and well able to withstand abrasion. The trunk must also be strong and well supported to take the large side-loading forces. The centerboard may also be used as a brake, to slow the vessel in shallow water, and as a "parking brake" for temporarily holding her on a beach or bank. Choose a windward beach, (*never* a lee beach), and gently nose the bow ashore, drop the board, and luff the sails. Watch the tide if you intend to step off the boat, and

let the sheets go completely. This is very useful when waiting for bridges to open. Another use of the centerboard is to check and turn the boat in reverse: With the foresail down or slack-sheeted, use the mainsail to steer by pushing the boom to the side. You can use this technique to back a sharpie into a shallow slip and "park," rather like the family car, but entirely under sail. Let me caution you that this takes practice. Make sure no one is watching the first few times!

Sprits and Snotters

In *The Fore and Aft Rig in America*, E. P. Morris explains use of the sprit, furling methods, and anchoring stern-to. Pay particular attention to the use of snotter tension to control sail shape:

> The sprit was of the usual kind; the outer end was fitted into a cringle at the clew, the other end had a deep slot cut in it [or hole, or sheave], through which a lanyard was run from the mast. With this, acting as tackle, the sail could be stretched flat, or, by slacking the lanyard, could be given a hollow draft. The halyards were single, running through a small block or over a sheave in the mast. On the earlier and smaller boats the sail was furled by unshipping the sprit and wrapping the halyard spirally about the mast and sail together; larger boats lowered the sail and furled it on the sprit as on a boom. The sheets were light and simple, and, since the foot of the sail was cut high, they could be allowed to run out freely....On the oystering grounds they are anchored by the stern,...the sheet is allowed to run out, and the sail swings forward over the bow. To one who does not know the rig it is an extraordinary and scarcely intelligible spectacle.

In general, you set the snotter (a lanyard run from the mast; see Chapter Five) up tight to flatten the sail when beating to windward, and slack it a little when reaching and running. A flat sail (less draft) will allow you to point higher, with a sacrifice to power; a fuller sail (hollow draft) will give you more power with less pointing ability.

The height of the snotter on the mast also controls sail shape by determining the angle at which the sprit pushes on the clew of the sail. Raising the snotter up the mast will flatten the sail aloft, preventing twist, luffing, and spilling of the wind aloft—just as a vang would. Since the sheet also does this to a degree, the two controls should be used together. Lowering the snotter creates more foot tension, allowing the sail to twist and spill wind, which might at times be desirable. In general practice, the snotter is placed in one position and left there, once the optimum location is found by trial and error. The snotter locations shown on the sail plans should be close to optimum—adjust them to get your sail shape just right. Thus, sharpies with sprits don't require vangs, as the foot of the sail automatically performs that function.

Those of you who are familiar with windsurfers and wishbone booms will also note that snotter tension (particularly when combined with sheet tension) pre-curves the mast, which

also flattens the sail shape. The sprit-rigged sharpie is the direct ancestor of the modern windsurfer.

The pure racing sharpies of the Connecticut coast were completely radical. They carried square sails on the foremast and had double sprits (one above the other) on the sails. The sprits on the foresail were often so long that they had to be eased by slacking the snotters when tacking or jibing, or they would break against the mainmast. Two planks were carried, about 16 feet long, which were run out to windward as "springboards." Eleven of the 12-man crew sat out on these to keep the boats from capsizing. One of the 35-foot racers described by Chapelle carried 2,250 square feet of sail, so you can see why they reached speeds close to 20 knots. Oh, how I would dearly love to build one of these hot rods, train a crew to avoid death and maiming while sailing it, and go out and kick butt on all those Tupperware tubs. Wouldn't that be fun!

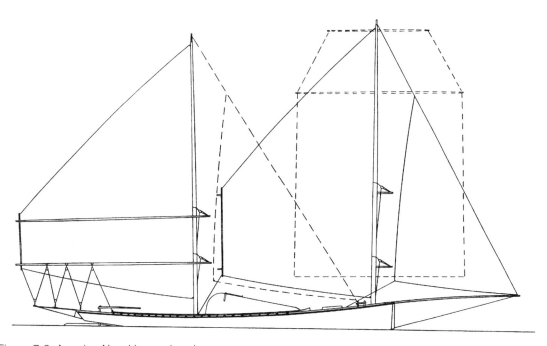

Figure 7-2. A racing New Haven sharpie.

Tips for Smooth Sailing

There are a few general rules for sailing sharpies that I should mention. First: *The mainsail (or mizzen—the aftermost sail) should be the first to go up and the last to come down.* This keeps your nose into the wind while you do whatever else you have to do, such as raise anchor, drop anchor, or handle another sail. When you raise a second or third sail, *leave their sheets slack until you gain headway*, thereby avoiding falling way off or even capsizing in a puff of wind with no way on (forward motion). In gentle wind, with no likely surprises, the mainsheet may be made off to hold the vessel's head to the wind. Otherwise, it's best to leave all sheets slack until you are ready at the helm, when you generally sheet in the aftermost sail first to avoid falling way off.

Second: *Reef early.* The old rule is this: As soon as you think about the need to reef, *do it.* Most craft, sharpies included, sail better if they are not over "on their ear"—you will have less weather helm, expose more sail area to the wind, be more comfortable, and court less risk of capsizing if you reef on time.

Third: *Safety comes first.* Equip your boat with proper life jackets, a throwable life ring, fire extinguishers, flashlights, flares, a knife, and fresh water. This last item comes first on my list—right up there with a good pair of oars and oarlocks. I won't go anywhere, even across the harbor, without a gallon jug of water somewhere in my boat. You also need adequate ground tackle (larger boats should carry a spare anchor), extra rope, and whatever spares are appropriate to your boat. Even though many of us feel antagonistic toward the U.S. Coast Guard these days, keep in mind that these guys don't make up the rules, and they are doing their job; it is far easier to *have all USCG-required equipment on your boat*, in acceptable condition, and to be polite and professional while your boat is being torn apart for pot seeds. Believe me; I'm experienced. I also like to carry fish hooks and a handline, and especially in the tropics sunscreen and sunglasses are important, although in the old days loose clothing and floppy hats did the job. If you sail in cold weather, have some warm clothing and watch caps (wool stays warm when wet) on board. Foul-weather gear is essential; I even like wearing a wetsuit at times. Finally, have a bail scoop, bucket, and hand pump (bigger boats) on board. Tie the scoop and bucket on lanyards so they can't get away.

There are many rules and wisdoms for sailing, and this book is too short to talk about them all—indeed, so is any single book. There is no substitute for experience, but you can do a lot of homework by reading everything you can get your hands on. Then you have to remember all that knowledge when the poop hits the fan—no easy task. Start *now*.

I have only capsized a sharpie once, but I also capsized my 44-foot cat-schooner, *Teresa*, which might be considered a large, arc-bottomed sharpie (with a draft of 2 feet 8 inches), in the 1985 Mayor's Cup Schooner Race in New York Harbor. In both cases, I can only blame myself, but it goes to illustrate that sharpies require careful handling.

In Islamorada, in the Florida Keys, I capsized my 19-foot sharpie *Gato Negro* in 20 to 25 knots of wind by doing several stupid things, starting with carrying full sail in that much wind while alone—I just wanted to go fast! I neglected to slack the fore sheet when I should have, and over I went. I had a bad time getting the boat upright and bailed out in that wind, and a strong current complicated things (I had to anchor, finally). Had I not been in two feet of water, it would have gone even worse than it did. The hull had no flotation, which would have helped me.

In general, it is necessary to pull the masts out of a sharpie after a capsize. *Tie them to the boat*, along with the oars and sprits and anything else that can drift off. With the masts, sprits, and sails tied off in the water on the lee side of the boat, and with an anchor out if there is a current, right the boat and bail her out. With no flotation, you will have to start bailing from overboard. Use a five-gallon pail if you have one, and bail from the lee side, using your weight to keep the windward side high—this keeps waves from sloshing in and makes it easier to lift the bucket over the side. When the boat is high enough in the water, climb in (carefully) and continue. When she is dry, retrieve your masts and sails, and either put the rig back together or row home.

Capsizing a big cruising boat is a very serious matter, and if *Teresa* didn't have several water-tight bulkheads, including the vital one between her cabins, we might have lost her. The galley sink through-hull was open (port side), and there was no gasket around the bridge deck ice hatch. The ice hold doglegs into the galley, such that water can get into the cabin from the outside hatch when capsized on the port side, which we were. We were tacking off Brooklyn when a dramatic wind shift, heralding an approaching squall line, locked us in irons. My mate and I jumped up to back the sails to get out of irons when the gale-force gust hit us (65 knots). Of course, the sheets were made off—big mistake—and over we went. *Teresa* was brand-new at that time—not even finished—and lacked 2,000 pounds of ballast. A local small tugboat, run by Joe Maddison, an old cohort from South Street Seaport, came to our rescue. We took a line around the mainmast, the tug hit reverse, and up we popped. The experience was very educational, and I confess I've never been the same since. We sailed *Teresa* another couple thousand miles, including out to the Bahamas, before eventually adding a lead shoe to the bottom of her keel after we got back home to the Keys.

The lesson here: If you get caught in irons (stalled out in the wind while coming about), *let the sheets go* before doing, or even thinking about, anything else. Many, many accidents are caused by this little oversight, including those in which lives are lost. A famous example is the capsizing of the schooner yacht *Mohawk*, at the time (1876) one of America's largest yachts. This 140-foot schooner was weighing anchor off Staten Island when hit by a sudden gust of wind.

Being dead in the water *with her sheets made off*, she heeled rail-down, was hit by another stronger gust, and capsized, taking the owner, his wife, the cabin boy, and two guests to their deaths. The vessel was condemned by those who were proponents of the deep-keeled, heavily ballasted yacht type, and a great controversy ensued, even though *Mohawk*, renamed *Eagre*, went on to serve many years as a U.S. Coast and Geodetic Survey vessel without mishap in much severe weather.

I almost hesitate to tell *Teresa*'s and *Mohawk*'s stories, but I feel a responsibility to make my readers clearly aware that all vessels can be dangerous if not properly handled. Extremely shoal-draft vessels in particular are rarely "self-righting" and must be handled skillfully and attentively, with *safety* being your highest priority.

Tales of *Kingfish* and *Egret*

As we have seen in Chapter One, Commodore Ralph M. Munroe did much to develop the sharpie for such diverse roles as mail carrier and cruising yacht. It was he who introduced the sharpie to Florida, bringing *Skipperee* to Key West in 1881, *Kingfish* to St. Augustine in 1883, and *Egret* to Coconut Grove in 1886. Of course, he sailed those three sharpies all over Florida waters, having many adventures and greatly shocking the populace with sharpie antics. He also designed and built many more sharpies, including what he came to call "round-bilged sharpies," or "Presto boats," after his good little ship *Presto*.

The following account is from *The Commodore's Story*, by Munroe and Gilpin, of a journey from St. Augustine to Coconut Grove in the sharpie *Kingfish* in December 1883:

> Toward evening an offshore breeze tempted us out of Matanzas Inlet, but it soon died out and left us knocking about in some sea. After midnight it began breezing from the north, was shortly a fresh northeast gale, and by daylight a hard one, putting

us under close reefs. The rapidly rising sea would have induced visions of an outside run, instead of the Mosquito Inlet and Indian River route, but for the fact we had a sharpie under us.

It was near low water, which made conditions worse for an ordinary boat, though even at high tide the bar would have been impassable. At that time the channel crossed the bar at the extreme south end of the opening, and ran through in a northwesterly direction, between two lines of breakers, and no craft, sail or power, could have negotiated it that morning.

With the sharpie, however, we picked out the shoalest looking spot at the north end, clear of the old boiler, took in the mainsail and headed for it. Good luck carried us in, just behind the first breaker, and before the second caught us we were safe in a foot or so of water, and an instant later high and dry, about half a mile from land. It was a precarious-looking position to an onlooker ashore, and so thought Captain Pacetti, the pilot, who immediately took steps toward a rescue. Had he known the possibilities of sharpies, and that we were making coffee, he would have been saved much trouble.

By the time we had breakfasted the tide was springing fast, and we got overboard on each quarter and held her stern to the sea. In a short time she had driven over the shoal, and away we went up the river, passing Pacetti on his way to help us, and singing out our thanks for his good intentions. We could just catch his answer—"What in hell kind of boat have you there?" It is apparent that I introduced the type on the Florida coast.

Munroe used *Kingfish* to go offshore regularly from Miami, meet the New York liners rounding Cape Florida, collect mail, small cargoes, and periodicals, and distribute them to the lighthouse keepers and inhabitants of the bay. He also transported passengers, sick patients, food, and cargo, captured giant crocodiles, made rescues, and salvaged wrecks. Go back to Chapter One and take another look at the photo of

Kingfish running wing-and-wing (Figure 1-15).

Don't try a stunt like the one Munroe described until you are both an experienced sailor *and* experienced with sharpies. First, you need to understand the cycles of the weather patterns common to the Gulf Stream off Florida. In a "norther," when a cold front presses down into Florida, the wind comes up strong from the north, veering to northeast. Often the wind shifts all the way around the clock: An approaching front is frequently heralded by a shift of the wind to the south from the prevailing easterly tradewind. The wind clocks all the way around to the west, when it may start to blow harder, and as it works its way to northwest, north, and finally northeast, it blows steadily harder and colder. Squalls and rain may or may not come with the westerly, but it frequently becomes clear and cold with the norther. After a day or so, it eases up and drops back to the easterly tradewind. This cycle of wind is used to great advantage by sailing vessels to run up and down the Keys, fetch the Bahamas, or generally head "down island." Here is how to use it: When the wind hauls southerly, run out your inlet and head east, having first a close reach (steering a little southerly to compensate for the Gulf Stream), and finally a screaming run onto the Bahama Banks or into the Northwest Providence Passage and toward your chosen destination. To come home, simply run before the prevailing easterly trade wind.

It is important for smaller craft to avoid the Gulf Stream when the wind hauls north, as the gale winds blowing against the powerful current whip up some of the nastiest seas, for their size (usually 5 to 10 feet), to be found anywhere on Earth. These seas (really large, short, steep wind chop) are the biggest reason the Gulf Stream has such a bad reputation, and they are easy to avoid if you memorize the preceding paragraph. I promise you that you don't want to meet them in a small sharpie. This is what Munroe meant by saying "...visions of an outside run, instead of the Mosquito Inlet and Indian River route, but for the fact we had a sharpie under us." The Mosquito Inlet was indeed impassable to most craft at most times, and was probably risky to run in even a sharpie in those conditions, but the run in the Stream would have been even more harrowing: The next inlet was below Canaveral, many miles away around the Cape—a hard choice.

Munroe took in his mainsail, or aftermost sail, so that the sharpie would not be overpowered and would keep her head going downwind and across the bar. He got her between breakers and kept her there—no mean feat—so she would not be pooped (swamped from astern) or capsized. He doesn't say, but you can be sure he had his centerboard all the way up, so as to keep *Kingfish* pointing downwind, to ensure that she wouldn't broach or "trip," and so as not to ground out prematurely. There is really no other boat type that could perform such a feat. A surf dory might try it, but she would be hard pressed to maintain enough speed to stay ahead of the following breaker. On the inclined face of a following sea, the wide, flat, keel-less bottom of the sharpie acts exactly like a giant surfboard.

Munroe designed the 28-foot double-ended sharpie *Egret* specifically for running the shallow Florida inlets and handling the rough Gulf Stream offshore waters in almost any weather. It was *Egret* that ran mail in all seasons on the east coast of Florida. The following is one of Munroe's accounts of *Egret* from *The Commodore's Story*:

> I remember beating out of Lake Worth Inlet one morning in a strong east wind, with all of north Dade County taxes in a salt-bag, the collector sitting in the bottom of the craft and hanging onto both sides while we worked our way through two lines of breakers. Though we started rather late, we were home at the Grove in time for supper.

And here's another tale of *Egret*, describing her windward ability in foul weather:

We wonder…if *Egret*…didn't often think of the night in the Gulf Stream off Hillsboro when the wind suddenly hauled from northwest to northeast and came on a gale. The two boats with us turned on their heels and ran back for the Cape [Cape Florida, to the south]; should we follow? No! we were bound for Lake Worth. So we tucked in a reef or two and stood offshore. Harder and harder it came down on us, but the little boat never whimpered. The sea? Well, just the Stream in a northeaster, as any skipper can describe it— capping, and phosphorescent in the darkness, with little foot to it.

There were hours of this, offshore and on, trying to locate landmarks against the western sky line. We picked up the first glint of Jupiter's flash [Jupiter lighthouse], and then its full glare, showing our sure gain to windward. Then we hunted for the treeless beach of the old Lake Worth Inlet, a mile or two below the present one, making short tacks just clear of the surf. Dick at last identified it with his unusually keen sight, and then, stooping head to gunwale, strained his eyes for the gleam of the breakers on Lake Worth Rocks at the inlet. Finally it appeared, and when well to windward and sure of the channel, it was down mainsail and up stick [centerboard], and with one wild rush we were through the breakers and foam, over the bar, and inside the point of beach.

It happened that young Will McCormick of Palm Beach was spending that night at the inlet, fishing, and had his lines out in the cut when we swooped past him out of the roaring turmoil on the bar. No one ever dreamed of running Lake Worth Inlet either at night or in a gale, there being only a foot or so on the bar at low water, and no room to swing inside. The apparition of *Egret*, under these conditions, sweeping past him and rounding to under the sand-spit, scared him half to death, and for a moment convinced him that there really were ghosts!

On this visit *Egret* was called on to demonstrate sharpie possibilities to some of the Lake Worth folk in a lively afternoon. All were interested in any new type of sailboat (the reader must remember that all traffic on the Lake was then by sail, even the mail and the butcher going from house to house in catboats) and a party including "Doc" Brelsford and Mr. Stone Smith was invited to go sailing. The wind was mild southwest, with signs of a norther coming, and away we went up the Lake putting *Egret* through all the sharpie tricks, some of which are rather startling to those unhandy with that handy rig. Meanwhile a heavy squall was rising in the north, and all the scattered sailboats on the Lake made for their moorings in a hurry, while the party on *Egret* grew more and more uneasy, and made several suggestions as to turning back. I wanted to show off the boat, however, and paid no attention, further than to serve out oilers all around, maintaining an air of entire unconcern while the clouds rapidly rose and a white squall swept down the Lake on the first burst of the norther, and the party fumed and scanned the deserted waters. The squall struck like the blow of a club, the little boat was carefully jockeyed through the first puff, and then squared away before the wind, for Dimmick's. She would run under whole sail in anything, and swooped down the Lake like an arrow from the bow, finally running down on the wharf wing and wing, and ended the performance with a sensational jibe and round-up possible only to her light and nimble type and rig, which turns and stops like a polo pony. It was all a revelation to her guests, and led to much talk, and in Mr. Smith's case to the building of the sharpie *Yosida*.

I should explain further why *Egret* was a unique sharpie, and what aspects of Munroe's design enabled her to sail in the Gulf Stream during northers and run Florida's wild, breaking inlets. Among her features that allowed such antics were her narrow, somewhat deep bottom, making her nearly a cross between dory and sharpie; her duck's stern, pointed and raised high to separate, and lift to, following seas and breakers; and her short, gaff-rigged, cat-schooner sail plan. Hence, she was deeper-bodied than other similar-sized sharpies and carried her ballast lower, making her self-righting; she could hardly be pooped, having no wide, low transom and deck to trap water like most sharpies had; and her sail plan was low-aspect ratio (low center of effort), being gaff-rigged on very short masts instead of marconi-rigged on very lofty masts, like most sharpies. *Egret* is widely acknowledged to be the most seaworthy sharpie ever designed and built, and those are the reasons why. Bill Smith's *Egret* (*Lahoma*), while modified, bears out all the Munroe stories. I highly recommend this model if you intend to use your sharpie as Munroe did, though most of the other models are faster sailers.

I also think that larger versions of *Egret* could be designed and built for extended cruising, in sizes up to 50 or 60 feet. Another advantage of the *Egret*-type hull over the other sharpies is that standing headroom can be achieved in smaller boats because of the deeper, narrower bottom. So, an *Egret*-type cruiser could have standing headroom in a 45-footer, whereas most of the other sharpies would have to be 55 feet or more.

Maintenance

Maintenance will vary greatly depending on where your boat is kept, how she is used, and how she was built and finished. The important thing is that you maintain her. She will give you more service, less trouble, and she will look and feel good if she is maintained. This means work. But you built this thing, you are responsible for her, and you have invested your time, energy, money, and Earth's precious materials in her. To protect your investment, she must be maintained.

Cruising sharpies covered with fabric and epoxy should get a haulout every year. Generally, a pressure wash and coat of bottom paint or two will be all that is necessary; but it is vital to thoroughly inspect the boat for corrosion, water violation of the hull skin, gouges, scrapes and abrasion (particularly on the centerboard, skeg, gripe, and rudder), rot, and worm damage. Scrubbing the bottom once in a while, anchored out or nose to the beach, helps slow down marine growth and simplify your haulout. I like to anchor in a strong tide, then don fins, mask, snorkle, and T-shirt, jump in the water with Scotch scrubby pads (the kind with a handle), drop some lines over the side to hang onto—and scrub away, staying upstream from the water-borne toxic bottom paint. I also like those plastic handles you can buy with the rubber suction cups for hanging onto awkward areas.

Paint and varnish work should be maintained; a little touch-up now and then will go a long way. Catching problems early is much easier than letting them go. If your boat is finished with polyurethane or another hard-gloss paint or varnish, you can wax or polish it periodically for a longer life. I find that window cleaners (like Windex) work well on gloss varnish and paint.

Carefully examine areas where fresh ("sweet") water can collect, and where air circulation is poor, for mildew and rot. You can buy paint additives to discourage mildew, which loves the undersides of decks and coach roofs. Clean these areas often and look for rot. If you find rot early, you can dig it out, epoxy the area or glue in a dutchman, find the cause and eliminate it.

Good air circulation is vital to wooden boats. Design and build your boat in such a way that there are no dead-air traps. If you build-in air-tight flotation boxes, it is best to fill them with foam. In any case, thoroughly seal the wood with several coats of epoxy, and paint it with epoxy paint if you don't use foam. Make sure water can't get in, and provide a watertight access if the compartment is large.

Sails and rigging should be checked often. Periodically, end-for-end your sheets, halyards, anchor rodes, and docklines to minimize chafe. Check the stitching in your sails as they age, as

well as the fabric. Ultraviolet light is the big enemy of synthetics, including rope. Good sail covers made of acrylic fabric (like Sunbrella) are nearly essential, unless you take your sails off (a major nuisance with laced-on sails). For sprit-rigged sails, sew a patch of Sunbrella along the foot of each sail, tapering from about 6 inches aft to 24 inches forward. Furl the sail on the sprit, detach the sail tack and fold the foot over the sail as a cover.

Blocks and hardware should be inspected. Varnish, oil, or paint your block cheeks periodically. Don't grease roller bearings in blocks, as the grease traps dirt and may do more damage than good. Use silicone spray, if anything, and clean out corrosion and dirt once a year. A toothbrush and mineral spirits work well. (If you blow them out with compressed air at your local gas station, you won't have to dismantle the blocks.) Winches need to be dismantled, cleaned, and greased once a year; follow the manufacturer's recommendations. A sticking dog in a winch can cause the handle to come around and break your arm.

Finally, take good care of your oars. If you row around shallow rocks and coral a lot, cover the tips of your oar blades with copper. Keeping your blades painted white helps; they won't deteriorate as fast as if treated with oil or varnish, and you can see them in the dark. Use tallow (rendered animal fat) or a grease that won't attack leather, like mink oil, on your oar leathers to keep them from drying out and cracking. Use it on your oarlock pintles also, to lubricate them and stop them from squeaking. And use it in the maststep.

The most important thing of all is this: *Use your sharpie.* Boats that are used are loved, understood, cared for—and they last longer and look better.

Great Sailing!

APPENDIX I
TABLES OF OFFSETS FOR ADAPTED SHARPIE DESIGNS

Complete plans for the author's designs in Chapter Six can be purchased from: Parker Marine Enterprises, P.O. Box 3547, Fort Pierce, FL 34948-3547, or by writing to International Marine, P. O. Box 220, Camden, ME 04843. Lines to outside of planking.

Sail dimensions should be scaled off the full-size plans by your sailmaker. If you choose, you can scale the sail dimensions yourself by enlarging the sail plans in this book to a scale of ⅛" or ¼" to the foot.

Station	Transom	3	2	1	Stem	
Heights above Baseline	1·9·2	1·7·1	1·7·0	1·11·0	2·4·4	Sheer
	1·1·6	0·7·1	0·4·3	0·6·7	0·9·2	Chine
Half~ Breadths	1·1·3	1·9·3	2·1·0	1·6·7	0·0·6	Sheer
	0·10·4	1·4·5	1·8·1	1·2·4	0·0·6	Chine

Baseline to L.W.L.= 9 ⅛"
Stations spaced as noted

14-foot Cape Cod Oystering Sharpie Skiff.

Station	Transom	3	2	1	Stem	
Heights above Baseline	2·0·7	1·10·3	1·10·0	2·2·0	2·8·2	Sheer
	1·7·2	1·1·1	0·7·4	0·8·1	1·1·2	Chine
Half~ Breadths	1·7·3	2·1·6	2·5·7	1·8·2	0·1·2	Sheer
	1·4·2	1·8·4	2·0·0	1·2·5	0·1·2	Chine

Baseline to L.W.L.= 12 ¾"
Stations spaced as noted
Ht. of keel top @ #3: 10 ⅜"
Ht. of keel top @ Transom: 13 ⅜"

16-foot Eastern Shore Stick-up Skiff.

Station	Transom	2	1	Stem	
Heights above Baseline	1·9·1	1·5·3	1·7·6	2·3·0	Sheer
	0·6·7	0·0·6	0·1·4	0·6·2	Chine
Half~ Breadths	1·7·2	2·3·0	2·0·0	0·1·0	Sheer
	0·8·0	1·3·6	1·2·0	0·1·0	Chine

Baseline to L.W.L.= 5 ¼"
Stations spaced as noted

15-foot Mississippi Yawl River Skiff.

Station	Transom	3	2	1	Stem	
Heights above Baseline	2·7·4	2·4·3	2·4·4	2·9·6	3·4·2	Sheer
	1·9·3	1·5·0	0·10·0	1·1·0	1·4·0	Chine
Half~ Breadths	1·6·5	2·0·7	2·8·4	1·9·2	0·1·2	Sheer
	1·4·5	1·8·1	2·1·6	1·2·1	0·1·2	Chine

Baseline to L.W.L.= 1'3 ½"
Stations spaced as noted
Heights of Keel top: @ #
1~0·11·3/2~0·7·2/3~1·1·3/Transom~ 1·4·6
Half~breadth @ Keeltop: 0·1·2

18-foot Modified Sharpie Skiff.

Station	Transom	4	3	2	1	Stem	
Heights above Baseline	1.9.6	1.7.5	1.6.1	1.9.1	2.3.2	2.6.1	Sheer
	0.9.6	0.6.6	0.0.5	0.1.7	0.6.2	0.7.6	Chine
Half~	1.8.7	2.1.3	2.9.0	2.5.3	0.11.2	0.1.2	Sheer
Breadths	1.4.5	1.7.1	2.1.0	1.9.6	0.6.1	0.1.2	Chine

Baseline to L.W.L. = 6¾"
Stations spaced as noted

19-foot Small Ohio Sharpie.

Station	Transom	3	2	1	Stem	
Heights above Baseline	3.0.4	2.7.3	2.7.1	3.0.2	3.70.4	Sheer
	1.10.6	1.2.4	0.10.6	1.1.3	1.7.6	Chine
Half~	2.2.0	3.0.2	3.4.6	2.10.5	0.1.2	Sheer
Breadths	1.6.5	2.2.5	2.7.5	2.0.2	0.1.2	Chine

Baseline to L.W.L. = 1'7¾"
Stations spaced as noted

25-foot Maryland Fishing Sharpie.

Station	Bow	1	2	3	Stern	
Heights above Baseline	2.1.6	1.9.4	1.5.1	1.7.0	1.10.2	Sheer
	0.9.0	0.6.0	0.4.0	0.5.7	0.8.7	Chine
Half~	0.1.2	1.8.0	2.6.0	1.7.1	0.1.2	Sheer
Breadths	0.1.2	1.0.4	1.11.3	1.0.6	0.1.2	Chine

Baseline to L.W.L. = 8¾"
Stations spaced as noted

20-foot Maryland Crabbing Skiff.

Station	Stern	4	3	2	1	A	Stem	
Heights above Baseline	1.11.7	1.8.6	1.6.6	1.8.2	2.2.7	2.5.3	3.2.3	Sheer
	1.1.5	0.9.2	0.2.0	0.0.0	0.3.5	0.5.2	0.9.5	Chine
Half~	1.9.4	2.0.6	2.8.4	2.11.5	2.4.0	1.10.7	0.1.6	Sheer
Breadths	1.3.0	1.6.0	2.1.3	2.4.0	1.8.6	1.4.7	0.1.6	Chine

Baseline to L.W.L. = 8 5/8"
Stations spaced as noted

27-foot New Haven Sharpie.

Station	Transom	4	3	2	1	Stem	
Heights above Baseline	2.2.1	1.11.4	1.9.7	2.0.7	2.6.5	2.11.4	Sheer
	1.2.5	0.11.6	0.5.5	0.7.2	0.10.5	1.1.0	Chine
Half~	1.7.2	2.0.6	2.8.7	2.9.2	1.9.5	0.1.2	Sheer
Breadths	1.2.6	1.5.7	2.0.4	2.0.2	1.2.4	0.1.2	Chine

Baseline to L.W.L. = 12¼"
Stations spaced as noted

22-foot Cedar Keys Sharpie.

Station	Stern	6	5	4	3	2	1	Stem	
Heights above Baseline	3.7.2	3.1.6	2.9.6	2.10.1	3.0.7	3.4.7	3.8.6	4.2.0	Sheer
	1.8.0	1.1.1	0.5.3	0.2.7	0.3.0	0.5.3	0.8.5	0.11.0	Chine
Half~	0.1.2	1.10.1	3.3.5	3.8.6	3.5.6	2.8.0	1.8.0	0.1.2	Sheer
Breadths	0.1.2	1.0.4	2.1.5	2.5.4	2.2.3	1.6.4	0.10.3	0.1.2	Chine

Baseline to L.W.L. = 11"
Stations spaced as noted

28-foot Munroe *Egret* Double-ended Sharpie Yacht.

Station	Transom	4	3a	3	2	1	Stem	
Heights above Baseline	3.8.3	3.4.1	3.2.3	3.2.4	3.5.1	4.1.3	4.8.5	Sheer
	2.7.2	2.0.3	1.3.3	1.1.4	1.1.6	1.8.7	2.1.1	Chine
Half~	2.5.4	3.0.7	3.7.5	3.9.1	3.8.7	2.2.3	0.1.2	Sheer
Breadths	2.1.2	2.5.3	2.10.7	3.0.1	2.11.4	1.5.7	0.1.2	Chine

Baseline to L.W.L. = 2'½"
Stations spaced as noted
Height of Keel top @ #'s:
3~1.0.2 / 3a~1.1.0 / 4~1.7.0 / Transom~1.10.6
Half~breadth of Keeltop: 0.1.2

24-foot Chesapeake Flattie.

Station	Transom	5	4	3	2	1	Stem	
Heights above Baseline	2.5.7	2.7.5	1.11.6	2.7.1	2.7.6	3.1.4	3.7.7	Sheer
	1.4.0	0.10.6	0.0.5	0.0.1	0.4.7	0.8.7	1.0.7	Chine
Half~	2.6.2	3.1.5	4.0.5	4.2.2	3.7.2	2.3.6	0.1.6	Sheer
Breadths	2.1.0	2.5.1	3.2.3	3.3.7	2.8.5	1.8.2	0.1.6	Chine

Baseline to L.W.L. = 10¾"
Stations spaced as noted

33-foot North Carolina Sharpie.

Station	Stern	7	6	5	4	3	2	1	Stem	
Heights above Baseline	2.5.6	2.2.3	2.2.7	2.1.3	2.2.2	2.5.5	2.8.4	3.4.4	4.0.1	Sheer
	1.6.0	1.0.3	0.9.7	0.2.7	0.2.2	0.3.2	0.4.7	0.9.5	1.1.2	Chine
Half-Breadths	2.4.0	2.7.6	2.10.6	3.7.3	3.8.5	3.7.7	3.4.1	1.11.6	0.1.6	Sheer
	1.9.0	2.0.0	2.2.7	2.10.0	2.10.7	2.9.3	2.5.7	1.3.6	0.1.6	Chine

Baseline to L.W.L. = 12"
Stations spaced as noted

35-foot New Haven Sharpie.

Station	Stern	5	4	3	Mid	2	1	Stem	
Heights above Baseline	3.10.5	3.5.7	3.2.5	3.4.0	3.5.6	4.0.3	4.11.3	5.10.3	Sheer
	2.0.0	1.5.2	1.1.0	0.10.0	0.10.0	0.11.5	1.4.0	1.8.0	Chine
Half-Breadths	0.1.6	2.0.7	3.8.7	4.9.6	4.10.2	4.5.7	2.9.6	0.1.6	Sheer
	0.1.6	1.4.3	2.9.2	3.7.5	3.10.2	3.4.6	1.9.3	0.1.6	Chine

Baseline to L.W.L. = 1' 11¾"
Stations spaced as noted

36-foot San Juan Island Double-ended Sharpie.

Station	Transom	5	4	3	Sa	Pb	Po	2	1	Stem	
Heights above Baseline	3.9.4	3.5.4	3.2.3	3.2.4	3.3.3	3.4.1	3.5.6	3.8.6	4.5.0	5.1.6	Sheer
	2.1.6	1.7.0	0.6.6	0.5.6	0.5.4	0.5.6	0.6.7	0.9.2	1.3.6	1.8.0	Chine
Half-Breadths	3.1.5	3.10.3	4.10.3	4.11.7	5.0.6	5.0.5	4.10.5	4.6.1	2.8.0	0.1.6	Sheer
	2.8.1	3.0.3	5.8.6	3.9.6	3.10.3	3.10.1	3.8.3	3.4.1	1.8.2	0.1.6	Chine

Baseline to L.W.L. = 18"
Stations spaced as noted

36-foot Ohio Pound-Net Boat (Great Lakes Sharpie).

APPENDIX II
THREE MODERN SHARPIE DESIGNS

Here are three contemporary sharpie designs by prominent American designers who are also sharpie fans. Plans for these boats can be purchased by writing to the addresses provided below.

Norwalk Islands 26-Footer

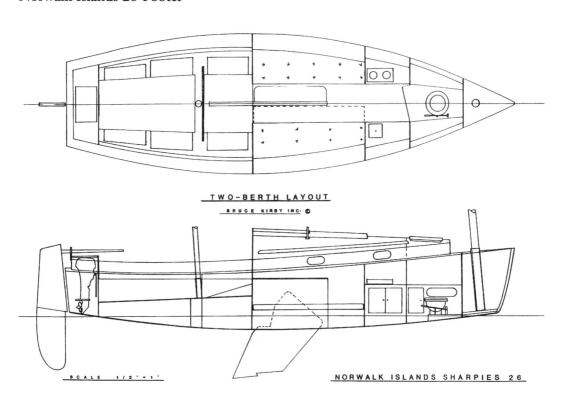

TWO-BERTH LAYOUT
BRUCE KIRBY INC. ©

SCALE 1/2" = 1'

NORWALK ISLANDS SHARPIES 26

LOA: 26 feet 3 inches

DWL: 22 feet 6 inches

Beam: 7 feet 11 inches

Draft: 10 inches (centerboard up) and 5
feet 9 inches (centerboard down)

Displacement: 3,700 pounds (w/3 150-
pound crew)

Trailer Weight: 3,100 pounds
(excluding crew, engine, fuel)

Sail Areas (including roach):
Large Rig: 340 sq. ft. (main 251 sq. ft., mizz. 89)
Small Rig: 302 sq. ft. (main 213 sq. ft., mizz. 89)

Designer: Bruce Kirby
213 Rowayton Avenue
Rowayton, CT 06853

Floridays

LOA: 19 feet 8 inches

LWL: 15 feet 10 inches

Waterline Beam: 4 feet 4 inches

Draft: 8 inches (centerboard up); and 2 feet 3 inches
(centerboard down)

Weight (at mooring): 1,200 pounds

Sail Area: 150 sq. ft.

Designer: Mark Fitzgerald

P.O. Box 763

Camden, ME 04843

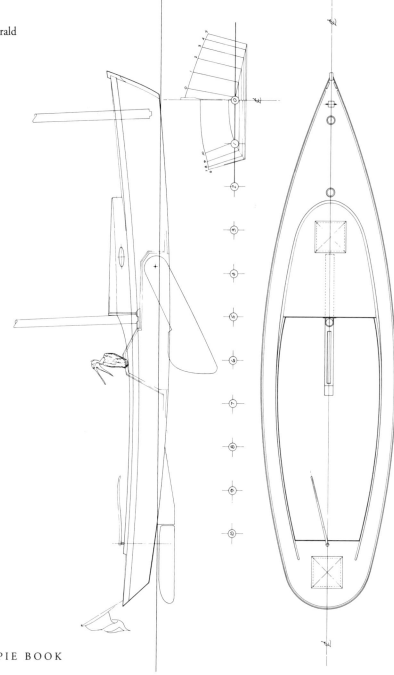

- FLORIDAYS -

A 20' SHARPIE SCHOONER
- for -
NATHANIEL BUCKLER

Birdwatcher

LOA: 23 feet 6 inches

Beam: 5 feet 7 inches

Displacement: 1,500 pounds

Sail Area: 226 sq. ft.

Designer: Philip C. Bolger

29 Ferry Street

Gloucester, MA 01930

Plans Available From:

H.H. Payson and Co.

Pleasant Beach Road

South Thomaston, ME 04858

or

Common Sense Designs

11765 Ebberts Court

Beaverton, OR 97005

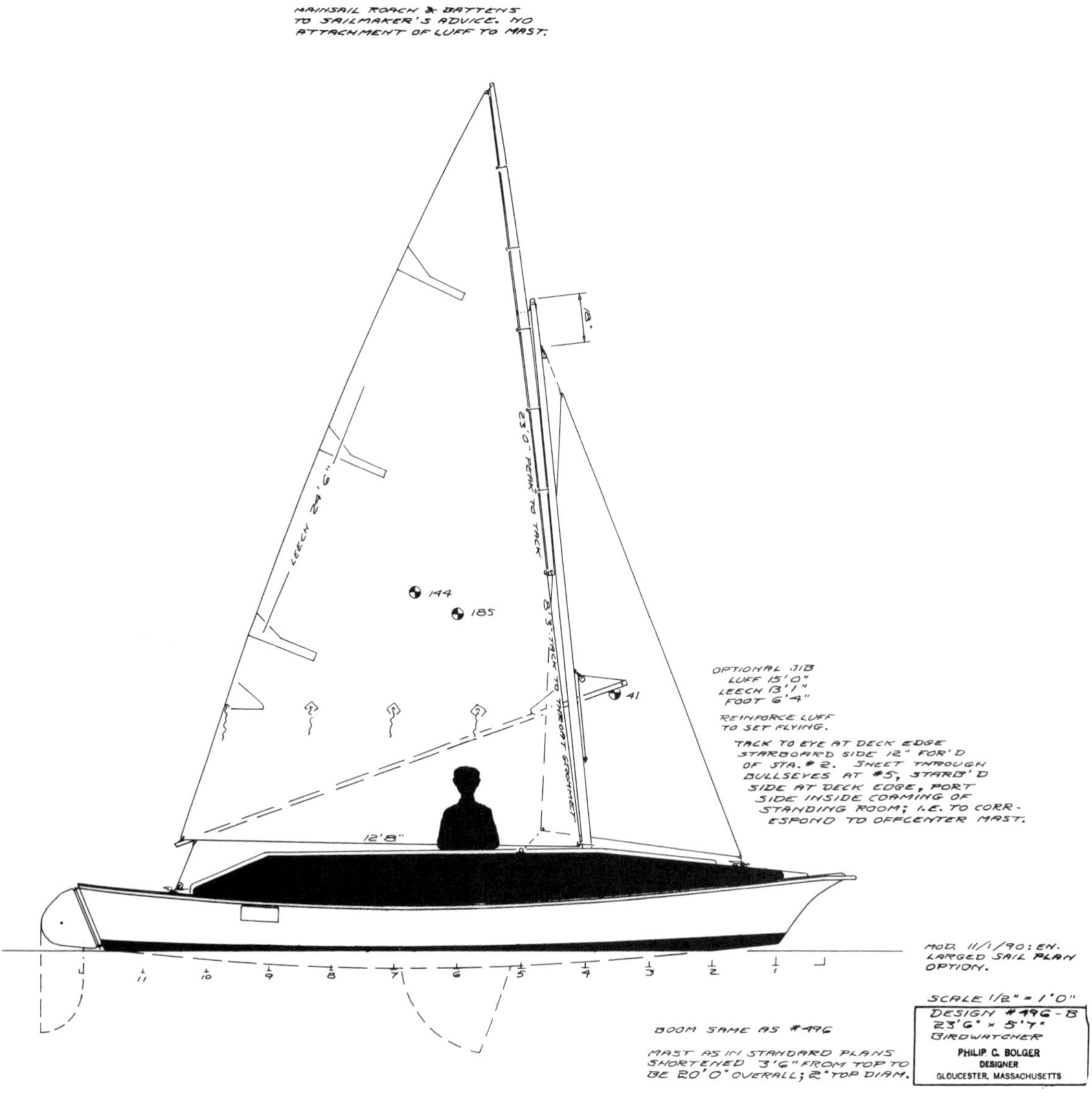

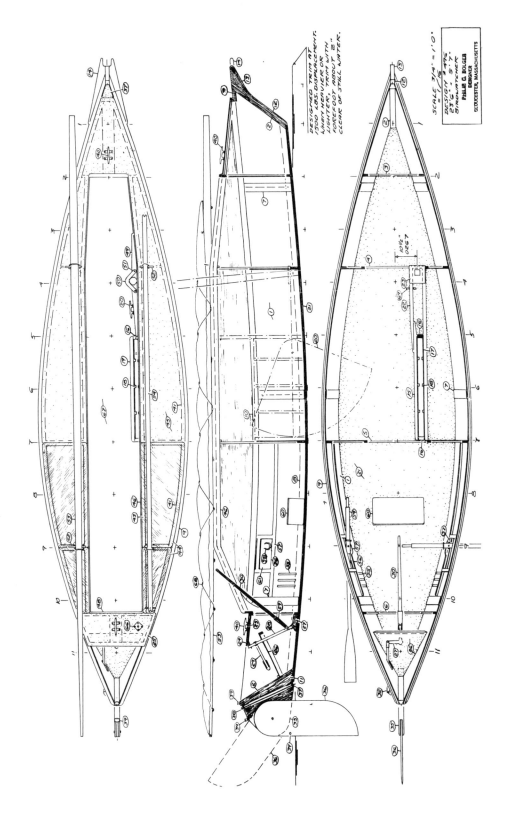

SCALE 3/4" = 1'0"

DESIGN # 496
23'G" × 5'6"
STARWATCHER

PHILIP C. BOLGER
DESIGNER
GLOUCESTER, MASSACHUSETTS

DESIGNED TRIM AT
1500 LBS. DISPLACEMENT.
WHEN HEAVIER OR
LIGHTER, TRIM WITH
FOREFOOT ABOUT 2"
CLEAR OF STILL WATER.

APPENDIX III
MATERIALS SUPPLIERS

Suppliers

The following suppliers are listed by material categories. I suggest trying local sources first, but certain specialty items will probably need to be ordered. There are many more suppliers than I have listed here; these are meant to provide known alternatives, or in some cases, sole sources for unusual items.

Epoxy and Glue

Doc Freeman's, Seattle, WA (arabol lagging compound, marine hardware, fabrics)

E-Bond, 501 NE 33 Street, Ft. Lauderdale, FL 33334; (305)566-6555

Glue Products, 4011 Georgia Avenue, West Palm Beach, FL 33405; (800)771-1863

Gougeon Brothers, P.O. Box X908, Bay City, MI 48707; (517)684-7286 (WEST Epoxy)

Joe's Auto-Marine Supply, 3285 SE Dixie Highway, Stuart, FL 34994; (407)283-6704/(800)881-9202/(800)881-6704

System Three Resins, P.O. Box 70436, Seattle, WA 98107; (206)782-7976

Fabrics

Defender Industries, 255 Main Street, P.O. Box 820, New Rochelle, NY 10801; (914)632-3001 (sole source for Xynole-polyester fabric)

Doc Freeman's (see "Epoxy and Glue")

J.R. Sweet & Co., U.S. 220, South Mustoe, VA 24468; (703)468-2222 (polyester-fabric tapes)

Fasteners

Chesapeake Marine Fasteners, P.O. Box 6521, Annapolis, MD 21401; (301)268-8973 (stainless-steel deck screws, etc.)

Jamestown Distributors, 28 Narragansett Avenue, Jamestown, RI 02835; (401)423-2520 or (800)423-0030 (outside RI)

Parker Merrick, 245 SW 32 Street, Ft. Lauderdale, FL 33335; (305)761-1677 or (800)432-3700 (FL only)

Hardware

A & B Industries, 1160-A Industrial Ave., Petaluma, CA 94952; (800)422-1301

Doc Freeman's (see "Epoxy and Glue")

Jamestown Distributors (see "Fasteners")

Sailorman, 350 East State Road 84, Ft. Lauderdale, FL 33316; (305)522-6717 (new and used marine equipment)

West Marine Products, P.O. Box 1020, Watsonville, CA 95077; (408)728-2700 or (800)538-0775 (outside CA)

BIBLIOGRAPHY

American Sailing Craft by Howard I. Chapelle. New York: Crown Publishers, 1939.

American Small Sailing Craft by Howard I. Chapelle. New York: W. W. Norton, 1951.

"Chesapeake Crabbing Skiffs" by Steve Redmond. Brooklyn, ME: *WoodenBoat*, March/April 1986.

The Commodore's Story by Ralph Munroe and Vincent Gilpin. New York: Washburn, 1930, and reprinted by the Historical Association of Southern Florida, 1966.

The Fore-and-Aft Rig in America by E. P. Morris. New Haven: Yale University Press, 1927.

Forest and Stream, Jan. 23, 1879, vol. 11, no. 25, p. 504.

Good Boats by Roger C. Taylor. Camden, ME: International Marine, 1977.

The National Watercraft Collection by Howard I. Chapelle. Washington, DC: Smithsonian Institute Press and Camden, ME: International Marine, 1966.

The New Cold-Molded Boatbuilding, from Lofting to Launching by Reuel B. Parker. Camden, ME: International Marine, 1990.

Paper 25: The Migrations of an American Boat Type by Howard I. Chapelle. Washington, DC: Bulletin 228: Contributions from the Museum of History and Technology, U.S. Government Printing Office, 1961.

Report on the Ship-building Industry of the United States by Henry Hall. Washington, DC: Tenth U.S. Census report, 1880–1885, pp. 29-32.

"The Sharpie" by W. P. Stephens. New York: *Yachting*, January 1927.

Le Sharpie, Son Histoire et Son Evolution, by Maurice Amiet.

Simplified Boatbuilding: The Flat-bottom Boat by Harry Sucher. New York: W.W. Norton.

Simplified Boatbuilding: The V-Bottom Boat by Harry Sucher. New York: W.W. Norton.

Small Yachts: Their Design and Construction, Exemplified by the Ruling Types of Modern Practice by C. P. Kunhardt. New York: 1886 (rev. ed., 1891, pp. 287-289).

"Thomas Clapham—An Appreciation" by William J. Starr. New York: *Yachting*, December, 1915.

"Thomas Clapham, 1839-1915" by G. Criffith Clapham. New York: *Yachting*, December 1938.

INDEX

A

Adhesives, 46-47
    aliphatic-resin carpenter's glue, 47
    epoxy, 46-47
    fiberglass tape, 47
    plastic resin glue, 47
    polyester tape, 47
    polyurethane-type adhesives, 47
    suppliers of, 172
    thixogens, 47
    Xynole-polyester fabric, 47
Aluminum
    masts, 46
Anchors, 39

B

Ballast, 95
Bandsaw, 43
Beam shelves, 66
Bevel square, 45
Birdwatcher, design for, 170
Blocks, maintenance of, 162
Bostik, 47, 52, 68, 132
Bubble rollers, 44
Bulkhead aft, 32
Bulkheads
    modern construction of, 53-55
    traditional construction of, 30

C

Cabins, 78-83
    boom tent type, 78
    cuddy cabin, 78
    furnishings, 82
    hatches, location of, 79-80
    iceboxes, 83
    permanent, construction of, 78-82
    pop-top type, 78
    sinks, 82
    skylights, 82
    storage areas, 82
    stove, 82
    water system, 83
Cab-O-Sil, 47, 91, 92
Cape Cod oystering sharpie (14-foot), design for, 102-104
Capsizing, 157-158
Carolinas, history of sharpie, 16-18
C-clamps, 44
Cedar Keys sharpie (22-foot), design for, 116-118
Centerboards
    centerboard slot, layout of, 62-63
    modern construction of, 68, 72
    traditional construction of, 30, 37
    uses of, 155
Chainplates, 94
Chalkline, 45
Chesapeake, history of sharpie, 10-12
Chesapeake flattie (24-foot), design for, 118-121
Chine logs, 30
    installation of, 58-59
Chisels, 44
Chocks, 39, 94-95
Circular saw, 43
Clapham Nonpareil sharpie yacht (38-foot), design of, 148-151
Cleats, 36, 39, 94-95
Clench rings, 39
Clevis, 37
Cockpits, construction of, 75-78

Cold-molded construction, 50-51
  advantage of, 50-51
Compass, 45
Cove strip, 34

D

Daggerboards, 37
Decking
  construction of, 33-34, 67
  deck beams, installation of, 65-66
  deck substructure, construction of, 66-67
Deck screws, 47-48
Designs for sharpies
  Birdwatcher, 170
  Cape Cod oystering sharpie (14-foot), 102-104
  Cedar Keys sharpie (22-foot), 116-118
  Chesapeake flattie (24-foot), 118-121
  Clapham Nonpareil sharpie yacht (38-foot),
    148-151
  Eastern Shore stick-up skiff (16-foot), 106-108
  Floridays, 168-169
  Maryland crabbing skiff (20-foot), 113-116
  Maryland fishing sharpie (25-foot), 121-124
  Mississippi yawl river skiff (15-foot), 104-106
  Munroe *Egret* double-ended sharpie yacht (28-
    foot), 128
  New Haven sharpie (27-foot), 124-128
  New Haven sharpie (35-foot), 137-141
  North Carolina sharpie (33-foot), 133-137
  Norwalk Islands (26-footer), 166-167
  Ohio pound-net boat (Great Lakes sharpie—
    36-foot), 145-148
  Ohio sharpie (19-foot), 110-113
  San Juan double-ended sharpie (36-foot), 141-
    145
  Sharpie skiff (18-foot), 108-110
Doorskins, planking round stern with, 60-61
Drawing battens, 44-45
Drills, electric, 43

E

Eastern Shore stick-up skiff (16-foot), design for,
    106-108
Electric drill, 43
Engines, attaching to sharpie, 72-73
Epoxy, 46-47
  suppliers of, 172

Exhaust fans, 43, 49
Eyebolts, 48
Eyestraps, 89, 94-95

F

Fabric/epoxy covering, application of, 63- 64, 68,
    91-93
Fabrics, suppliers of, 172
Fairleads, 39
Fasteners, 47-48
  suppliers of, 172
Fiberglass tape, 47
Fillets, 92
Flanges, 37
Florida, history of sharpie, 18-22
Floridays, design for, 168-169
France, history of sharpie, 9-10
Furnishings, cabins, 82

G

Glue. *See* Adhesives
Grapples, 39
Great Lakes, history of sharpie, 13-16
Gripe, construction of, 63

H

Hammer, 44
Hand tools, 44-45
Hardware
History
  Carolina Sounds (1881), 16-18
  Chesapeake (1870), 10-12
  colonial era, origins of sharpie, 1
  Florida (1881), 18-22
  France (1870), 9-10
  Great Lakes (1870s), 13, 15-16
  modified sharpie (1890s), 23-28
  New Haven (1850), 6-8
  New Jersey (1860), 9
  New York City/Long Island (1855), 8-9
  North Carolina (1874), 12-13
  20th century, 28-29
  use in oyster fisheries, 2-6
  Vermont/Lake Champlain (1870), 13
  Washington State/San Juan Islands (1880s), 22-
    23

Hull
     fabric/epoxy covering, 63-64
     modern construction of, 52-53
     traditional construction of, 30-34
Hydrodynamics, basic aspects of, 97-98

I

Iceboxes, 83
Interior, traditional construction of, 34-37

K

Keelson
     construction of, 30, 34, 41
     modern construction of, 60

L

Lag-eyebolts, 48
Lake Champlain, history of sharpie, 13
Lazyjacks, 90
Levels, 45
Line and anchor lockers, 82-83
Lofting, 98-101
     design elements, 99-101
Long Island, history of sharpie, 8-9

M

Maintenance, 161-162
     blocks, checking, 162
     checking for mildew/rot, 162
     inspection of boat, 161-162
     oars, 162
     paint/varnish, 162
     scrubbing bottom, 162
Mallet, 44
Maryland crabbing skiff (20-foot), design for, 113-116
Maryland fishing sharpie (25-foot), design for, 121-124
Masts, 33
     aluminum, 46
     mast taper, layout of, 88-89
     materials for, 46
     operation of, 153
Maststeps, 36
     modern construction of, 69

Materials, 45-47
     suppliers, listing of, 172
Mattresses, 83
Microballoons, 47
Mildew, 162
Mississippi yawl river skiff (15-foot), design for, 104-106
Molds
     construction of, 53-55
     setting up of, 55
Munroe *Egret* double-ended sharpie yacht (28-foot), 128

N

Nails, ring-shank nails, 48
New Haven, history of sharpie, 1-8, 41-42
New Haven sharpie (27-foot), design of, 124-128
New Haven sharpie (35-foot), design of, 137-141
New Jersey, history of sharpie, 9
New York, history of sharpie, 8-9
North Carolina, history of sharpie, 12-13
North Carolina sharpie (33-foot), design of, 133-137
Norwalk Islands (26-footer), design for, 166-167

O

Oars
     leathering of oars, 75
     maintenance of, 162
     oar sockets, location of, 75
     size requirements, 75
Ohio, history of sharpie, 13-16
Ohio pound-net boat (Great Lakes sharpie—36-foot), design of, 145-148
Ohio sharpie (19-foot), design for, 110-113
Orbital sander, 43
Outer stems, construction of, 63
Oyster industry, use of sharpie, 2-6

P

Painting, 93-94
Pintles, 94
Pivot pin, 37
Planes, 44
Planking
     bottom planking, 61-62

materials for, 46
modern method of, 57-58
sides, 57-58, 100
Plans for sharpies
body plan, 99
design stations, 99
load waterline, 99
lofting design stations, 99-100
sheerline/chine line/baseline, 99
stem line, 100
table of offsets, 99
for specific designs, 163-165
Plastic resin glue, 47
Pliers, 44
Polyester cloth, covering vessel with, 63-64, 91-92
Polyester tape, 47
Polyurethane-type adhesives, 47
Power plane, 43
Power tools, 43-44
Pressure-treated wood, 45-46
Protractor, 45
Putty knives, 44

R
Rafter squares, 44
Rasp/file, 44
Rigging
construction of, 89-91
operation of, 153
standing rigging, 91
Ring-shank nails, 48
Ripping guides, 43
Roller frames, 44
Rolling bevel, 53
Router, 43
Rowlock sockets, 39
Rubrails, 34, 39
materials for, 46
Rudders
modern construction of, 70-72
options for, 153-154
traditional construction of, 37

S
Saber saw, 43
Safety guidelines
for construction, 48-49
for sailing, 157

Sailing guidelines, 157-158
Sanders, orbital sander, 43
Sanding block, 44
San Juan double-ended sharpie (36-foot), design of, 141-145
San Juan Islands, history of sharpie, 22-23
Sawhorse, 45
Saws, 43-44
Scantlings
in modern construction, 66
in traditional construction, 40-42
Scarfs, 44, 46
Screwdrivers, 44
Screws, deck screws, 47-48
Scuppers, 30
Seacocks, 95
Shackles, 95
Sharpening guide, 45
Sharpening stone, 44
Sharpie construction (modern method)
bulkheads, 53-55
cabins, 78-83
centerboards, 72
centerboard slot, 62-63
centerboard trunk, 68
chine logs, installation of, 58-59
cockpits, 75-78
cold-molded construction, 50-51
deck, 67
deck beams, 65-66
deck substructure, 66-67
engines, use of, 72-73
fabric/epoxy covering, 63-64, 91-93
gripe, 63
hardware, 94-96
hull, 52-53
keelson plank, 60
maststeps, 69
molds, 53-55
oars, 73, 75
outer stems, 63
painting, 93-94
planking, 57-58
planking bottom, 61-62
planking round stern, 60-61
planking sides, 57-58
rigging, 89-91
rudders, 70-72
sheer clamp, 64-65
skeg, 62

spars, 83-88
stem, 53
stern, 55-57
sternpost, 62-63
strongback, 51-52
tiller, 72
compared to traditional method, 50
thwarts, 69
Sharpie construction (traditional method)
centerboards, 37
hardware, 37, 39
hull, 30-34
interior components, 34-37
rudders, 37
scantlings, 39-42
spars, 39
stern, 41
Sharpie skiff (18-foot), design for, 108-110
Sheer clamp, construction of, 64-65
Sikaflex, 52
Sinks, 82
Size of sharpie, construction problems of, 40, 41
Skegs
construction of, 62
and performance, 154-155
Skylights, 82
Snotters, 89
use of, 155-156
Spars
construction of, 83-88
double-tapered spars, 85-88
traditional construction of, 39
Sprits
materials for, 46
use of, 155-156
Stanchions, 55, 56, 64
Staple guns, 43-44
Staples, 48
Staving, 41
Stem, modern construction of, 53, 63
Stern
modern construction of, 55-57
planking round sterns with doorskins, 60-61
round stern, 56-57, 58
traditional construction of, 32, 41
transom sterned, 55-56
Sternpost, construction of, 62-63
Storage areas, cabins, 82
Stove, 82

Strongback, construction of, 51-52
System Three, 46

T
Table of offsets, 99
Table saw, 43
Tape measure, 44
Thimbles, 95
Thixogens, 47
3M 5200, 47, 52, 68
Through-bolts, 48
Thwarts
for interior components, 36
modern construction of, 69
Tie-rods, 39
Tiller, modern construction of, 72
Tiller hardware, 94
Titebond, 47
Titebond II, 47
Toerails, 34
materials for, 46
Tools
hand tools, 44-45
power tools, 43-44

V
Vent holes, 32
Vermont, history of sharpie, 13
Vise, 45
Vise-grips, 44

W
Washington (state), history of sharpie, 22-23
Waterlines, 54-55
Water system, 83
Weldwood, 47, 52
WEST System, 46
Wet-wells, 32
Windlasses, 95
Wood for construction, types of, 45-46
Wood vise, 45

X
Xynole-polyester fabric, 47